KU-717-152

Church and State after the Dreyfus Affair

By the same author

GATHERING PACE: CONTINENTAL EUROPE, 1870–1945

Church and State after the Dreyfus Affair

The Separation Issue in France

MAURICE LARKIN, M.A., Ph.D. (Cantab.)
Senior Lecturer in History, University of Kent at Canterbury

Macmillan

First published 1974 by
THE MACMILLAN PRESS LTD
London and Basingstoke
Associated companies in New York
Dublin Melbourne Johannesburg and Madras

SBN 333 14703 0

Printed in Great Britain by
HAZELL WATSON & VINEY LTD
Aylesbury, Bucks

Contents

List of Illustrations

Acknowledgements

It was a commonplace of nineteenth-century fiction that criminals about to be hanged saw in their mind's eye a succession of faces of those who had helped and hindered them along the road to perdition. So it is when a book reaches completion and its defects reflect the prophecies and warnings of wiser men.

The central part of this book started life as a Ph.D. thesis for the University of Cambridge, when I was particularly fortunate to have Professor Sir Denis Brogan and M. Adrien Dansette as my supervisors. I wish to give them my very grateful thanks and also the many others who have helped me then and in the later stages of this cautionary tale. I must particularly mention M. Yvon Bizardel, Mrs J. E. C. Bodley, Mlle Geneviève Boegner, M. Marc Bonnefous, Canon Fernand Boulard, M. Denys Cochin, Fr Joseph Dehergne, S.J., Fr Pierre Delattre, S.J., M. Marcel Faucon, His late Eminence Cardinal Feltin, M. Jacques Gadille, the late M. Paul Grunebaum-Ballin, Mlle d'Haussonville, the Abbé Patrick Heidsieck, Professor Douglas Johnson, M. Jean Jolly, Fr Angelo Martini, S.J., M. Jean-Marie Mayeur, Mlle Louise Violette Méjan, Dr Peter Morris, M. Pierre Sorlin, Fr Pierre Touveneraud, the Abbé de Vigan, Mr J. M. K. Vyvyan, Dr James E. Ward, and the indefatigable Mrs Waring and her band of typists. Nor can I sufficiently thank my parents for their constant help and encouragement.

As with all work abroad, finance might have been a major problem. The initial postgraduate research was kindly made possible by Trinity College, Cambridge, with an Exhibition and the Earl of Derby Studentship. The British Institute in Paris subsequently awarded me a Leverhulme Scholarship, and I was thereafter the recipient of several research grants from the University of Kent, for which I am very grateful. More recently the British Academy provided me with a generous Visiting Fellowship in the spring of 1972.

As everyone knows, the wives of academics lead the life of Eurydice. Seeing little but their husbands' backs, they must often feel nostalgia for the pleasures of the Underworld. With more cause than most for such longings, my wife has shown a patience and endurance that has become something of a local legend.

June 1973 M.J.M.L.

The extract from *Portrait of the Artist as a Young Man*, by James Joyce, is reproduced by kind permission of Jonathan Cape Ltd and the Executors of the James Joyce Estate.

Introduction

Many historians still speak of 'the Dreyfusian Revolution'. They see the Affair and its aftermath as an episode which consolidated the Republic and set the stage for 'a new deal in French politics'. It broke up right-wing subversion and emancipated the younger generation from the influence of clerical education. Once this was done – and the Catholic Church disestablished – the way was open for the serious business of economic and social development.

It could be argued, however, that the so-called Dreyfusian Revolution was not a revolution at all, but a counter-revolution, a revival of old concerns which deflected France from the path of social progess.[1] Far from clearing the decks for social reform, it littered them with the old bric-a-brac of the constitutional and clerical issues. The mid-1890s had seen a certain smoothing-out of French politics along economic and social lines. Many monarchists, both Catholic and agnostic, were tired of supporting lost causes and were glad enough to join forces with conservative Republicans against left-wing demands for a graduated income tax and old-age pensions. 1893 found some fifty Socialists in parliament; and politics were now increasingly concerned with the sort of issues that divided most democratic countries at the turn of the century. French politics had come of age – or so it seemed.

The Affair and its aftermath, however, destroyed this situation. From 1899 to 1906 parliament was realigned once more on the issues that had divided it in the eighties – religion and the regime. The conservative Republicans were split in two. Those who regarded the Church as an integral part of the social status quo, feared that reprisals against it would weaken the whole social structure; and they therefore voted with the Catholics and the extreme Right against the Government's programme of Republican defence. Others, however, who conceded the need for this programme, found themselves in the uncongenial company of the Radicals and Socialists who made up the rest of the Government's majority. For seven years parliament wandered in an anticlerical wilderness, where political relationships were forced and retrogressive.

The benefits that this period brought to France are far from obvious.[2] Sections of the clergy had undoubtedly played a divisive, when not subversive, role during the Affair; and there was an urgent need to counter clerical influence of this kind. Yet many of the measures that were taken revived rather than settled the underlying issues, and did much to alienate moderate Catholic opinion. The most drastic item in the Government's programme was the campaign against Catholic private schools – in which nearly a quarter of the country's children were educated. Many agnostics found it intolerable that the minds of these children should be subjected to 'irrational' concepts such as Revelation; while Republicans feared that the children would be tainted by the anti-Republican sympathies of many of the teachers. It is an open question whether religious instruction should be prohibited in the name of truth; people will answer it according to their convictions. But few politicians dared base their campaign on this premiss. They preferred the safer ground of alleged political subversion; and, taken on this criterion, there is little doubt that the innocent not only suffered with the guilty, but far outnumbered the guilty. As a result of Combes's ministry (1902–5), one in three of these schools was forced to close, while the others had nominally to be run by laymen – though the law was unevenly applied.

The most durable achievement of this iron age of Republican defence was to come in 1905. Rouvier's ministry of that year saw the end of Napoleon's Concordat and the Separation of Church and State.[3] It was a highly paradoxical achievement in that Separation was wanted by none of the premiers who had ruled France since 1899, least of all by Rouvier under whom it became law. And yet, ironically, it was the only major act of those years that has survived the passage of time.

The historian has difficulty in assessing the advantages to France of this and other legislation, in that the outbreak of war in 1914 cut short the period in which its effects could be observed. In the short run, it undoubtedly made for bitterness among the Catholic population, and was a divisive not a unifying force. The Church's new-found freedom to choose its own bishops resulted in a new intransigent generation of bishops, many of whom were openly hostile to the government and lacked the *souplesse* of their predecessors. The fact, moreover, that Catholics now had to finance the clergy out of their own private funds increased their sense of solidarity and self-reliance.

Relations between Church and State improved between the wars; but it would be difficult to attribute this to the long-term effects of 'the Dreyfusian Revolution'. The First World War and its attendant problems eclipsed, if they did not extinguish, old quarrels; and the alignments of post-war parliaments were clearly based on social and economic issues. It is significant that when men like Edouard Herriot attempted to raise the anticlerical banner, they were rapidly made to realise that they were guilty of anachronism. And if one turns to contemporary France, the anticlericals of 1900 would find it hard to discern the fruits of their labours. Not only are the monks, friars and nuns back in their tens of thousands, but the State gives subsidies to Catholic private education – something that even Charles X had never envisaged. It is true that the secular clergy are no longer salaried – except in Alsace-Lorraine. But the Vatican consults with the Government before making episcopal appointments. In Alsace-Lorraine, moreover, the Concordat is still in operation – the Second Reich having preserved it from the anticlerical high tide of 1899–1906. The Alsatian clergy continue to be given state salaries; and the French Government still nominates bishops to the sees of Strasbourg and Metz, as it did in the time of Napoleon.

It would be hard to prove that France is necessarily the worse for this. Freethinkers may regret what they see as the Church's freedom to mislead the young; and the older among them may wonder what has happened to the intellectual ideals of 1900, when France for many was '*la République des professeurs*'. Yet the opportunities for self-fulfilment among the mass of the population are greater today than most of them would have dared hope; and it is arguable that if this has happened, it has done so *despite* 'the Dreyfusian Revolution' – rather than because of it. The improvement in educational opportunities and material conditions, which have brought about these changes in the last fifty years, owe little to Radical anticlericalism. After

1906, parliament reverted to the pattern that had characterised it in the mid-1890s – a cleavage on social and economic lines, rather than Republican defence. Once the common enemy was defeated, the Radicals and Socialists drifted apart. It is true that old-age pensions (1910) and a general income tax (1914) owe a lot to the Radical spade work of these years; but thereafter the Radicals were an obstacle to social reform. Dominated by rural interests and wedded to a doctrinaire individualism, the Radicals had little to offer other than anticlericalism – and economic protection for the peasantry and lower middle classes. The menopause of French Radicalism was well under way.

Even so the Radicals in the 1906–14 period helped to achieve reforms which could have been effected earlier, but for the Dreyfusian Revolution. This is not to deny that the strength of rural and middle class interests would undoubtedly have prevented the dramatic improvements that took place in some of the more industrial countries; this would continue to be a problem in France until the urban working class became a larger section of the nation. Yet there is no reason to suppose that the years 1899 to 1905 could not have seen the sort of social legislation that other states, more rural than France, were introducing about that time. One can argue, it is true, that the Dreyfusian Revolution helped to pave the way for the predominantly Radical ministries which subsequently introduced old-age pensions and a general income-tax. Yet such ministries did not necessarily require 'the Dreyfusian Revolution' to bring them into being. A Radical cabinet had briefly come to power in 1895–6 – despite the tacit entente in parliament between conservative Republicans, Catholics and former monarchists. It even succeeded in persuading the chamber to debate a graduated income tax; and although this particular venture failed, the proposal was in the logic of current developments. The same could be said of old-age pensions, likewise favoured by the Radical government of 1895. Sickness insurance was also a partial if indirect victim of the anticlerical programme, despite the example of other, more rural, countries.

The theme just outlined provides the background to this book. My main purpose, however, is to show how the Separation of Church and State came about and what led the Vatican to prohibit Catholics from accepting its principal advantages. Despite much valuable work in print, there still remains a need for such a book.[4] Somewhat surprisingly, this is the first history of the Separation to be based on a wide range of archival material – Italian and Belgian, as well as French. The voluminous private papers of Émile Combes and the sparser fragments of Francis de Pressensé's notes and letters have never been used before; nor have the rich archives of the Assumptionists in Rome for the post-1899 period. New material has likewise come from the unpublished minutes of the parliamentary Separation commissions and from the originals of the Montagnini papers.[5] Other archives, hitherto unused for the Separation, are those of the French, Belgian and Italian foreign ministries, as well as most of the privately owned papers listed on p. 243.

What emerges from this evidence is the major role of Francis de Pressensé in the creation of the Separation Law, and the predominance of international factors in shaping Vatican policy towards France. It likewise shows how the nature of the Roman Question changed between the pontificates of Leo XIII and Pius X. Other issues that it clarifies are the part played by the Assumptionists in the bizarre events of 1899, the origins of the system of delation in the army, and the enervating effect of the Concordatory regime on the life of the Church.

In presenting new evidence, one is under some compulsion to be precise and detailed. This poses problems of balance in a book which also attempts to give a comprehensible general outline for the non-specialist reader. The papal rejection of the *associations cultuelles* is a case in point. It still remains a matter for bitter speculation in France, involving as it did the permanent loss of nearly half a milliard francs' worth of property. The bulk of historians appear bewildered by it, and generally leave the reader to make his choice from a catalogue of possible explanations. The evidence assembled here, however, should leave little room for further serious doubt. The subject is nevertheless an emotive one; not only did it involve a vast economic loss, but it has since raised questions in many minds concerning the propriety of the Vatican's behaviour. In these circumstances it is obviously desirable to present as much of the evidence as is compatible with the size of this book – even at the risk of overweighting the relevant chapters.

1 Grass-roots Catholicism and the Secular Drought

Addressing the Eldest Daughter of the Church in 1892, Leo XIII called France 'a Catholic nation . . . by virtue of the faith of the great majority of her sons today'.[1] Like King Lear, fathers often entertain fond illusions about their eldest daughters; and if there were traditional reasons for still giving France this title, the faith of her sons in 1892 scarcely remained one of them. Admittedly the vast majority of Frenchmen had been taken to a Catholic church as unsuspecting babies to be baptised – perhaps well over 90 per cent.[2] And of the two or three million who escaped the brief alarm of having water poured on their heads and salt put in their mouths, some 600,000 underwent similar experiences in Protestant churches. A church wedding was still the dream of most women, over 80 per cent of French weddings being blessed in church as well as in the drab solemnity of the *mairie*. And finally, when life had no more to offer, the vast majority of people were taken feet first to church, to be buried according to the rites of their ancestors.

Yet in most cases these were no more signs of faith than the similar social conventions of the English, where committed Christianity was arguably stronger in numerical terms. 'He's an agnostic? All right, put "C. of E."' was to become a familiar enough cliché in the English armed services. Faith is not an easy commodity to measure; and the activities of the religious demographer may sometimes seem like those of the medieval schoolmen of popular legend, debating the size of the heavenly host in numerical terms. But while religious demography cannot attempt to concern itself with the quality and depth of religious practice, it can at least provide data on the outward signs of religious conformity. It is here, moreover, that the student of Catholicism has a distinct advantage over his Protestant colleagues. The Church regarded non-attendance at Sunday Mass as mortal sin – unless there were mitigating personal circumstances; and at the turn of the century few priests would have sought to qualify this verdict.[3] Catholics were also under a similar obligation to go to holy communion at Eastertide.[4] Consequently the statistics of church attendance and Easter communions provide a useful if imperfect guide to the numbers of practising Catholics in a given area. Statistics for the 1890s are unfortunately rare; and those that exist are often based on different criteria from modern censuses, thereby making it difficult to assess the rate or even the direction of change.

It was only in the 1950s that comprehensive surveys began to be made; and much can change in sixty years. It would appear that in the late 1950s nearly a quarter of the total adult population regularly attended Sunday Mass,[5] while nearly a third fulfilled their Easter duties.[6] Given the world-wide decline in religious observance during the course of the century, it is tempting to assume that the level in France in the 1890s was higher than in the 1950s. But, as the bewildering evidence in Figure 1 indicates, no demographer worth his salt would be prepared to make such an assumption, regional and class differences being so great. There nevertheless seems a fair measure of agreement that working-class observance fell during much of the nineteenth and twentieth centuries, while middle-class observance rose. Similarly the proportion of women making up the total appears to have diminished since the 1890s.[7] While they provided two-thirds of church attendance in the 1950s,[8] their contribution was probably much higher sixty years previously. Given these contrary movements, one would still be risking the derision of experts if one made even the cautious suggestion that somewhere between 15 and 35 per cent of French adults could be regarded as practising Catholics in the 1890s. An injudicious historian, worth no one's salt, might wish to pitch it more narrowly between 20 and 30 per cent, with a leaning towards the higher figure.[9]

As in other Western countries, however, church attendance among children was much higher than among adults. The front rows of any congregation were filled with fidgeting ten-year-olds, adapting their anatomy to the sharp-edged, over-high wooden kneelers and returning each other's pinches. Most

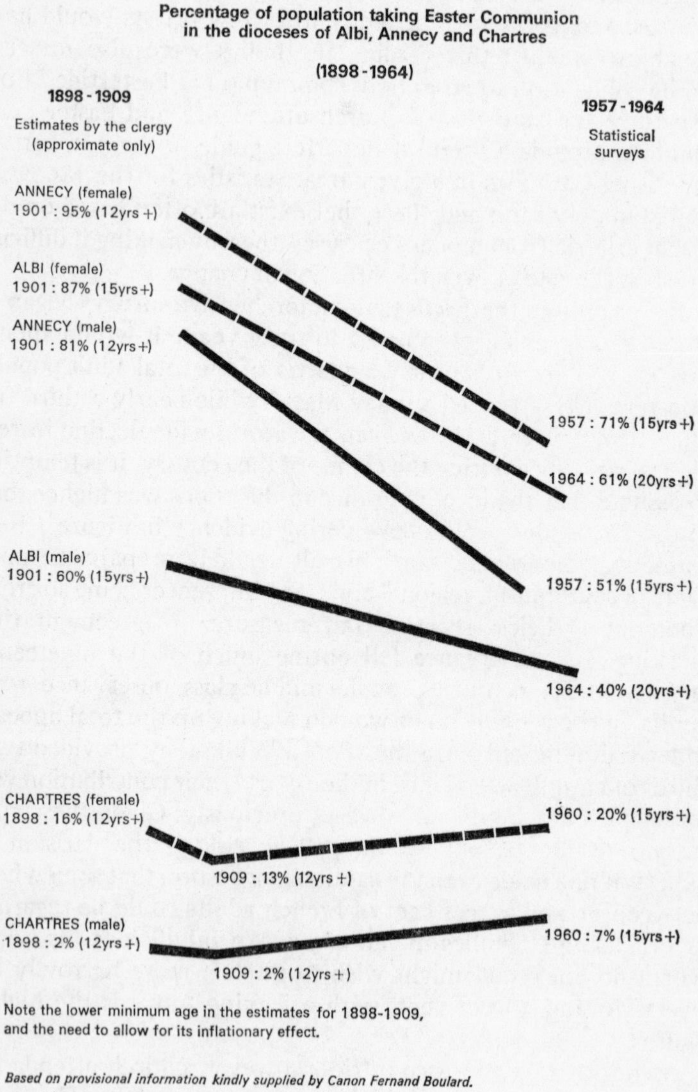

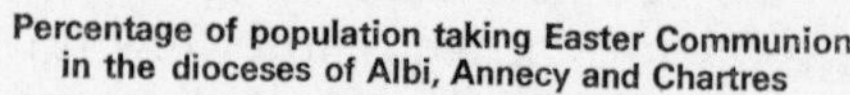

Percentage of population taking Easter Communion
in the dioceses of Albi, Annecy and Chartres
(1898-1964)
1898-1909
Estimates by the clergy
(approximate only)
1957-1964
Statistical
surveys
ANNECY (female)
1901 : 95% (12yrs +)
ALBI (female)
1901 : 87% (15yrs +)
ANNECY (male)
1901 : 81% (12yrs +)
1957 : 71% (15yrs +)
1964 : 61% (20yrs +)
ALBI (male)
1901 : 60% (15yrs +)
1957 : 51% (15yrs +)
1964 : 40% (20yrs +)
CHARTRES (female)
1898 : 16% (12yrs +)
1960 : 20% (15yrs +)
1909 : 13% (12yrs +)
CHARTRES (male)
1898 : 2% (12yrs +)
1960 : 7% (15yrs +)
1909 : 2% (12yrs +)
Note the lower minimum age in the estimates for 1898-1909,
and the need to allow for its inflationary effect.
Based on provisional information kindly supplied by Canon Fernand Boulard.

Fig. 1

French children made their *communion solennelle* – at the age of eleven or twelve – and this usually involved up to three years' attendance at preparatory catechism classes. This in turn subjected them to strong pressure to go to Sunday Mass in this period, the result being that for at least a year of their childhood, perhaps half of the French population had a fairly sustained contact with the Church. In the 1950s some two-thirds of all French children made their *communion solennelle*,[10] the number attending Mass in the preparatory months being slightly lower. What the figure was in the 1890s is still a matter for speculation; but 'upward of a half' may not be a gross travesty.

Like baptism, marriage and death, the significance of the *communion solenelle* for most families was social rather than religious. For many manual-class children in the 1890s it marked the passage from the ink-stained protection of school, with its thumps and chalkdust, to the harsher realities of long hours over fast-moving machinery, or humping root-crops in all weathers. But like the other major events of life, it called for festivity and an elaborate social ritual, the white satin, sashes and *dragées* being in effect, if not in intent, a last celebration of childhood before the onset of darker responsibilities. Its religious significance tended to be overshadowed by the fact that most children had already made their first holy communion, an event which spiritually meant more to the committed Catholic than the *communion solennelle*.[11] Nevertheless the preparatory classes for the *communion solennelle* were for most of the population the only period of their lives when they had any systematic contact with religion – a time for ever linked with the sharp sacristy smell of candle wax and fading flowers.

However problematic the number of believers in France, their distribution over the face of the country poses fewer difficulties. No one disputed that church attendance was highest in the windswept western peninsula and amid the pointed belfries and clinking cowbells of the Massif Central and the eastern uplands. The distribution maps for 1877 and the 1960s show remarakable similarities – despite some puzzling differences, some of which stem from the fact that the map for 1877 is based on the opinions of bishops and prefects, with little or no statistical evidence to guide them.

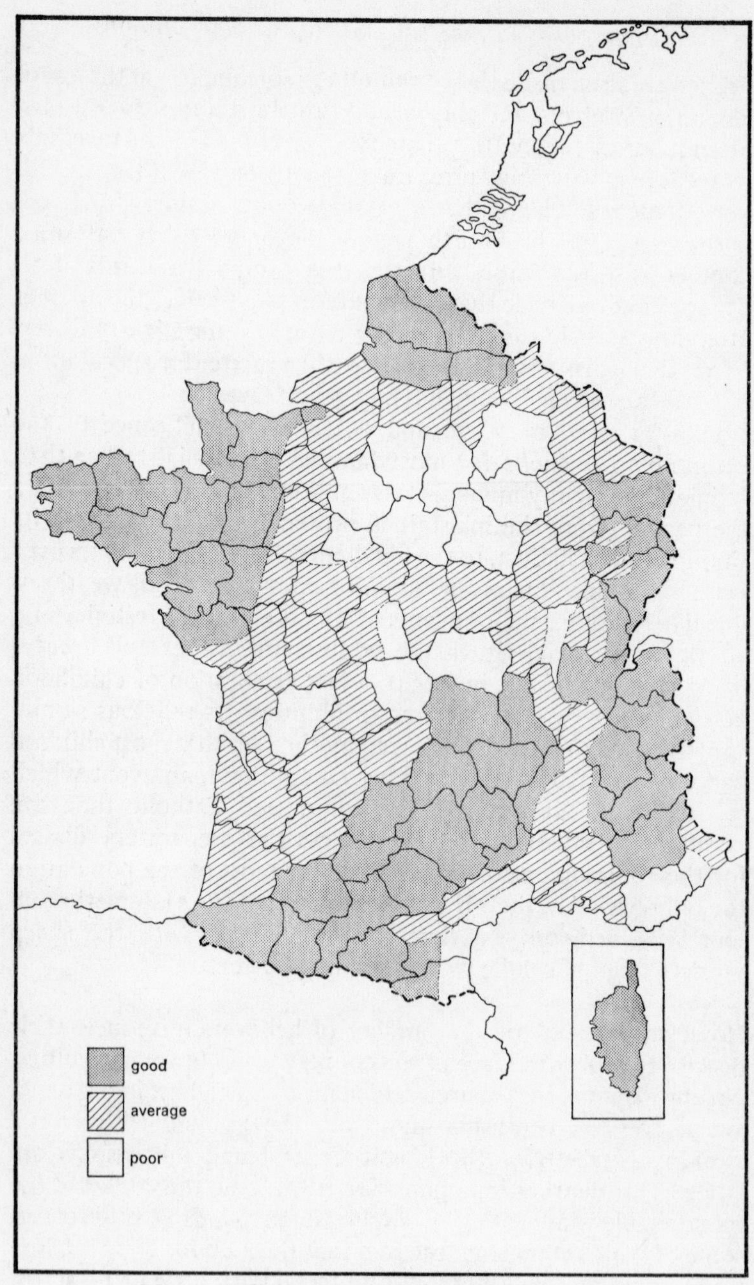

Map 1 Religious observance in France in 1877
(source: see p. vi)

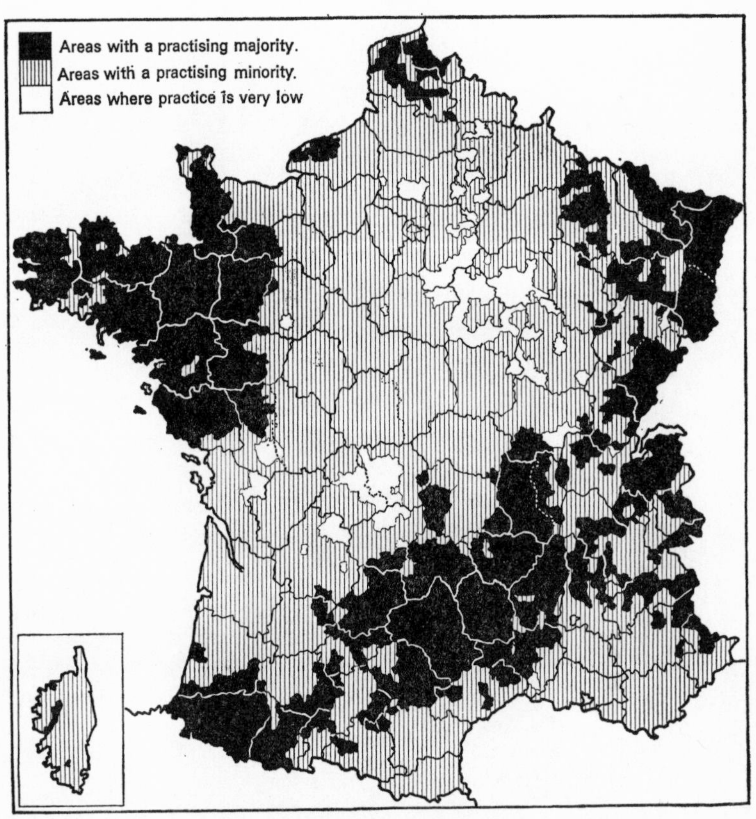

Map 2 Religious observance (Easter Communion) in France in the late 1960s (source: see p. vi)

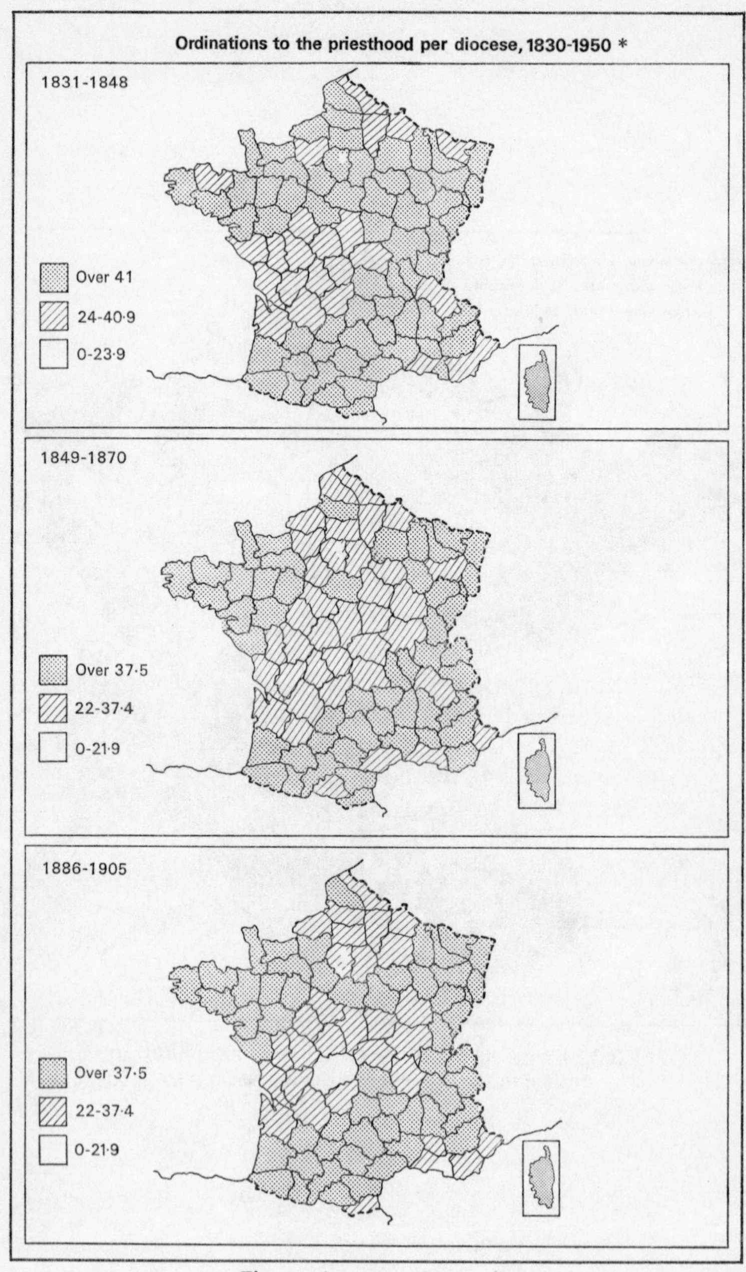

Fig. 2 (source: see p. vi)

* Ordinations of secular priests per 100,000 Catholic inhabitants

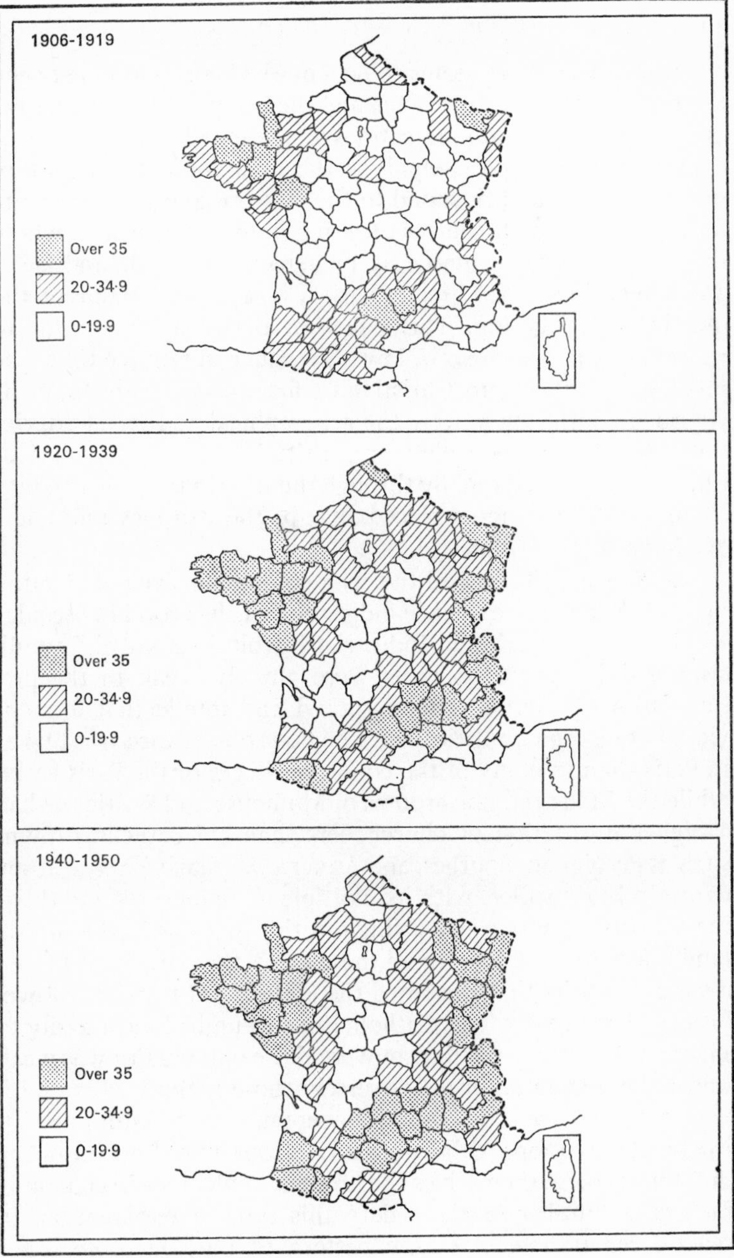
1906-1919
Over 35
20-34·9
0-19·9
1920-1939
Over 35
20-34·9
0-19·9
1940-1950
Over 35
20-34·9
0-19·9

At first sight there seems to be a marked correlation between the regions of high observance and the backward pastoral areas of France, where communications were difficult and the level of education low. Conversely it is the areas of low observance which seemed to correspond to the cultural and economic hinterland of the main centres of population – the regions where there was a constant and easy movement of people and ideas, and where there was a greater variety of secular demands on the individual's attention. This equation obviously has a lot to recommend it. The areas of low observance in modern times are precisely those where Christianity first made headway in its vigorous youth. These were the geographical and social arteries through which new beliefs and attitudes flowed; and just as Christianity moved rapidly through them, so in turn Christianity came to be diluted and replaced there by the attitudes and beliefs of a later, more secular, age.

The danger is to regard this as a comprehensive explanation in itself. Yet all the evidence indicates that the scorching secular winds of the French and Industrial Revolutions killed Catholicism mainly where its roots were already weak in the pre-Revolutionary period. Urban sprawl and intellectual ferment were not enough on their own. Religious observance was higher in Paris than in many of the country villages of the Paris basin, while the industrial mushrooms of Mulhouse and St Etienne had a higher proportion of churchgoers than old cathedral towns such as Perpignan, Bourges, and Auxerre. Similarly church attendance in Montpellier, with its multiple manufactures and thriving university, was twice as high in the 1950s as in the marshland museum of Arles.[12] In all these cases, the paradox reflected a state of affairs that pre-dated the French and Industrial Revolutions. The areas where Catholicism succumbed most easily to nineteenth-century secularism were those where faith was weak under the *ancien régime*. Conversely those regions where faith was strong before the Revolution were most successful in resisting secular erosion. Although many of these pre-Revolutionary differences were themselves the product of older socio-economic factors, a number of them defy this type of explanation. In several remarkable cases the pattern of religious observance corresponds to old diocesan boundaries that were abolished at the Revolution. Surviving to this day, and amenable to no other suggested explanation, these patterns of religious behaviour would seem to be a living monument to the success and failure of differing diocesan methods in past centuries.[13] Unfashionable though this genre of explanation may be, it is a type of factor that needs investigating.

If the roots of the modern distribution of faith lay buried in earlier centuries, the secular drought of the nineteenth century was none the less real. Under the *ancien régime*, much of what had passed for religious observance was little more than social convention, enforced by fear of employers and local magnates, or of what people would think. Underpinning the whole structure was the traditional alliance between throne and altar. The situation is eloquently reflected in some of the letters Voltaire wrote from his seigneurial estates in 1761. 'I am not obliged to attend Mass on anyone else's property, but I must on my own.' 'I am sixty-seven, I go to Mass in my parish, I set an example to my people, I am building a church, I take communion.' 'If I had 100,000 soldiers, I know what I would do; but I don't have them. I shall make my communion at Easter, and you are at liberty to call me a hypocrite.'[14]

In so far as religious observance was more than this, love of God probably played less a part than did a vague apprehension of what might happen after death. It is probably true that in all ages only a minority of people are temperamentally 'religious', in that they experience a positive desire for prayer or to 'feel at one' with nature or humanity. Many others have endeavoured to achieve this state through a sense of duty, based on the conviction that the teachings of religion are true and must be observed. Admitting their failure to achieve much personal 'satisfaction' from prayer, they have taken some comfort in the notion that the merit of their efforts is the greater for not having had the consolations of 'spiritual' experience.

When the Church was persecuted under the Revolution, only the convinced Catholic was prepared to hear Mass said by a virtual outlaw. And it was only in those areas of France that resisted the Revolution that social convention kept the churches full. Elsewhere, however, the habit of church-going, once broken, was not easily mended – even under the Bourbon Restoration. Although the timid Catholic resumed church attendance under Napoleon, the indifferent one remained lost to the Church.

What the French Revolution had begun, the Industrial Revolution continued. The growth of industrial towns took young men from their families and settled them in communities where social conventions had no traditional roots, and where there was little social incentive to go to church. At the same time the Industrial Revolution accelerated the whole process of communication. Railways and newspapers put the rural provinces in increasing contact with the secular attitudes of the main centres of population. City newspapers were dumped on the platforms of country railway stations on the day of printing; and the Homais of the local press were able to model their editorials and political comment on the latest Paris opinion. It was above all the local press which provided the vocabulary and shaped the attitudes of the emancipated petty bourgeoisie – the shopkeepers, bar-owners and primary-school teachers – men whose livelihood was independent of the local landlords. The lugubrious potted plants of the Café de la Gare and the somnolent cats of the entrance hall of the Hôtel du Commerce witnessed a constant interchange between these local luminaries and the commercial travellers and visiting *inspecteurs* whose boots and *bonhommie* brought the savour of distant places. Similarly the main-street and market-place bars saw the products of this learning disseminated among the poorer peasants, who could not, or did not, read the local press, and who listened passively to the loud disputes of the local literates.

As far as urban life was concerned, displacement was the main factor in dechristianisation. A close second was the creation of an industrial proletariat whose needs were alien to the Church's experience. The country-bred worker who settled in urban employment was uprooted in every sense. He was removed from the influence of both his family and the community that had provided the sum-total of his previous experience. Knowing few people other than his fellow workers, the rent-collector and a handful of shopkeepers and barmen, there were none of the social incentives to church-going that might still exist in his former village. The fact that the working-class lived in one area and their employers in another meant that there was no longer even the dubious motive of impressing a pious employer. The population was constantly on the move, shifting from one insanitary rented room to another, and thereby increasing the anonymity of life. His neighbours neither knew nor cared if he went to church or not; and in such circumstances, only the committed Catholic was likely to continue.

Symptomatically, defection was greatest among the generation that actually made the move; it was much less marked among the descendants of those whose faith survived it. As elsewhere, the family was the most important factor in preserving religion; and as long as children continued to live in the same neighbourhood as their parents there was a fair chance that the faith of their immigrant parents or grandparents would be preserved.

While displacement was the principal cause of defection in the growing towns, the character of most urban churches was a closely related factor. The village church, despite the hierarchical spirit which might pervade it, was a community institution, where everyone knew each other. Urban churches, however, were mostly geared to middle-class attitudes – unless they happened to be in a largely working-class area. The sermons were mostly delivered in the urbane understatements that were pleasing to middle-class congregations; and even the familiar language of the Bible, with its agricultural similies, became remote and unreal in an environment where work was anonymous and mechanical.

Another half-century was to elapse before the Church made a conscious effort to adapt the externals of the Church to the needs and understanding of the working classes. A vernacular liturgy and a visible action, with the priest facing the people, represented a belated attempt in the 1950s to come to grips with some of these problems. Even then, as an English Dominican has said:

> it does not necessarily follow that the working classes regarded a priest and a few student-acolytes, dressed as garage-hands, standing around a trestle-table, as a preferable alternative to the bright lights and unctious music of a nineteenth-century service. To a cold bedraggled slum-dweller, of the last century, liturgical solecisms, such as Perpetual Exposition of the Blessed Sacrament, with its banks of flowers and candles, and the unashamed sentiment or jollity of the organ-accompaniment, had some of the warmth and attraction of a well-

appointed bar, with its shining brass and engraved mirrors and glass work.[15]

Even so, there were many senses in which the nineteenth-century worker felt an outsider in the urban parish church. It was only under Leo XIII (1878–1903) that the Vatican started to take serious official notice of the predicament of the industrial working classes. And as long as the Church continued to regard better working-class conditions as charity rather than social justice, its appeal was always at risk from the much beefier promises of the secular champions of working-class interests. Indeed the more fashionable city-churches, with their well-washed congregations, must often have seemed like a property-owner's club which had condescended to open its doors to the less fortunate.

From a religious point of view, the basic ingredient in all these environmental changes was the lessening of family influence and the intrusion of alternative modes of behaviour. This factor was particularly acute in matters of sexual morality. For most Catholic children, the onset of adolescence was a time of crisis, for it brought them their first encounter with the Church's teaching on these issues. 'Mortal sin' was no longer a term that children could exclusively associate with the violent, alien, situations described in newspapers and sensational fiction – murder, robbery, and the like. With adolescence, the occasions of 'mortal sin' became not only relevant to their personal experience, but positively attractive. And when they were told that an unrepented 'act of self-abuse' might mean eternal damnation, a point of genuine crisis was reached in their lives.

The moment of trauma might well be the Lenten mission, preached by a visiting Redemptorist, who came and went like the wind, leaving it to the parish priest to pick up the pieces in the confessional. Or for the bourgeois adolescent in a Catholic secondary school, the avenging angel might be a visiting Jesuit, conducting the annual school retreat – James Joyce's distillation of such sermons having plenty of living counterparts in France.

A holy saint (one of our own fathers I believe it was) was once vouchsafed a vision of hell. It seemed to him that he stood in the midst of a great hall, dark and silent save for the ticking of a great clock. The ticking went on unceasingly; and it seemed to this saint that the sound of the ticking was the ceaseless repetition of the words – ever, never; ever, never. Ever to be in hell, never to be in heaven; ever to be shut off from the presence of God, never to enjoy the beatific vision; ever to be eaten with flames, gnawed by vermin, goaded with burning spikes, never to be free from these pains; ever to have the conscience upbraid one, the memory enrage, the mind filled with darkness and despair, never to escape; ever to curse and revile the foul demons who gloat fiendishly over the misery of their dupes, never to behold the shining raiment of the blessed spirits; ever to cry out of the abyss of fire to God for an instant, a single instant, of respite from such awful agony, never to receive, even for an instant, God's pardon; ever to suffer, never to enjoy; ever to be damned, never to be saved; ever, never; ever, never. O, what a dreadful punishment! An eternity of endless agony, of endless bodily and spiritual torment, without one ray of hope, without one moment of cessation, of agony limitless in intensity, of torment infinitely varied, of torture that sustains eternally that which it eternally devours, of anguish that everlastingly preys upon the spirit while it racks the flesh, an eternity, every instant of which is itself an eternity of woe. Such is the terrible punishment decreed for those who die in mortal sin by an almighty and a just God.[16]

A child belonging to a strong Catholic milieu had the best chance of surviving this period without loss of faith. Others, however, became a prey to self-torment. Too embarrassed to question a priest, they might resort to one of the many gloomy manuals of Catholic morality, where the principal of safety first generally dictated a sharp uncompromising line. Sins were sins – and were put in bold Gothic type to prove it. To add to the child's consternation, explicit sexual terms were often given in latin, thereby adding uncertainty to his alarm. The eventual outcome in a large number of cases was that he rejected what he took to be the Church's teaching as too harsh to be credible, and finally lumped it with the threats of impotence or blindness fondly attributed to free-thinking schoolmasters, desperate for some sort of sanction.

For the survivors, a parallel test of faith was the exchange of school for regular employment, with its secular atmosphere and loosening of parental influence. Even more disruptive was military service, which became quasi-universal, following the legislation of 1872 and 1889. The fact that the officers' mess generally included a sizeable number of practising Catholics had little or no impact on the ordinary soldier, whose dreary three years of drill and kit-cleaning had virtually nothing to enliven it, other that the *louche* entertainments offered by garrison towns. The exemplary church-going of a coldly remote lieutenant was no counterweight to the pneumatic charms of the girls of the local establishment.

For Catholic women, the main test of their religion came with marriage. A Catholic match brought mutual support and the need to give children an adequate example – all of which strengthened church-going habits. Family influence thereby became two-directional and self-perpetuating. 'Mixed marriages', however, posed problems. A non-practising husband, who rejected the Church's teaching on birth control, might well object to its intrusive presence in his married life; and although many priests advised Catholic wives to 'submit' to their husbands' contraceptual stratagems, 'submission' was scarcely the ideal frame of mind for the dionysian delights of a double bed. This problem was particularly acute among the French peasantry who had pressing economic reasons for limiting their families.

When the austere architects of the Code Napoléon stipulated the division of land between heirs, they unknowingly set the scene for some bizarre marital practices among the peasantry. With the passing of each generation, farms became smaller and more numerous, thereby putting the peasant under strong pressure to keep his family small, if his children's holdings were to be economically viable. Consequently the second half of the century saw a dramatic decline in the peasant birth rate – especially in regions where Church influence was weak. Clergy and patriotic Nationalists alike shook their heads as they compared this situation with the proliferation of the peasant in Germany, where the inheritance laws were less egalitarian and the influence of the churches stronger. Available evidence indicates that peasant birth control mainly took the form of conjugal Onanism – what the Dutch peasantry called 'leaving church before the singing'. The use of contraceptive appliances, on the other hand, was mainly confined to a small section of the middle and upper classes, it not being until the First World War that mass-produced sheaths became available at a working-class price. This far-reaching development was itself largely the result of armies issuing them, in order to reduce the incidence of venereal disease among their troops. The first really reliable sheath to be mass-produced for the civilian market did not appear until 1929, when an American firm produced one under the reassuring trade-name of 'The Dreadnought'.

Condemned by the Church, the use of these various methods often inhibited women from going to confession. Either they feared close questioning by an over-zealous priest; or their husbands, resentful of clerical intrusion into their married lives, discouraged them from going. Women who no longer went to confession found it difficult to go to communion – especially in small parishes where their absences were noted. And once Easter communion was missed, it became progressively likely that they would cease attending Sunday Mass altogether.

'Le style, c'est l'homme; le langage, c'est le métier.' The language of religious demography has largely reflected the preoccupations of its pioneers. These for the most part, were practising Catholics, concerned at the religious indifference of the mass of the population; and their phrases not only implied regret for any current religious decline, but largely seemed to equate it with negative factors. Faith is 'weak', people 'succumb' to scepticism; and the irritated agnostic is constantly put in mind of that most arrogant of Catholic epithets, 'a lapsed Catholic'. Even so, it would be unrealistic to assume that the decline of religion was principally the outcome of the sort of intellectual emancipation that Positivism – and other -isms – celebrated in the nineteenth century.

The middle classes have been saddled by historians with various familiar adjectives. In the first half of the nineteenth century, they were not only 'rising' (as always), but were 'Voltarian'. The term, however, suggests a degree of cerebral application which only a minority were prepared, or able, to indulge. It becomes more acceptable if it is thought of as an attitude, adopted as much through fashion as personal conviction. Undoubtedly the middle and upper classes produced the bulk of the writers whose work challenged the premisses of the Church's intellectual position. But then, as now, it was only a minority of men who were seriously preoccupied with such questions as the nature of man and his purpose, if any, in life. Under the *ancien régime,* the scepticism of the eighteenth-century rationalists had been kept from spreading as widely as it might have done by government restrictions and social convention. The Revolution, however, broke down many of these restrictions; and nineteenth-century Positivism was merely the most coherent expression of an attitude which could now advance on a broad front through Western intellectual circles.

Its main inspiration – and that of its allies – was science; and science increasingly saw Man as the product of heredity and environment, an animal no different from other aimals, except in his complexity. Steely nerved evolutionists were now portraying life in all its forms as a struggle for survival, a continual conflict in which the wastage and suffering were enormous. Moralists looked into this furnace, and were appalled at what they saw. Not only was the suffering enormous, but it seemed to serve no 'moral' purpose, other than to perpetuate a material existence which itself had no apparent *raison d'être*. Nature red in tooth and claw offered them little proof of a loving Creator; and they became increasingly scornful of traditional Christian claims that even the suffering of children and animals had its place in the economy of salvation. Poetry and fiction gave birth to a growing literature of protest against the moral outrageousness of a creation that belied the gospel virtues. Indeed, Jesus in conflict with the Creator became an overworked poetic cliché, especially in France; '*le silence de Dieu devant la misère du monde*' proved to them that God was either a monster or a void – and the void was the preferable explanation. The Christian churches gradually learnt, after a fashion, to assimilate the unpalatable evidence of science, and to ward off the attacks of moralists and men of sensibility. But it created doubts in the minds of many thinking Catholics; and the casualties on the way were great.

Secular thought responded in varying ways to the harsh vision of life that science had produced. A pessimistic stoicism characterised the attitude of many of the more sensitive creative writers. Others, however, especially those who were conscious of the great advances made in science, saw hope in human progress. Though an animal, man's intelligence and self-consciousness would enable him to advance far beyond the imagination of traditional Christianity – provided that he followed the light of reason and knowledge and ignored the irrational prohibitions and beliefs taught by the Church. This was the view of many Positivists, and was a major reason for their prominence in the anticlerical movements of the later nineteenth century.

These attacks on the intellectual foundations of Catholicism were matched by a mounting campaign to reduce clerical influence in politics. In France an acute situation had arisen in the 1870s in the early years of the Third Republic, when a largely pro-monarchist government had attempted to impose its will on a Republican Chamber of Deputies. The Church had openly sympathised with the monarchists; and when the Republicans eventually won decisive control of government in 1879, the Church paid a heavy price for its ill-judged partiality. The Republicans' prime concern was to maintain their recent hard-won victory, which meant that a large part of their energies were directed to excluding pro-monarchists from positions of influence. Taking a long-term view of the problem, the answer lay in the field of education. Many Republicans saw the prime purpose of the Republic as the formation of future generations of Frenchmen who would think rationally and would be equipped to lead society on to a higher level of material and moral well-being. At the same time it was argued that if every child was educated on true rational principles and filled with ideas of civic virtue from an early age, future generations of Frenchmen would see a democratic republic as the only form of government acceptable to an adult-minded nation. The chief obstacle to such a programme was the extensive control of education by the Church. In 1879 one-fifth of the children of France were educated in Catholic schools, over which the State had no direct control. This meant that a large percentage of the future generation was not only cut off from contact with the principles of Republican virtue but was left to the mercy of 'irrationalist' Christian concepts such as Revelation. Furthermore, since the Church was known to be largely monarchist in sympathy, it was suspected that these children would emerge as bigoted reactionaries, all straining to vote for the monarchists as soon as they were old enough. So the battle of Church and State under the Third Republic was largely one for intellectual control of the new generation.

The majority of the clergy and many of the practising laity were biased against the Republican form of government for three principal reasons. First, they objected to the secular basis of Republican thinking. Secondly, there was the anticlerical record of the first French Revolution and the anti-religious activities of the Commune of 1871. Although most thinking Catholics realised that the Commune of 1871 and the ruling Republicans of the 1880s had little in common, many thought that the activities of the Commune indicated what could break out, once a strong monarchical government was replaced by a seemingly weak Republican regime. Thirdly, and most important, many of the Republicans had included in their electoral programmes their intention to press for the disestablishment of the Church and the abolition of Catholic schools. It was therefore not surprising that the Church had broadly sympathised with schemes to restore the monarchy.

In consequence, the ruling Republicans of 1879 considered it essential to close down as many Catholic schools as was politically feasible. The new Minister of Education, the high-minded, mutton-chopped, Jules Ferry, therefore issued decrees in 1880 ordering the expulsion of various religious orders that had not obtained government permission to reside in France. Although the decrees were only half-heartedly applied, they and other measures increased the anti-Republican attitude of the Church, and partly account for the sympathy which many Catholics felt for the political intrigues of General Georges Boulanger in the late 1880s. The result was that many liberals, who had no quarrel with religion as such, found themselves involved in unedifying anticlerical conflicts. Each side tended to become more extreme in its utterances, the outcome being a political cleavage which caused much heart-searching among Catholics who found their loyalties divided. A fair number painfully learnt how to reconcile their faith with a refusal to accept the political influence of the clergy; but others found this schizophrenic existence too demanding. If they already entertained intellectual doubts about Catholicism, this was often the decisive issue that left them their Sunday mornings free.

Others decamped for reasons of professional expediency. The Republican victory of the 1870s had been a close-run thing; and, like most victories, it had its darker side. Perhaps its most unpleasant aspect was the systematic vetting of the civil service, in the interests of Republican defence. Too often the watchdogs of official orthodoxy equated a staunch Catholicism with anti-Republican sentiment; and there were many civil servants in the provinces who feared that their promotion prospects might be prejudiced if they displayed this faith too openly. Apprehension of this sort was most acute in those rural areas such as the Paris Basin and Limousin where church attendance was low, and where their presence at a sparsely attended Mass was more likely to attract attention. In these circumstances the way out for a lukewarm Catholic was both obvious and hard to resist.

In the final alalysis, however, it was amid the flaking walls and acrid stove-fumes of the class-room that politics had the greatest impact on religious observance. The triumphant Republicans of 1879 found a challenging situation – as will be seen from Table 1.

TABLE 1

The Church and Education

The French Primary-school Population in 1881–2
(boys and girls)

Children in private schools run by religious orders	764,000	(27%)
Children in private schools run by laymen	174,000	
Children in state schools staffed by religious orders	1,009,000	
Children in other state schools	3,349,000	(73%)
Total	5,296,000	

The French Male Secondary-school Population in 1876

Boys in private schools run by religious orders	46,816	(31%)
Boys in private schools run by laymen	31,249	(20%)
Boys in state schools	75,259	(49%)
Total	155,324	

(Adapted from information in A. Prost, *Histoire de l'Enseignement en France, 1800–1967* [Paris, 1968] p. 218, and Robert Anderson, 'The Conflict in Education', *Conflicts in French Society* [London, 1970] p. 59.)

Not only did the religious orders run a large number of private primary and secondary schools, but their rustling robes and soap-scented hands were a dominating presence in many state primary schools staffed by laymen, the net effect was that over a quarter of the nation's primary-school children were given a specifically Catholic education. In secondary education the proportion was much higher. Of the privileged 5 per cent of French boys who spent their adolescence in a school, instead of supplementing the family income, just over half did so in Catholic schools.

As far as the remaining school population was concerned – the three-quarters who were taught by secular state teachers – they too were reared on the catechism and New Testament, Catholic religious instruction being an integral part of their curriculum. This was intolerable to the Republican idealists of 1879. Within three years of their victory, denominational instruction was formally banished from all state primary schools (law of 25 July 1881), it now being left to parents to send their children to Monsieur le Curé on a Thursday afternoon, if they were so minded. But old routines died hard; and the fact that R.I. periods were now replaced by *instruction morale et civique* did not mean that middle-aged teachers were going to scrap overnight the formulae that had served them well for thirty years. In regions such as Brittany and the Massif Central, the catechism was taught as before, the *inspecteurs* turning a blind eye to what surrounded them.

A more dramatic gesture was the progressive exclusion of nuns and brothers from state primary schools (law of 30 October 1886). But although the number on the state payroll was cut by half in the next five years, most of them merely migrated to the private sector, displacing laymen who in many cases took their place in the state schools, bringing with them much the same denominational baggage at the bottom of their suitcases. Nevertheless now that state primary education was free (law of 16 June 1881) and obligatory (law of 28 March 1882), state schools expanded rapidly, taking in a new generation of teacher, more attuned to the secular ideals of the new reign of virtue. In their hands, *instruction morale et civique* became in many cases a forceful alternative to traditional Catholic teaching, and was arguably a significant, if overrated, factor in dechristianisation

– despite its theoretical neutrality and its nominal commitment to teaching 'the laws of God, as revealed by conscience and reason'.

Secondary education raised problems of a different order – for it was in the *lycées* that the cadres of the new France were being nurtured. To ensure their dominance, the Government dealt a damaging if short-lived, blow to the rival system of Catholic colleges, by expelling the Jesuits and a number of other unauthorised orders in 1880 (see p. 24). These measures, however, were loosely observed; and many schools continued much as before, under nominal lay auspices. Within a few years, moreover, the clergy who had taken the hard road of exile were back in augmented numbers, until they and their more fortunate colleagues controlled over two-fifths of the entire secondary school population (see pp. 83–4). Many families of unimpeachable Republican loyalty sent their children *chez les bôns pères* or *chez les bonnes soeurs*, because of the closer attention they received there. Without families or *thèses de doctorat* to occupy their thoughts, the teaching clergy generally devoted more time and concern to their pupils than the clock-watching *professeurs* of the *lycées*. Academically inferior to the better state schools, a good Catholic college had something of the ethos of an English public school, with its attention to character development and behaviour.

It was through these schools, moreover, that a growing number of the bourgeoisie were indirectly brought back to religious practice. The mid-nineteenth century had already seen a certain church-ward drift among sections of the propertied classes. This is often attributed to unease at the growing restlessness of the working classes – though the process by which this unease produced the drift has not been adequately analysed. To give opium to the masses was one thing; to smoke it oneself was another – which requires more than disillusion and nostalgia as a satisfying explanation. A more straightforward, if less important, factor was the spread of Catholic secondary education. This itself had its origins in the Falloux law of 1850, removing many of the existing government restrictions on the opening of Catholic schools. Apart from the intrinsic merits of these new Catholic colleges, the fact that the better-known were frequented by the Catholic nobility gave them a *cachet de snobisme* which many middle-class parents found irresistible (see pp. 83–4). An attraction of an opposite kind were the lower fees of many Catholic schools when compared to those of the *lycées*. A celibate clergy, vowed to poverty, was cheaper to employ than a salaried secular staff, *bons pères de famille*. Even so, there was an unexpected price to be paid, in that the non-practising parent often found himself going to Sunday Mass during the holidays, so as not to upset his adolescent children, carefully schooled in the faith he had lost. Once he became known at his local church, it was less easy for him to stop going in term-time; and in this way outward conformity soon became an established feature of his life. It was therefore not only the younger generation that the growing colleges were harvesting.

Yet the State too was making converts – and, in the long term, at a steadier rate. A major innovation of these years was the institution of state secondary education for girls (law of 21 December 1880). Given the entrenched and respected position of convent schools among the bourgeoisie, with their starched nuns and polished floors, the Government's 'godless' rival was slow to make its mark. Even so, state secondary education was arguably the main intellectual spearhead of secularism among the middle classes. With girls beginning to appear at this fountainhead of secular thinking, it is plausible that this development was a factor in the relative decline of female religious practice in the twentieth century (see pp. 7–8). Like so much in this field, however, it still remains a matter for speculation.

2 The View from Rome

The Eldest Daughter of the Church was fortunate in having an indulgent father. The fact that Leo XIII's francophilism was far from disinterested was an added advantage; mere fatherly affection might not have produced such generous favours. This former Archbishop-Bishop of Perugia, Cardinal Gioacchino Pecci, was eminently a man of common sense. A scholar, of considerable culture, he combined breadth of knowledge with a sturdy sense of what was politically possible. His errors and his blindspots were mainly rooted in an over-optimistic nature, which assumed too often that what was self-evident to him was equally apparent to others. A patrician of the Roman *campagna*, he had the limited perspectives of a man of his time, most of whose life had been spent in the genial but hierarchic atmosphere of the Papal States, where spiritual and material influence often went hand in hand. Nevertheless he succeeded in transcending many of the instincts and prejudices of a man of his milieu. And more than most of his curial colleagues, he realised that a church without understanding for the aspirations of modern society would forfeit much of its influence.[1]

His frail appearance and delicate health portended a short reign – a consideration that may have won him extra votes at the 1878 conclave. After thirty-two years of Pio Nono, a robust physique was no longer an electoral asset. Contrary to all expectation, however, this autere nobleman from Carpineto was to outlive all but one of his electors, eventually to die at the age of ninety-three, after a pontificate of twenty-five years, the second longest in papal history. His face in death had every reason to smirk, as indeed it did in life – for 'this pope with the face of Voltaire' had wanted to be pope. As *camerlengo* in the last months of Pio Nono he had unobtrusively prepared the ground for his candidature, and had allowed his friends to undermine the claims of his principal rivals. His alabaster skin, stretched over the bones, and his deep-set gleaming eyes, suggesting a man at death's door, were trump cards. Imaginative writers even claim that a major rival, Cardinal Alessandro Franchi, agreed to withdraw his candidature in Pecci's favour, on the understanding that Pecci would make him Secretary of State, with strong claims to the succession on Pecci's anticipated early death. Pecci perhaps suspected that his own undoubted gifts were not alone in winning him the election. As he was being robed to give the traditional maiden benediction to the crowd, he allegedly said to those dressing him, 'Hurry, or I shall die before you have finished'. Whatever the truth of the matter, he duly made Franchi Secretary of State. A man of the world and a connoisseur of Havana cigars, Franchi enjoyed the company of diplomats, and fulfilled his functions ably enough. Provided he offended none of his colleagues, he seemed well placed for the next conclave. But anyone who had voted mainly for Leo's cadaverous countenance might more properly have noted Franchi's florid face. Although nine years Leo's junior, apoplexy intervened and struck Franchi dead, within a few weeks of taking office – thereby giving Leo an unambiguous freedom in choosing his chief collaborator.

Leo had a very clear idea of how he wanted to govern. He abandoned many of the endearing but time-consuming customs of Pio Nono and was available only to those he wanted to see. Being the Prisoner in the Vatican had advantages for a pope who liked to work in private. Even so, there remained pilgrims and official visitors who could not be avoided; and on Mondays and Thursdays he would grudgingly change out of his tobacco-stained soutane to receive deputations of foreign visitors.

At the same time he remained a patrician, who respected material comfort, both for himself and others, and who respected the economic factors that made such comfort possible. He inherited a kingdom without land, whose income would have to come from new resources. The faithful in other countries were encouraged to be generous; and Leo liked to receive their offerings in person, even when engagements pressed on him. The Vatican household-staff were not markedly more honest than those of other Italian households, and Leo made a point of wearing a soutane with capacious pockets.

His essentially practical order of priorities could be disconcerting. One priest recalled coming to Rome with his diocesan offering of Peter's Pence, at a time when the pope was particularly busy. Leo entered the audience-chamber on a litter – born by his sturdy attendants – en route for an important engagement. Smiling benignly, he took the priest's offering with a sweep of his claw-like hand; and then, with a cheerful 'Avanti' to his litter-bearers, disappeared in the direction of his appointment – leaving the priest to take the train home.[2]

These and other moneys Leo kept in a huge cupboard in his bed-room, which no one was allowed to open and which he himself opened only when no one else was present. He likewise always remained in ear-shot when his bed was being made and the furniture dusted. It was from this cupboard that the Secretary of State was given each month whatever extra he needed to run the Universal Church – the regular revenue being kept in a safe near the archives.

Leo's own family income was partly spent in helping out a scapegrace nephew. Although Leo regularly used to explode into fits of anger when he came for money, he nearly always capitulated by obliging him once more with a timely sum. After one such gift, the nephew shamefacedly sent his wife to beg for more. An accomplished singer, she tried to shock Leo into generosity by saying that poverty would drive her on to the stage. To which Leo replied, in his nasal voice, 'I am only sorry for one thing, my dear; I shall not be able to come and listen to you'. Even so, the interview ended with the usual substantial gift.

At the same time Leo was not a man to leave fund-raising entirely to others. It was perhaps symbolic that his name and likness should be used to advertise Mariani Tonic Wine and Bovril. A Bovril poster depicted him drinking Bovril under the slogan 'Two Infallibilities – the Pope and Bovril'. He drove careful bargains. The secretary of the Archbishop of Reims once came to warn him about the intentions of the French Government; but the Pope, weary of such warnings, cut him short by showing him a box of jewels which he was anxious to place on the French market. While the unhappy abbé tried to outline the hazards ahead, Leo sat fondling the jewels with hands half-covered with woollen mittens, repeatedly murmuring '*bellissime, bellissime*' and occasionally questioning the abbé on particular Paris dealers.[3]

Like most Italian landowners, Leo also enjoyed providing for

his own table. In the first years of his pontificate, he used to net finches in the Vatican gardens. Concealed in a small wooden gazebo, he would wait at day-break until a large quantity of birds were feeding on the bait provided; and then, clapping his hands, he would cause the startled birds to fly into the nets he had suspended between the trees. He would then have the choicest roasted for lunch, which he took with his favourite red Bordeaux in the seclusion of his study, accompanied only by his caged canaries whose singing provided a constant background to his working day. The press, however, eventually got wind of these early-morning forays; and solemn critics within the Curia suggested that these Papageno-like activities were not befitting the Supreme Pontiff. So the netter of birds became exclusively a Fisher of Men, and left the provision of lunch to a professional bird-catcher.

THE CONCORDAT AND THE ROMAN QUESTION

Leo was greatly attached to the French Concordat. It is generally assumed that both Church and State gained more than they lost when France abolished it in 1905. This was not the view of most ecclesiastics at the time – nor was it the unqualified view of most anticlericals.

To anyone familiar with the history of Church–State relations in France, Napoleon's Concordat appears at first sight as something of an oddity in the late nineteenth century. The Republic's campaign to reduce church influence would seem to have implied its ultimate abolition. But here there were difficulties. The opponents of the Church were divided between two policies. Those who considered the Church a declining force insisted that the Concordat must go. They believed that the Church in France would quickly fall to pieces once it was deprived of state support – for the Concordatory regime not only subsidised the Church, but it also buttressed the Church's hierarchical structure. Others thought, however, that the Church still had much life in it. They feared the results of leaving it free to choose its personnel and organise its activities outside the close supervision of the State. For them the only solution was a tighter application of the Concordatory regime, until it held the Church in a massive bear-hug, which would cripple development and smother initiative. The hostile governments of the Third Republic had all preferred this second policy; and every government, including the most moderate, had recognised the value of having some means of keeping the Church under control.

The Church too was anxious to keep the Concordat, despite its shortcomings. Rome and the French clergy were both equally insistent on this – though for different reasons. The Vatican was mainly concerned for its international standing, while the eyes of the clergy were sharply focused on their own economic survival.

Legend has it that when Randolph Churchill visited Pius XII some thirty years ago, he began the audience by saying, 'Well, Your Holiness, I expect you know Evelyn Waugh. He's an R.C. too.' Leo XIII might have found such a remark upsetting, in that he reigned in a period of acute papal sensitivity on matters of prestige. International respect was perhaps the Vatican's major preoccupation between 1870 and 1929, when it had no territorial sovereignty in Rome. The occupation of Rome in 1870 had deprived the papacy of its last vestige of temporal power. The Temporal Power had been no obstacle to serious military atack – as Napoleon and the Italian armies had proved. Yet it had at least provided the Pope with sufficient geographical independence to enable him to rule the Universal Church, without being accused of subservience to any particular country. Since 1870, however, the Papacy was now theoretically at the mercy of the Italian Government; it felt open to claims that it had lost its moral independence. For this reason the Vatican not only refused to recognise the Italian occupation of Rome, but demonstrated its defiance by forbidding Catholics to participate in Italian national politics. Pio Nono was determined to convince the world at large that he was not under the influence of the Italian Government; otherwise other states might affect to believe that he was, and make it an excuse for ignoring him when dealing with the Church in their own territories. At the same time, lest there still be room for doubt, the papacy went out of its way to be rude to the rulers of Rome. Admittedly it never quite emulated Garibaldi, who had called Pio Nono 'a cubic metre of dung'; but by rejecting every olive branch with scornful words of protest, the Vatican hoped to show other states that it was in no way a tool of Italy. Twenty years later, when tension was slacker, the Vatican secretly assured the Quirinal that 'the Pope . . . as head of the Catholic Church has to bear in mind the opinion of Europe and America, and therefore must keep up appearances. That is why he sometimes has to speak unfavourably of Italy'[4] – a gross understatement, but a fair explanation of the position. In fairness to the Vatican it should also be added that Italy's various olive branches held not a grain of Roman soil – the only gift that would have made them acceptable.

For the same reasons the Pope rejected the financial compensations offered him by the Italian Law of Guarantees of May 1871. He likewise refused to appear outside the Vatican – thereby acquiring the inappropriate if romantic title of 'the Prisoner in the Vatican'. The situation was later well summed up in the daily patter of an itinerant guide for English tourists: 'You see that-a building? That where-a the Pawp work. He called "the Prisoner in the Vatican". He could-a come out if he want to – *but he no want to*!' The Vatican may also have hoped that the role of 'Prisoner in the Vatican' would bring the Pope some sympathy – which he certainly needed after the difficulties surrounding the proclamation of Papal Infallibility in 1870 – but, as Queen Victoria likewise discovered, people often lose interest in a figure they seldom see. It needed the insatiable Pius XII of a later age (1939–58) to make up lost ground on this score. Through his countless appearances and endless addresses, he won a place in the public affection which none of his self-immured if perhaps more deserving predecessors had ever enjoyed. And as a subject of popular legend he outdid them all. His regular injections of sheep-glands became monkey-glands in the public imagination, while the accumulated level they had supposedly reached towards the end of his life caused the amateur theologians of the satirical press to speculate on whether technically he could still be regarded as Pope. No such rumours surrounded the captive popes of earlier decades – despite the opportunities for the imagination that periodic invisibility may engender. It needed intellectuals such as André Gide and Jules Romains to celebrate in fiction the dark possibilities of the Vatican cellars, and the yet darker goings-on at Castel Gandolfo.

This negative policy of protest had a positive corollary. The

Vatican in these years was anxious to increase the respect it enjoyed internationally; for respect was the only secular power it had. Without it, there was nothing to inhibit foreign governments from sequestering their Catholic subjects from contact with Rome; nor would there be any safeguard against Italian pressure on the Pope – or, what was more dangerous, the appearance of it. One outcome of this preoccupation was an increasing attachment to the outward signs of respect. Traditional marks of deference to Rome were mentally docketed with papal preservation orders, with the result that a bizarre collection of old customs and agreements were rescued from the tide of convenience and common sense. They included, however, a number of important items, notably the various concordats and treaties made with sovereign states, many of which conferred on the Church a privileged position.

The French Concordat was a notable example. It admittedly fell short of Roman ideals, by recognising Catholicism merely as 'the religion of the great majority of French citizens' – an overconfident assertion even in 1801. France, moreover, gave parallel concessions to three other religious bodies, representing Calvinists, Lutherans and Jews. Even so, with all its shortcomings, the French Concordat was a secular monument to papal authority in Catholic matters. It signified that Napoleon had sought papal approval for his restructuring of the French Church; and it also implicitly recognised Rome as the fountainhead of episcopal authority – whatever ambiguities it might contain on the matter of choosing candidates (see pp. 48–50). Cold-eyed realists might point out that the anticlerical record of the Third Republic scarcely suggested respect for Rome; yet even at times of greatest tension the Vatican still received an outward show of formal deference from the French Government. There was still a full-blown French embassy to the Holy See, which periodically presented the Pope with the nation's respects and 'filial devotion', while in Paris the Papal Nuncio was doyen of the diplomatic corps, and led the ambassadors of the great powers on processional occasions. All of this meant much to an organisation that felt desperately insecure. If France abolished the Concordat, the embassy might also disappear. And even if the embassy stayed, the death of the Concordat might well deprive Rome of what little respect it still received from France – as well as set a dangerous example for other nations.

Of course, Rome also had more formal reasons for wishing to keep the Concordat. A close alliance between Church and State was a commonplace of Catholic teaching, enshrined in many encyclicals.

Such documents do not make compulsive reading. Popes, like celebrated wits, labour under a great difficulty: people expect something new and memorable from them. But unlike wits, their memorable novelties are also expected to be true. When not actually infallible, they should at least be demonstrably plausible; and plausibility and novelty are not an easy combination to achieve. Such chemistry needs ample room to fulfil itself. And so Rome's teaching was dispensed, not in epigrams, but in encyclicals of many pages – Ronald Knox's imaginary exemplar, *Tedium interminabile*, having plenty of historical counterparts.

Leo's encyclicals were among the better ones of recent times. Unlike Pio Nono's Syllabus (1864) or Pius X's *Gravissimo officii* (1906), they were memorable for the right reasons. The notoriety of the Syllabus needs no emphasis; but in its treatment of Church and State Pio Nono merely reiterated traditional teaching on the need for a close alliance: Church and State being divinely ordained institutions, they must work in harmony to serve God. Leo, however, chose a different ground, less remote from the political realities of the time. He took as his point of departure the individual man, whose spiritual and temporal needs were reflected in the institutional dualism of Church and State. Consequently the necessity for the 'orderly relations' of the two powers did not primarily lie in the principle that they were 'parts of the one Christian Commonwealth'.[5] It lay mainly in the fact that 'they both have power over the same men' who were themselves both Christians and citizens. 'If the two that rule man are "separated", he will be torn apart.' This in fact represented a return to primitive concepts that predated the centuries of powerful papal influence in the high Middle Ages. It was a belated recognition of the fact that the nature of the Church's political influence had changed. The Papacy was no longer in a position to deprive rulers of the allegiance of their subjects; it had been a risky enterprise at the best of times. The Church's influence now rested on the earthy fact that Catholics formed part of the electorate within each country. If secular governments rode roughshod over the Church, a price might have to be paid at election time.

As far as France was concerned, Leo also made appeal to the fond supposition that its people were overwhelmingly Catholic; in such a situation, the Separation of Church and State was unthinkable. More realistically he pointed out that any Separation in France would be a harsh one – given current government attitudes. The Church could not expect the cosy benevolent neutrality practised in certain Separatist countries where 'the legislator, by a happy inconsequence, is guided by Christian principles'.[6] In any case 'one must not conclude that America exemplifies the best kind of existence for the Church'.[7]

Even so, Leo was sufficiently pragmatic to admit the dark possibility that the Concordat might be used as 'a chain to shackle the freedom of the Church'.[8] But he insisted that he alone was competent to decide what should be done if this happened. It was not for the rank and file to call the Concordat in question. In any case Leo's optimism envisaged a sea-change in French policies. Ministries were as short-lived as May flies in France; and although parliamentary attitudes took longer to change, Leo hoped that more moderate attitudes might gradually prevail – as for a time they did.

It was partly to encourage such a change that Leo publicly advised French Catholics to proclaim their allegiance to the Republican regime. Officially launched in an encyclical of February 1892,[9] the papal policy of a *ralliement* to the regime was the work of several years, and had its roots in two very different sets of factors. On the one hand the collapse of Boulangism in 1889 had confirmed Leo's sturdy conviction that the current republic was there to stay – and that until the bulk of French Catholics accepted the fact, the Church could not expect better treatment from the Government. Such a view was already widespread among percipient Catholics – and among disillusioned monarchists, many of whom were looking for an occasion to join forces with conservative Republicans against left-wing demands for social reform.[10] But fears of splitting the Catholic opposition in parliament had inhibited positive moves. The papal lead was therefore welcomed by many as a respectable reason for dropping old loyalties which were progressively felt as an embarrassment. Even so there were a large number of Catholics who resented the Pope's advice; and of those who followed it, many did so merely to stand on firmer ground in their fight against Republican ideals – as will be shown in Chapter 4.

The second set of factors behind the Ralliement sprung from the Pope's own difficulties in Rome. Like Leo III eleven hundred years earlier, Leo XIII looked to France to rescue Rome from the hands of Italian usurpers. Quite how France was expected to do this was an open question – even in Leo's mind. And France was not his first choice for the role of Charlemagne. In 1888 he specifically compared Wilhelm II of Germany to Charlemagne;[11] – the comparison was lost on no one who was intimately acquainted with Leo's diplomacy during the previous months.

Count Soderini, who knew Leo well, claimed that 'there were times when he believed in the possibility of almost total restitution of the temporal domain, and others when he hoped to recover only a small portion'.[12] His predecessor, Pio Nono, had been more modest. Speaking to the French ambassador in 1871, he had said 'All I ask is a little corner of land where I should be master. If I was offered the return of the Papal States, I should refuse, but as long as I am without this little corner of land, I cannot exercise my spiritual functions in their plenitude'.[13]

The Law of Guarantees of 13 May 1871 offered the Pope sovereignty of his person but only *extraterritoriality* for those of his former possessions left to him – the palaces of the Vatican and the Lateran, and the summer residence of Castel Gandolfo. Since the Law was a purely internal measure with no international or even national guarantee against repeal, it left the Pope's status at the mercy of the changing majorities of the Italian parliament. As Leo XIII wrote in 1895, 'It is not a real independence, but only an apparent and transitory one, for it is subject to the will of others. Those who conferred it yesterday can cancel it tomorrow'.[14]

Whatever the merits and shortcomings of the Law, the Vatican refused to accept it, both Pio Nono and Leo remaining firm in the attitude that they were the victims of an unlawful usurpation. The Vatican further maintained that any ruler of a Catholic country who accepted the hospitality of the King of Italy at the Quirinal was *ipso facto* condoning the usurpation and gravely insulting the Pope. Heads of Catholic countries could not therefore visit the King of Italy in Rome without offending the Vatican, and either had to avoid an invitation altogether or arrange to be entertained by the King in a locality other than Rome. In 1875, for instance, the meeting of the Emperor Francis Joseph of Austria with Victor Emmanual II had to take place in Venice.

A diplomat by instinct, Leo XIII was undoubtedly more preoccupied with the Roman Question than Pio Nono – despite the fact that it was Pio who was Pope in 1870. To a large extent, his protests were a calculated policy, designed to convince other nations that the Pope was morally independent of Italian influence (see pp. 33–4). But, in Leo's case, the Roman Question also acquired something of an obsessive quality. He issued no less than sixty-two formal protests against the Italian usurpation; and when he spoke of it, his animation became positively frightening. In July 1899, at the age of eighty-nine, he startled the French ambassador by shouting out, 'For twenty-two years I have been a prisoner!' And as the ambassador afterwards reported, 'It is hard to convey the animation with which Leo XIII expressed himself. The fire of his eyes burnt with a brilliance, which was only enhanced by the tears which he could not restrain.'[15]

Although the Roman Question for Leo was primarily a matter of the Church's moral independence, one must not discount the personal effect of so long a self-imposed captivity, however congenial the prison. Years of pacing the same pathways, watching the lizards rippling past, had reprived him of all direct contact with the outside world, except the Rome that was visible from the higher parts of the Vatican. The fitful clamour of trams and the plash of distant fountains were a constant reminder of the Rome that was lost, while the world beyond lived only in newspapers, despatches and the eyes of visitors. It was scarcely surprising that the Roman Question had an emotional content for Leo that was personal as well as stemming from what he saw as the needs of the Church.

Nor was it surprising that the City of Rome – not something less – was his main objective. In October 1888 he told Herbert Bismarck that the Italian Government ought to pack its bags and return to Florence, 'this Athens of Italy' – while 'Rome must be reserved for the papacy'.[16] Bishop Bonomelli of Cremona on the other hand thought that the Pope should strive for 'a miniature state' on the right bank of the Tiber, linked to the sea by a narrow strip of territory – a proposal that Leo symptomatically put on the Index.[17] Bonomelli's fault, however, was not so much the suggestion, but its propagation in print. The Papacy in fact was to settle for something similar to Bonomelli's proposal in 1929 – minus the maritime corridor – but in the meantime Leo wished his claims to remain intact.

An important development at this time was the appointment of Cardinal Rampolla as Secretary of State. A Sicilian – with a Leonine smirk like his master's, but delivered from a fuller less humorous mouth – Rampolla was a relentless worker. Rising at five and retiring at midnight, his day always included an hour on his knees meditating. While sharing a close identity of political views with Leo, he seems to have been less personally obsessed with the Roman Question, and to have been less subject to the feverish waves of optimism and desperation that drove Leo into unburdening himself to whichever foreign power seemed better placed to help him at the time. Thirty-three years younger than Leo and a foreigner to the Papal States, it was understandable that he should take a more detached view of the Roman Question. Like Leo, however, he recognised the need to prove to the world the Pope's moral independence of Italy; and the Roman Question was therefore always in the forefront of his policies. The similarities and differences between their attitudes is well suggested by Rampolla's remarks to the French *chargé d'affaires* in November 1887. 'In our view, it is the principle that is of greatest importance. The restitution itself is a secondary matter. If we ask for everything, we shall be given nothing; if we ask for little, it will result in our being given still less. We shall therefore formulate nothing precise, except in the matter of principle. Afterwards we shall see. The Roman Question is a real issue, however, and the Pope will never abandon it'[18]

It was in fact Rampolla who largely encouraged Leo to look to France. The Pope had hitherto pinned his hopes on Germany. When Wilhelm II visited Rome in October 1888, Leo proposed to the Kaiser that he should break off his alliance with Italy and create a new grand alliance of other nations, which should include the Pope. Considering that Wilhelm had made the long journey to Rome specifically to strengthen his ties with the Quirinal, the Pope's suggestion was nothing if not daring. Indeed the Kaiser had some difficulty getting a word in at all, as Leo held forth on his need to recover Rome. It was only when Leo paused for breath that Wilhelm had a chance to point out the impossibility of depriving Italy of her present capital. The interview ended as Rampolla feared it would, with the Pope feeling humiliated and the Kaiser astonished and ruffled.[19]

This debacle disposed Leo to listen more attentively to Rampolla's counter-proposals, involving France. Their main attraction lay in the fact that France and Italy were locked in a bitter tariff war. France had deeply resented Italy's entry into the Triple Alliance with Germany and Austria in 1882; and although Franco–Italian Trade had been a profitable affair, there was no longer the goodwill to exploit it. It therefore seemed to Rampolla that France was much more likely than Germany to sympathise with a scheme to strengthen the Pope at Italy's expense. Unlike Germany, she apparently had little to lose – and, in Rampolla's view, much to gain. If the Pope encouraged French Catholics to accept the Republic, France would be cured of an endemic problem – a rich reward for helping the Pope against Italy.

Rampolla had already pushed out feelers and dropped vague hints in the previous year. After puzzling the French *chargé d'affaires* with 'protestations of friendship which . . . seem to me too energetic to be disinterested', he at last came somewhere near the point: 'The Roman Question . . . is a question that interests the whole universe, and particularly France. . . . The Roman Question, there is the strength of France! . . . At the moment nothing can be done, but things change with time. Whatever happens, the Roman Question – believe me – is a great strength for France – against Italy.'[20] Leaving Monbel to ponder these intriguing words, Rampolla came back to the subject a year later, a few days after the Kaiser had shattered Leo's German hopes. 'An entente is necessary between France and the Holy See. We have a common enemy [i.e., Italy], and we must co-operate to fight him.'[21]

Rampolla's main hope was the growth of republicanism in

Italy. If the House of Savoy was replaced by a republic, the Pope would once more become the main focus of popular loyalty in Rome. The crowds who cheered a cockaded monarch would not turn out for a dreary group of frock-coated politicians, who represented high taxation, conscription and all the other evils that Unification had brought from the north. Even as things were, King Umberto complained that 'The Pope . . . is far more popular with Italians and foreigners than I am. They come to see him, not me. It is he who still rules in Rome; I have only the edge of the chair to sit on.'[22] How much truer this would be of an Italian republic. And once the Pope was re-established as the main focus of Roman loyalty, Italy would find it much more difficult to resist French demands that this situation be given a *de jure* basis.

This sanguine assessment obviously depended on two conditions – the fall of the monarchy and French willingness to help. 'The day when [Crispi] falls, the monarchy will fall with him', Rampolla told the attentive Monbel.[23] The Quai d'Orsay was not so sure; and even if Rampolla was right, a transfer of ownership in Rome was not necessarily in French interests. Italy was not her principal enemy; and a day might come when Franco–Italian economic interests might detach Italy from the Triple Alliance. Try as he would, Rampolla could elicit nothing from France but a sphynx-like smile.

Both Leo and Rampolla, however, were anxious to force the pace and prove to France that a papal alliance was worth having. Rather than wait for positive signs of a *quid pro quo* they launched the Ralliement in the hope that a conservative alliance between Catholics and moderate Republicans would produce a government that was readier to help. Such rewards as came in the short run were largely confined to France. 1894 found the French Minister of Cultes talking of '*un esprit nouveau*' in Church–State relations; but it was mainly reflected in domestic politics and government dealings with the French clergy. Gratifying though these improvements were, they were only indirectly relevant to Leo's Roman problems; and Leo was not disposed to wait indefinitely until the perfect government came to power. Business would have to be done with the men of the day.

Leo could scarcely reproach himself for want of trying. When

Paul Cambon was passing through Rome in November 1892, Leo treated him to a resplendent vision of what a Franco-Papal alliance might do. As Cambon reported to the Quai d'Orsay, 'The Pope, with a warmth of expression and an ardour of imagination, extraordinary in an old man of eighty-three, traced . . . the prodigious results that would arise from an alliance between the Pope and democratic France . . .'. With eyes flashing, he transfixed Cambon with a Mabuse-like exclamation, 'Together we would dominate the world'.[24]

Not only were these advances unrequited, but they increasingly exasperated those French Catholics who regarded Leo's conciliatory policies as a one-sided capitulation. The *loi d'abonnement* was a case in point. In 1895 the French Government reorganised the property-tax on the religious orders in France – and episcopal sympathy was in favour of resistance. But, as the Archbishop of Reims discovered (and his secretary noted), 'Vatican opinion in in favour of submission, and the matter of the religious orders is not taken seriously – or rather, it is made a secondary issue. The Pope clings to his ideal of the temporal power. He counted on Germany. Disappointed, he has turned to France. He does not wish to lose this last support; and, whatever is may cost, he does not wish to break with the French goverment; France will perish in this game if it continues.'[25]

As long as Italy remained an integral member of the Triple Alliance, it was hard to see what Leo could seriously expect. In his interview with Cambon in 1892, he had dismissed Italy's partners as having no political future; Austria was 'only an agglomeration of various races . . . destined to disintegrate', while Germany was the destined 'victim of socialism'. But even these predictions could offer little hope of compensation in the short run. The Franco-Russian alliance of 1894 undoubtedly strengthened France's diplomatic position in Europe; but no French government would challenge the Triple Alliance – or Italy on her own, for that matter – merely to oblige the Pope. Now that the Ralliement was launched, and had a life of its own, Leo had few tangible rewards at his disposal.

In so far as Leo's hopes had any specific shape left to them, they probably lay in Italy's low rating in the Triple Alliance. If she progressively became a Cinderella, for whom her partners were not prepared to act, she might succumb to a feeling of isolation. Spurned abroad, and with her domestic politics boycotted by committed Catholics, she might be readier to listen to papal demands.

Her diplomatic setbacks were always a matter of interest to the Vatican; and it was with particular curiosity that Leo awaited the outcome of Italy's humiliating defeat at Adowa in March 1896, at the hands of the Ethiopians. This traumatic experience was the nemesis of Italy's unhappy imperial activities in eastern Africa – and the blame was universally put on the serving premier, the ebullient Francesco Crispi. In order to raise his prestige in the country, this bustling Sicilian had tried to build up a head of steam by lighting a fire under popular jingoism. It was this that had led him to propel Italy along the barren track of African imperialism. At best he only had part of public opinion with him; and when the essential ingredient, success, was ineptly lost at Adowa, the drum-beaters were among the first to turn on him and secure his resignation.

Rampolla had already predicted that the monarchy would fall with Crispi (see p. 42); and other Vatican officials were prepared to go much further in their optimism. The future Cardinal Agliardi even envisaged Italy breaking up into three or four republics, loosely linked in a federation – with the Pope perhaps receiving part of Rome.[26] Although Agliardi was a trusted confidant of Leo, the Pope's own expectations are not clear. He shared with King Menelek of Ethiopia the same emblem of the Conquering Lion of Judah; and one of his favourite possessions was a sleek Ethiopian lion which Menelek had sent him in tribute to this fact. As he daily surveyed his garden menagerie, Leo may well have wondered whether this distant dusty victory in the scrubland of Adowa would bring the release that others hopefully predicted.

The prophets were routed by events. Not only did the House of Savoy survive the fall of Crispi; but Italy began to find a new friend in France. The Franco-Italian tariff war of the last ten years had been disastrous to Italy, costing her a fifth of her potential exports – since France had been her best customer. Common sense and material self-interest eventually triumphed over Italian national pride, and profitable relations were ultimately established once more with a Franco-Italian trade treaty of 21 November 1898.

This was a crushing blow to Leo. As Rampolla told the Archbishop of Reims, 'The pope has been very upset by the trade treaty signed with Italy. This *rapprochement* is a disturbing setback for the pope. The more Italy feels herself supported, the more critical is the position of the Holy See. Conversely, it is when Italy is hard pressed that she finds it most difficult to avoid the Roman Question.'[27] So desperate was Leo that he sent Agliardi to find out if France contemplated a political alliance with Italy. A former prophet of Italy's demise, Agliardi told the French ambassador to the Quirinal that 'a political alliance with [the Vatican's] worst enemy would put a very severe strain on papal fidelity to France'.[28] The ambassador made soothing noises, but Agliardi was far from satisfied.

From the papal point of view, the rapprochement could not have come at a worse time. Its gestation had coincided with Rampolla's efforts to get a seat at the Hague Conference – his aim being to raise the Roman Question on an international level.[29] Only a few weeks before the trade treaty, Rampolla had tentatively asked the French *chargé d'affaires* if France would sponsor papal membership;[30] and now it was clearly an impossibility. Italy would not have it at any price; and France was not disposed to annoy her. In any case, France had no desire to lumber the conference with an issue that she regarded as an irrelevant anachronism.

Leo's menagerie can have inspired little optimism in his last years, as his attendants carried him round the confines of his little quasi-kingdom. He was fond of the elegant gazelles that had been a gift of Cardinal Lavigerie, who had paved the way for the Ralliement in France. But like Menelek's lion, they too were now a reminder of disappointed hopes. To a Firbankian pontiff, consolation was rather to be found in his solitary kangaroo, whose hopping presence was perhaps a happy reminder of Archbishop Moran of Sydney, whom Leo had made a cardinal, the first red hat from down-under. And when his spirits were at their lowest ebb, there was always the troop of goats from his home town of Carpineto, whose milk provided his morning coffee, a source of solace on the worst of days.

Even so, Leo was never one to despair. Although the Dreyfus crisis and its aftermath had dispersed the warm aroma of the *esprit nouveau* in France, there remained traces of hope in his thoughts. This was apparent even as late as March 1902, when admittedly his ninety-two years must have weighed heavily on the lucidity of his perception. Speaking to a group of French bishops, he said:

> There are voices which tell me that it is France who will deliver me. What are these voices? Voices of history or voices from heaven . . . I firmly believe in them. The Holy See is not free. The Vicar of Jesus Christ cannot fulfil his mission without being independent. France will give the Pope freedom. How? I have no idea. By arms or diplomacy? I do not know. But I rely only on her. And then *these gentlemen* of the Quirinal will realise that it does not do to be the enemy of France! [31]

3 The Concordatory Regime

'Before Abraham was, I am.' To many Catholics, Leo seemed too old to die. A boy of five when Napoleon was defeated at Waterloo, Leo was only nine years younger than the Concordat. And as long as the preadamite Pope was firmly wedded to the Concordat, few French churchmen dared say that the treaty should go.

But it was not mere sentiment or respect that silenced clerical demands for Separation. While some churchmen personally held Separatist views, the vast majority could see no realistic alternative to the status quo. For them its advantages were mainly economic. The removal of state finance would probably mean a major cut in their evangelical work, and as dedicated priests they were determined to resist this as long as possible.

The 1890s were the last period of normality in the Concordat's working life. It was an average, middle-aged marriage of convenience – too much a matter of routine for either partner to waste energy in making accusations of indifference or frigidity. Bread-and-butter relationships are not the stuff of high romance; and Concordatory matters in the nineties make rather prosaic reading – mercifully so, for those concerned. Government policy had a reassuring air of circumspect moderation for much of the period; and it was only in 1899 that the Church came under direct attack. Even then, it was the religious orders who bore the brunt of government animosity; and the Concordat – which concerned only the secular clergy – was not itself at issue. Matters changed in 1902, however, with Combes's accession to office. The Concordat then entered its period of crisis, and its functioning was no longer typical of what it had to offer – either to Church or State.

Before this, however, its life was fairly uneventful.[1]

The appointment of bishops was inevitably the most sensitive issue. Although the Concordat allowed the Government to nominate bishops, Pius VII had warned Napoleon that he would refuse to accept unworthy men.[2] After the Restoration, the Government usually informed the nuncio in advance of the names of the candidates it had in mind, so as to avoid formal dispute. This gradually developed into an informal discussion with the nuncio on their suitability – the *entente préalable* as it was later called.[3] But the Government still insisted on its right to maintain its choice of candidate, unless the Vatican could show that the man was deficient in the qualities canonically required of a bishop. In practice, the French Direction des Cultes maintained a list of suitable candidates which it based on the various recommendations that it had received from civil servants, members of parliament, and certain of the more Republican bishops.[4] When a diocese fell vacant, the Government would submit to the nuncio a name drawn from the list. The nuncio would give the Government his opinion on the suitability of the candidate, and, if it were favourable, he would then forward the name to Rome. If Rome accepted, the nuncio would inform the Government; and the Government would then send letters patent to Rome, officially making the nomination. These letters patent introduced the formal stage of the process. The Government would then decree the appointment, and the Vatican would send the bull of investiture shortly after.

Between 1 January 1891 and the advent of Combes on 7 June 1902, the appointment of bishops created few prolonged difficulties. In this period forty-eight bishoprics became vacant through decease or retirement. At the risk of giving a tedious catalogue, it is worth noting that the succession to twenty-two of these was settled with the nuncio within three months of the vacancy; a further nine were settled within six months; seven within nine months; five within a year; and only one remained vacant for longer.[5] In addition to these, a further eighteen bishoprics became vacant through the translation of their bishops to other sees. For all except four, the Government and the nuncio had already reached agreement on the succession before the occupant had departed.[6] Of nineteen vacancies among the archbishoprics, five were settled within three months, six within six months, five within nine months, and only one remained vacant for longer.[7] The difficulties were confined to three episodes, only one of which was really serious.

This occurred during Combes's memorable début at the Ministry of Cultes, when Léon Bourgeois's Radical Government briefly held the stage (1 November 1895–23 April 1896). Although only a curtain raiser to his later three-year run, Combes lost no time in showing his mettle. A small-town Radical, whose roots lay in the Second Empire, he was already sixty when he took office; and he knew precisely what he wanted to do for France before death or the whims of parliament deprived him of the chance. His background and beliefs are discussed in later chapters (see pp. 91–4); but he was essentially a man who had witnessed the dangers of clericalism under the Second Empire and 'the Republic of Dukes', and was determined to prevent them re-emerging. An unhappy false start as a seminarist (see p. 92) also added a certain bitterness to this crusade, and gave his anticlericalism a markedly obsessive character. His brief winter in office found him conducting a massive inquiry into the clientele of Catholic private education. His private papers contain information on officers and public servants sending their children to Catholic schools; and it is clear that the policies of his later ministry were already present in embryo in his activities of 1895–6. Both his expulsion of the orders and the system of delation in the army (see pp. 138–9) owed something to this initial inquiry.[8]

As far as the Concordat was concerned, he saw it as a useful means of controlling the secular clergy, provided that the State insisted on its rights, especially in the choice of bishops. A key issue arose over the vacant Archbishopric of Toulouse. Combes's candidate, Mgr Fonteneau, was already Archbishop of Albi; and Combes claimed that Rome could not object to a candidate who had already held archiepiscopal rank. The nuncio suspected, however, that Fonteneau wanted Toulouse as an indirect means to paying his family's debts, and refused him.[9] As always in such cases, Rome was at a disadvantage, in that clerical loyalty prevented a frank statement of these suspicions. Combes for his part insisted that lateral transfers were entirely within the competence of the Government, since the candidate had already been accepted by the Vatican as worthy of an archbishopric.[10] This was an issue of principle that was to re-occur after Combes became premier in 1902. The Vatican and the Government were agreed that the only reason that the Vatican could have for opposing a government candidate was canonical unsuitability. The argument centred on the meaning of this phrase. For Combes it could only mean that the man was unfit for the rank. For the Vatican it meant that he was not suited to this particular see, whatever his general qualities might be. In Rome's view the relationship of a bishop to his diocese was that of husband to wife; and so the question of canonical suitability had to take into account the temperament of the bride as well as that of the eager groom.[11] An effervescent liberal with a social conscience might cause trouble in a conservative Breton diocese, while an industrial city with a *banlieu rouge* might not take a *grand seigneur* to its grimy bosom. The Government admitted these considerations, but regarded them as non-canonical, lying within the discretion of the Government, not Rome. As in his later ministry, Combes refused to fill other vacancies, until the issue was settled; and it was only the extinction of the Bourgeois cabinet in April that broke the deadlock. The new Méline government lived for the quiet life; and Fonteneau was left to sort out the family fortunes as best he could, amid the frustrating splendour of his official residence at Albi – later to be the home of the Toulouse-Lautrec museum.

It says something for the working of the Concordat that the French bishops were no worse than they were. The very condition of Church–State relations in France hardly suggested an episcopate that was subservient to the Government. The classified lists at the Direction des Cultes indicate that in 1896 only nineteen of the eighty-six listed bishops and archbishops could be regarded as '*satisfaisants*' from the Government's point of view. Twenty-nine others came into the doubtful category of '*habile*' ('crafty'), and the remaining thirty-eight were '*violents*' (including one '*dangereux*', Cardinal Langénieux of Reims). The situation was little better in the Government's eye in 1899, when the list for that year described twenty-two as '*satisfaisants*', twenty-six as '*douteux*', and the remaining thirty-one as '*mauvais*'. Moreover, the conduct of some had lowered their positions in their respective categories. Cardinal Lecot of Bordeaux who hitherto '*se gâte*' ('is deteriorating') now '*se gâte tout à fait*', and Cardinal Coullié of Lyons, at one time no worse than '*habile*', now suffered the double condemnation of being *'mauvais et malade'*.[12] As Aristide Briand once remarked, the Government in its choice of bishops was like a hen with duck eggs. As each hatched, 'she saw, with a surprised and saddened eye, the chick instinctively throw itself into the nearest pond. The wheedling candidate, once so full of promises, is no sooner a bishop than he flings his mitre over the Organic Articles', and becomes an intransigent like the rest.[13]

This was not the view of the royalist Mgr Maurice d'Hulst. According to him, the Government was 'poisoning the episcopate . . . Respect for the bishops is withering in the hearts of both priests and laity.' To be a bishop it was now sufficient to 'shout out loud, "*Vive la République. Vive Léon XIII*, the presiding genius of the new age!" '[14] His fellow royalist, Bishop Freppel of Angers, had earlier complained of 'the doses of chloroform which are being inflicted on the French episcopate'.[15] But the examples they chose of bad appointments were often liberals of considerable personal distinction. There is little doubt that a number of able bishops of liberal views would never have reached the episcopate if it had not been for the insistence of the Government. Although certain appointments were undoubtedly unfortunate, the Direction's list of likely candidates contained many men of considerable worth. The Abbé Louis Birot, the Abbé J.-B. Soulange-Bodin, and the Dreyfusard Abbé Joseph Brugerette were notable examples.[16] When the Vatican obtained control over episcopal appointments after the Separation, their chances of becoming bishops grew correspondingly less. The Abbé Birot was a case in point. His hopes were slender enough in the Rome of Pius X; but within a few months of the Separation they were systematically shadowed by the Assumptionists – with the help of a royalist bishop, the future Cardinal de Cabrières.[17]

The Government also had a say in the appointment of *curés*, though its rights were merely those of approbation, not nomination. This was usually a matter for the local prefect and one of the lesser lights in the Direction des Cultes. Ministerial intervention was rare, though sometimes necessary, as in 1891 with the Bishop of Séez. The minister complained that his latest nominations were 'hostile to Republican institutions', to which the bishop replied: 'If I knew any of my priests so wretched that he approved of Republican institutions, . . . I would put him under interdict.'[18] Most issues, however, were settled at a humbler level, and helped to while away the otiose summer afternoons in cathedral towns. They permitted many an exchange of letters between prefecture and palace, as each comfortably faced the other across the dusty squares of box-cut chestnut-trees and chirping sparrows.

The Concordat obliged the Government to provide the clergy with 'a suitable salary'. But 'suitable' is a subjective term; and, as will be seen from Table 2, the salary of most priests was similar to that of a probationary primary-school teacher (900 francs) – which was admittedly better than a textile-worker's wage (750 francs), but much below the income of a doctor (at

TABLE 2

State salaries under the Concordat in the 1890s[19]
(excluding Algeria)

	Number	*Annual Salary*
Archbishops	17	15,000 fr
Bishops	67	10,000 fr
Archdiocesan Vicars-General	17	3,500 fr
Archdiocesan Vicars-General / Diocesan Vicars-General	168	2,500 fr
Canons	variable	1,500 fr minimum
Curés	c. 3,450	
1st class	(c. ¼ of total)	1,500 fr minimum
2nd class	(c. ¾ of total)	1,200 fr minimum
Desservants (parish priests not recognised as *curés* within the meaning of the Organic Articles)	c. 31,000	900 fr minimum
Vicaires (curates)	c. 6,930	450 fr minimum

(It was open to parish councils – the *fabriques* – to supplement these incomes from their own resources; but such additions averaged only *c.* 100 fr even in a relatively *bien pensant* diocese such as Angers.)

least 5,000 francs). The priest was also entitled to Mass stipends and a percentage of the fees and offerings he received as a dispenser of sacraments and officiant at ceremonies. On the average, a parish priest probably received about 300 francs annually from these sources, though in a poor parish it would be very much less.[20] About sixty francs of his income went in taxation, and he probably gave his housekeeper 250 francs, plus board and lodging.[21] Often a desiccated and sour-faced woman, this 'sacristy spider' prepared his meals, stitched his ageing clothes and answered the door. Her other duties were to decorate the altar with flowers, occasionally change the greenish water in the vases, and cuff the front row of children at Sunday Mass into some sort of attentiveness. Like her master, she generally led a rather lonely and unpopular existence.

The state establishment, however, was not enough to meet the demands of parochial work. On top of the 42,000 state-paid priests, the Church had to employ another 15,000 out of its own resources. The state budget provided for only seven *vicaires* in Paris – but the requirements of this growing city obliged the Church to employ over five hundred, none of whom got anything from the Government. Nor was there any state provision for the staff of seminaries and *instituts catholiques*.[22]

Despite the inadequacy of these salaries, the clergy's main complaint was the practice of suspending salaries as a disciplinary measure. Most Catholic lawyers argued that the 'suitable salary' in Article 14 of the Concordat was an indemnity for the church property confiscated at the Revolution. For them it was in fact a *quid pro quo* for the Pope's agreement in Article 13 not to molest people who had bought this property. There was some historical argument for this. Three days before the signature of the Concordat, the Government's negotiator, the Abbé Bernier, had described this article as 'the natural compensation of the one before it'.[23] Appealing to this and other material, Catholic lawyers denied the Government's right to withhold any part of the indemnity, however small.[24] The Government for its part replied that the Concordat and subsequent documents clearly spoke of a salary and not an indemnity. As such, it could be suspended whenever the Government found the clergy abusing its authority.[25] In effect it was the only safeguard of discipline that the Government had, since the clergy could not be suspended from their duties without the consent of Rome.[26]

Between 1881 and 1892, 1217 salaries were suspended for periods of varying length, the commonest serious charge being interference in elections.[27] The elections of 1889 alone saw 181 salaries suspended,[28] while the municipal elections of 1892 resulted in six bishops being similarly punished for their pastoral letters on the electoral duties of Catholics.[29] The susceptibility of the Government in this matter was understandable if sometimes oversensitive. The Direction des Cultes paid very close attention to the wording of catechisms, laboriously querying statements such as *'Pontius Pilate était opportuniste'*.[30] Even so, in the eleven years before the Combes ministry, there were only sixteen cases of bishops losing their salaries – and most of these were old offenders, the average 'sentence' being a year on short commons and the charity of his flock.[31]

Some clergy, like Mgr d'Hulst, felt that the Church would fare better under a system of Separation where state salaries would be commuted for a lump sum in *rentes*.[32] This would certainly remove salary suspension from the State's armoury of sundry retribution; but it was expecting far too much of a French government in the 1890s to imagine that it would give the Church its freedom and a golden handshake. D'Hulst knew too well that the only alternative to the Concordat was poverty with whatever honour they could earn. Priests would have to live together in groups and travel out to the remoter parishes as best they could. He believed that living in community would bring them advantages which had hitherto belonged to the regular clergy; and this in turn might have a regenerating effect on parish life in general.[33] Cardinal Manning had recommended much the same idea to the Abbé Jules Lemire in 1888, for Manning, like d'Hulst, thought that the Church had a lot to gain from Separation.[34]

The Organic Articles, which supplemented the Concordat, had been a perennial source of embarrassment throughout the nineteenth century. The Church's attitude towards them was that of a wife to her husband's nocturnal caprices: she refused to sanction them, but was forced to live with them. They had never been accepted by the Vatican, yet continued with the Concordat as part of the package law of 18 germinal X. Several of them were entirely incompatible with the claims of the Vatican, and this was just as apparent in the 1890s as it had been in 1802. Yet the Concordatory regime had survived, in spite of them, and by the 1890s a lot had been learnt in the art of tactful oversight.

The Vatican had made its attitude perfectly clear from the start. In 1802 the Papal Legate told Talleyrand – then Foreign Minister – that since the Pope had had no part in their formulation, they could not hope to have his approval.[35] Two years later, he pointed out that several of the Articles 'cannot be reconciled with the principles and maxims of the Church'.[36] And nothing had changed by the 1890s – as the nuncio made abundantly clear.[37] The Government, for its part, realised that the articles would have to be applied fairly flexibly. As early as 1804 the wily Talleyrand, rich in the clerical experience of his double life, had sought to mollify Rome by saying that the articles were merely 'the method of implementing' the Concordat, and as such 'the method is open to change and improvement, according to circumstances'.[38] And so it was. Although the text of the Articles was to remain largely unaltered,[39] the way successive governments applied them genuinely reflected the ex-bishop's assurance.[40]

Despite variation from ministry to ministry, this application displayed a certain overall consistency of principle. To a large extent, this was due to Charles Dumay, who was Directeur (then Directeur-Général) des Cultes from 1887 to 1906. A man of 'robust corpulence' (to quote *Le Figaro*), his physical size was matched by what an aspiring subordinate called 'a mental and moral grandeur, springing from the unity of his vision of Church-State relations'. He had the keen eye of the demarcation expert, and possessed to a remarkable degree that peculiarly French *fonctionnaire's* confidence in the ability of existing regulations to solve all problems. The archives of the Direction des Cultes are full of clippings from the provincial 'bonne press', proudly reporting the movements of the local bishop – and acidly annotated by Dumay in terms of the number of Organic Articles the bishop was breaking. It came as no surprise to those who knew him that Dumay should survive the Organic Articles by only a few months. He was to oppose the Separation throughout its progress, and his sudden decline in health was not unconnected with the failure of his hopes. Yet only a fraction of the transgressions he noted led to retribution.

The Articles that raised most passion in the celibate breast were those that muffled the Church's voice. Papal statements on anything but 'interior faith' needed government authorisation before they could circulate in France (Article 1).[41] The Church ignored the Article as far as it dared, while the government contented itself with the odd desultory sally, to show the flag. A much more serious matter was the ban on unauthorised 'deliberative assembles' (Article 4). A crippling blow to co-operative thought and action, it was less regretted by Rome than by the French clergy. The Vatican still feared the ghost of Gallicanism, and disliked seeing bishops in droves. Fortunately for Rome's paternalism, the Government came down hard on any conference that might strengthen French church unity. By contrast, the Government generally turned a blind eye on meetings that did not correspond to the administrative divisions of the Church – unless they brought together a significant number of its key personnel. It would even tolerate semi-national gatherings such as the Bourges congress of *abbés démocrates* in 1900, provided that no administrative division of the Church was represented as such *en bloc*.[42] Despite the fact that few of these large congresses applied for authorisation, no warning would be sent to the organisers beforehand, and no action would be taken against them afterwards. All that happened was that the Prefect would send a confidential report to the Government – as he did with much smaller meetings. Even such bodies as the Meurthe-et-Moselle branch of the Chevaliers Cyclistes de *Le Croix* were entitled to assiduous coverage by the prefecture's informants – long before *La Croix* was classified as subversive.[43] And even when *La Croix* flirted with subversion in 1899, few thought of its Cycling Knights as a particularly sinister body, as they swept through the countryside of a Sunday afternoon, taking in fresh air and letting out wholesome *bien pensant* expletives.

The Government took a tough line on meetings that corresponded to the official divisions of the Church. Whenever it knew that a bishop contemplated marshalling his clergy for anything other than a retreat or ceremony, a warning note was sent. In fact most bishops preferred their own opinions to those of their clergy; but the Government's attitude had the unfortunate effect of encouraging them to trust implicitly in their own superior wisdom.

Inevitably, the Government's greatest concern was for meetings involving several bishops – as the bishops themselves well knew. When the Bishop of Soissons wrote to his colleagues in the Reims province, suggesting a meeting, he was coldly rebuffed by Fuzet of Beauvais. Speaking from the lofty eminence of his sixty years, Fuzet told the fledgling bishop, 'You are young, Monseigneur' – he was fifty-eight – 'You are ignorant of history. One does not do that sort of thing.' Despite his good sense and salutary influence, Fuzet was nothing if not ambitious; and success under the Concordat required a good relationship with the Direction des Cultes. To acquire this, Fuzet was not above shopping his colleagues; and he accordingly sent the bishop's proposal to Dumay, together with a copy of his own exemplary reply. The double loyalty of a Concordatory bishop was not an easy ideal; and it was not uncommon for the more Republican bishops to succumb occasionally to shabby temptations of this sort.[44]

A recurring feature of what the French bishops were to regard as their '*mémoires d'outre-Combes*' was the ease with which the breach of one Article entailed the breach of another. Infractions of Article 4 often involved infractions of Article 20, requiring bishops to remain within their dioceses. The Government did not usually bother to apply the Article to temporary absences within France, unless it knew that an illicit meeting of bishops was taking place. But it was more strict regarding visits abroad; and bishops were expected to ask permission for these. In effect, permission was always granted for the periodic visits to the palms and pines of Rome (*ad limina apostolorum*) which all bishops were canonically obliged to make. And when permission was sought to go elsewhere – for health reasons or a foreign conference – it was rarely refused. Nor were the sanctions crippling. The worst that happened was deprivation of salary, equivalent to the period of absence.[45]

In the case of *curés*, the Direction was supposed to be notified of any absence of thirty days or more;[46] but in practice days away too often passed quickly and uncounted.[47]

Although these restrictions made good grumbling material for the waiting-room of the Direction des Cultes, their effect was trivial compared with the steely grip which others had on the Church's growth. The Organic Articles had limited the Church's diocesan structure to a set number of specified sees, which subsequent governments had increased to sixty-seven dioceses and seventeen archdioceses – all predating the Third Republic.

At the beginning of the nineteenth century, transport could move no faster than a galloping horse – and bishops did not gallop. It was therefore inevitable that the criterion which decided the size of a diocese was distance rather than population. No matter how thinly populated a region might be, a bishop could not remain in contact with his clergy if he lived more than a day's journey from them, and in consequence the dioceses in the mountainous areas of France were extremely small. This factor of distance had an even greater influence on the size of parishes. The priest had to be able to reach even the most remote farmhouse in his parish with reasonable speed. A parishioner might meet with an accident and need his ministry quickly. The result was that in a diocese or parish where communications were bad, the proportion of clergy to people tended to be relatively high, whereas in a region where communications were good, the proportion tended to be low. In many cases this inequality was increased by the relatively high number of priestly vocations in the small *bien pensant* dioceses of the uplands. In the nineteenth century, dioceses continued to be self-contained, with ordinands living out their mortal span in the diocese which had seen them pass through the adolescent perils of the *petit séminaire* to the spartan learning of the *grand séminaire*. It was rare for a bishop to admit to being overstocked; and, even if he did, ties of family and friendship made most priests reluctant to become emigrants to the mission fields of urban dioceses.

Initial inequalities grew much worse during the second half of the century, when the population of certain of the principal towns grew enormously and industrial development brought about the creation of others. The population of many rural parishes, on the other hand, either remained relatively unchanged or actually decreased. Between 1871 and 1898, the population of France, excluding Algeria, increased from 36,200,000 to 38,700,000. Yet the population of six dioceses remained unchanged and that of forty-five decreased. Of the thirty-three dioceses that saw an increase. Paris grew by over 1,300,000, Cambrai by over 400,000 and Lyon by over 200,000.[48]

The ability of the Church to respond to these changes was tightly cramped within the strait-jacket of the Organic Articles. Not even a *succursale* could be created without government approval, let alone a *cure*.[49] The governments of the Third Republic were always parsimonious, when not actually hostile, and this prevented the reorganisation that was needed to meet the new situation. The Government was quick to withdraw its financial support from parishes that were clearly redundant; but it was extremely reluctant to finance new parishes, however pressing the demand.[50] In the arid diocese of Fréjus, for instance, the population had fallen from 402,445 in 1871 to 309,191 in 1898, despite the growth of its coastal resorts. Accordingly, its 36 *curés*, 202 *desservants* and 96 state-paid *vicaires* were reduced to 28, 142 and 67 respectively. In the heavily industrial diocese of Cambrai, however, with its mines and textiles, the population had increased from 1,392,041 to 1,811,868, yet only twenty *vicariats* were promoted to *succursales*, while twenty-nine others ceased to appear on the budget list altogether. The number of *cures* remained unaltered. In France as a whole, excluding Algeria, the number of *cures* and *succursales* during this period increased from 3407 to 3452, and 30,671 to 31,002; but the number of state-paid *vicariats* fell from 8934 to 6932. So although the population had increased by two and a half million, the number of state-paid clergy had dropped by 1626.

Paris remained the most striking example. In 1802 the population of the diocese was said to be 630,000, for which there were 116 parishes, of which little more than thirty were *cures* – the rest being *succursales*, mostly financed by the Church. The average size of a parish was therefore 5431 people. However, to shed light behind the leprous façades and sunless alleyways of pre-Haussmanite Paris, the Church provided these harassed parishes with an additional force of 259 *vicaires*, none of whom was state-paid.[51] There therefore existed one priest for 1682 people. As industry and commerce drew weary heards of plodding workmen to the capital, and filled the chilly spiralling staircases with their families, the population rose to 3,340,514 by 1898. But the number of *cures* was only thirty-nine, and the *succursales* 104, thereby making the average size of parish 23,360 – a fourfold increase. In France as a whole the average size was a mere 1133. Even with the help of 519 *vicaires* – of whom only seven were state-paid – Paris now had only one priest to 5046 people.[52] Apart from the occasional gaggle of seminarists, the *soutane* was a rare sight in the crowded streets.

Very different was the situation in the country's smallest diocese, Tarentaise, surrounded by the 12,000-foot peaks of Savoy. The inhabitants of its misty limestone valleys numbered only 68,000 in 1898, and yet the State supported eighty-six parishes, averaging only 791 inhabitants each. There were in addition twenty-five *vicaires*, of whom all but three were paid by the State, thereby giving the diocese one priest to 612 people. An even more striking example was the diocese of Bayeux. The coastal fringe of this benign region, edged with broad sands, was heavily populated in summer, when Cabourg, Deauville and Trouville drew their *jeunes filles en fleurs* from Paris. But its winter population was only 417,176. And yet, as perhaps befitted this former see of the battling Bishop Odo, it boasted a remarkable regiment of priests. With a liberality that the Norman dukes would have deplored, the Republic supported seventy-three *curés* no less than 640 *desservants*, and 120 of the 147 *vicaires*. The average size of a parish was therefore only 585, while there was a priest to 486 people.

It is clear that a large part of the problem was not so much the lack of priests, but their wasteful distribution. Now that the clergy could make use of bicycles, they could have been withdrawn from a large number of the smaller parishes without seriously reducing the religious amenities of the area. A few bishops still refused to let their priests bump about on bicycles, but the sight of clerical ankles no longer caused alarm. A number of dealers were already providently advertising strong lady's models at reduced prices for wearers of the *soutane*.[53] Clearly a priest with a bicycle could have easily served three of the tiny parishes that had in fact a priest each, whose duties were few. The men made available might then have been moved to the growing towns. Unfortunately the Concordatory regime scarcely encouraged such enterprise. Unless the Government uncharacteristically agreed to the creation of a new post, a priest who was moved in this way would have received no salary nor lodging allowance in his new situation. Furthermore, the income and presbytery he had enjoyed in his former parish would have been lost to the Church on his leaving there. When each move meant a severe material loss, the Church was hardly tempted to be adventurous.

The effect of all this on religious observance was clearly considerable. In the absence of comparative statistics, it has to remain a matter for guesswork; and the interplay of factors that produced this decline has already been considered in the first chapter. But as far as the urban proletariat is concerned, it has often been pointed out that this class was not dechristianised – it was born and reared outside the Church. Shortage of priests in the growing industrial communities was clearly one of the many reasons why the Church failed in its mission to the urban workers – though of more fundamental importance was the failure of the Church to realise in time the enormity of the new social problem. Religious demography, as practised today, did not exist.[54] Few ecclesiastics realised just how far the new urban populations were removed from religious influence of any kind. Not only was the Church more or less encouraged by the Concordatory regime to distribute its men wastefully, but the Church was largely unaware of how wasteful this distribution was.

This was shown after the Separation, when the Church was extremely slow to make use of its new-found freedom.[55] It is true that the possibilities revealed by modern transport and the telephone were not immediately apparent. It was likewise understandable that bishops should dislike withdrawing men from parishes that had always had a resident priest. Many thought that the wobbling priest on two wheels was a poor substitute for the resident who knew his people intimately and all their personal problems. This was certainly the view of Pius X who actively discouraged a reorganisation of the existing system (see p. 161). Yet perhaps more than anything else, this very slowness to adapt the Church to new requirements shows the stultifying effect of the Concordatory regime on the imagination and initiative of French churchmen. After four centuries of being part of a state-supervised organisation, they did not find it easy to think for themselves – and Rome scarcely encouraged them to do so. The separation burdened them with many urgent tasks, and it was understandable that they should feel, however mistakenly, that there were more pressing problems than the recasting of the administrative structure. In any case, to most of them, this structure had seemed almost immutable. At the same time any inclination that they might have had to think for themselves was to be gravely handicapped by Pius X's refusal to allow them to have regular episcopal assemblies. Though Gallicanism was long since dead in France, its ghost – as noted earlier – was still haunting the Vatican. Nevertheless the need for this reconstruction existed, and the Organic Articles had played a large part in preventing it.

In sum, however, there was very little in the application of the regime that suggested that it could not, or would not, continue for many years to come. The exchanges over episcopal appointments were perhaps an indication that what had been a source of occasional difficulty could become a threat to the regime under a hostile government. But this particular tourney-field was well trodden, and few doubted that what had always been eventually worked out in the past would not be likewise settled in the future, after the traditional posturing. The real danger of the Concordatory regime was the discouragement of any Catholic initiative outside the traditional pattern. This had never been sufficiently realised by churchmen in the past, and was scarcely better understood in the 1890s. And of those who came nearest to understanding it in the 1890s, few actually concluded that the regime was not worth keeping.

4 The Dreyfus Affair – Before and After

The chain of circumstance that brought about the Separation was less direct than most historians suggest. The decisive events took place during the ministry of Combes; and, despite his own personal hostility to Separation, his conduct of affairs was a major factor. Yet pressure came from many sides – from the Socialists for whom Separation was the threshold to social reform, from anticlericals who wanted it for its own sake, and from Combes's enemies among the Gauche Radicale and the Union Démocratique who thought that it would prove Combes's undoing. Diverse thought these factors were, the Dreyfus Affair was a common denominator in the genesis of many of them.

Basically the Affair added nothing new to French politics – it merely revealed with disturbing clarity the division that still existed between those on one hand who accepted Republican hopes for a humanity emancipated from 'irrational' beliefs and prejudices, and those on the other hand who felt that Republican policies ran counter to all that was great and good in the French tradition. Without the Affair, however, it is arguable that a tolerable *modus vivendi* between these two sides might have been established well before the First World War. The Pope's public advice to French Catholics to accept the Republican regime (1892) was a gesture that had been gladly received by many disillusioned monarchists. It enabled them to seek an alliance with conservative Republicans against the demands of Radicals and Socialists for a graduated income tax and old-age pensions.[1]

The election of some fifty Socialists to the Chamber of Deputies in 1893 promised an influx of new parliamentary issues, with a predominantly economic and social slant; and union between conservatives seemed doubly desirable, if the existing social order was to be adequately defended. It seemed to many politicians that there was now an alternative to the traditional parliamentary system of *concentration républicaine*. As long as the regime had been threatened by monarchists and right-wing revisionists, a general policy of 'no enemies to the left' had obscured the important differences that existed between the economically conservative Opportunists and the Radicals, especially their Radical-Socialist wing. But the arrival of a substantial contingent of Socialists in parliament introduced a new Republican element with whom no Opportunist was prepared as yet to be friends. Now that the republican form of government no longer divided the Opportunists and the Ralliés, the way seemed open for their co-operation on economic and social issues. The old formula of *concentration républicaine* no longer seemed relevant; and while it would always be misleading to talk about a 'two party' system in the context of French politics, the Ralliement made a broad 'two grouping' system a possibility – of the type that was to emerge, after a fashion, in the inter-war period.

The main obstacle to union on the Right were the so-called *lois intangibles* – the corpus of secularising laws of the 1880s. Most Catholic deputies hoped that these would ultimately be rescinded, once the Church and the Republic had learnt peaceful coexistence. The more realistic among them realised that this would be a long and difficult process, which could only be jeopardised by a premature insistence on Catholic demands. Others, however, believed that if Catholics did not insist on a rapid *quid pro quo* for this support, the Ralliement would be a mere dupery, a unilateral act of disarmament with all the advantages going to the Government.

THE RALLIEMENT ASKEW – THE 1898 ELECTORAL CAMPAIGN

This conflict of strategies came to a head in the general elections of 1898. Leo XIII was anxious to see Catholics present a united front, which would both convince the moderate Republicans of the value of the Catholic vote and encourage them to prefer the Ralliés to the anticlerical left-wing of the old Opportunist grouping. The powder needed would be a judicious mixture of strength and moderation: not an easy combination to achieve. It is always simpler to rally enthusiasm around the banner of militant indignation, rather than a vague conciliatory principle of wait-and-see. The Catholics lacked an obvious leader. There was no French Windthorst; and in any case the bellicose talents of a Windthorst would have been inappropriate to the task. Leo encouraged Catholics to follow the lead of Étienne Lamy, whose prime recommendation was his indisputable republicanism, which long predated the Ralliement. While this would facilitate an alliance with the Opportunists, it left uncertain the obedience of the more *exalté* elements of French Catholicism, who had accepted the Republic as a bitter pill prescribed by the Pope, not something that was attractive in itself. Nor was Lamy's hesitant self-questioning personality of a kind to win over men who did not share his republican commitment. Nevertheless the Catholic *avant-tout*, having swallowed the Republic, were prepared to swallow Lamy – as long as the Pope told them to.

After considerable difficulty, a Catholic electoral federation was eventually formed, in which it was agreed that the constituent elements would retain their separate identities, but would follow a common electoral strategy (April 1897). The main problem for Lamy was that the most effective instrument of propaganda at the federation's disposal was *La Croix*, which was the centre-piece of the Assumptionist press empire.

The Assumptionists have been described as 'the last of the papal Zouaves'.[2] Their mentality belonged to the period of the Syllabus and the last years of the Temporal Power. In 1871 their founder, Emmanuel d'Alzon attributed the problems of the time to the spirit of the Revolution. 'The struggle is between the Church and the Revolution, and, if you want to go deeper, it is between God and Man who wants to make himself God.'[3] The three men who were most responsible for Assumptionist policies in the 1890s were already active priests in the 1860s. Vincent de Paul Bailly, who edited *La Croix* from its inception to 1900, had been a chaplain in the papal Zouaves during the crucial years 1867 to 1869. As a French chaplain in the Franco-Prussian War, he had followed the beleaguered army of Metz into captivity; and, on his release, he had returned to Paris at the most violent period of the Commune.

François Picard, Superior-General of the order from 1880 to

his death in 1903, had likewise witnessed the Commune and its suppression; and the two men were convinced that France could only be saved by national penitence. The recognition of God must be brought back into French public life; and in the meantime the faithful must atone for the nation's sins by prayer and expiation. The pilgrimages they personally led to the Holy Land and elsewhere were strenuous affairs, on which illness and death were not infrequent. And the order of priorities they represented was never in doubt. When a young girl died on one of these excursions, and was buried at sea, Vincent Bailly wrote of 'the excellent effect' it produced on the other pilgrims.[4]

The *lois laiques* of the 1880s intensified their crusading spirit. *La Croix* regarded the dechristianisation of France as essentially the work of the political and intellectual enemies of the Church – the Freemasons, Protestants and Jews. It was dimly aware that a connection existed between dechristianisation and economic change – even to the point of urging a Chester–Bellocian solution to France's difficulties. If the proletariat were given little plots of land, and the factories closed down and split up into small workshops, 'the social question would be solved'.[5] But the prominence of Jews and Protestants in high finance enabled even this theme to be absorbed in *La Croix*'s general onslaught on the foreign bodies in Catholic France. They were much easier and more satisfying to pillory than the impersonal forces of economic change – as the dictators were to discover in the depression of the 1930s.

La Croix likewise understood 'acts of God' in a deeper sense than the insurance companies. Natural disasters were the retribution of sin, just as narrow escapes were the reward of prayer. A 'flu epidemic in the winter of 1889–90 was attributed to the fall in religious observance;[6] and Vincent Bailly firmly believed that 'in the 1870–71 war . . . no place which offered up public prayers was occupied'.[7]

In politics, the overriding concerns of *La Croix* were religious. Vincent Bailly's personal predilections were Bonapartist and plebiscitary; but these betrayed themselves only very indirectly in *La Croix*. The Ralliement posed few problems for it on the institutional level. The outward form of government mattered little to the Assumptionists; and a clear papal directive appealed to their military sense of obedience. What *La Croix* found more difficult to accept were the men who represented the Republic; and it was here that its loyalty to papal policy suffered most strain. The ruling Opportunists were heirs to the twin-headed beast of the Assumptionist apocalypse – the French and Industrial Revolutions. With their big business connections, the Opportunists were riddled with Jews, Protestants and Freemasons; and the Assumptionists found them uncongenial partners for any political understanding – unless they were prepared to make substantial concessions to the Church.

By 1896 the national edition of *La Croix* had a daily sale of 180,000, with the Assumptionist illustrated weekly, *Le Pèlerin*, averaging 110,000. *La Croix* also had over a hundred local weekly editions, which probably brought the total readership of the Assumptionist press to somewhere near half a million.[8] No other Catholic publication came anywhere near this. Although *L'Univers* was the paper that reflected papal policy most faithfully in the 1890s, its circulation was less than 20,000.

The pen was not the only sword wielded by *La Croix*. In January 1896 it founded an electoral committee, the Comité Justice-Egalité, with a view to opposing 'Jews, Masons and Socialists' in elections at all levels. A network of local committees was quickly established all over France; and it rapidly became clear that Justice–Egalité was the only organisation with enough teeth to give bite to Lamy's campaign.

It would be hard to imagine two men more different than Lamy and Vincent Bailly. The Assumptionists were constantly to be complaining of Lamy's lack of drive – and rightly so. Conversely Lamy maintained – with equal truth – that the Assumptionists never really entered into the spirit of the exercise. In fairness to them, however, it must be admitted that the spirit of the exercise was not always clear – an uncertainty which resulted from the Pope's desire to offend nobody. The protocol of a papal audience tends to inhibit straight talking; and the role of the benevolent father which every Pope has to play may soften or obscure the criticism or reproof he is trying to administer. In such cases, it is usually up to the Secretary of State to put things bluntly.

In the case of the Assumptionists, however, the matter was complicated by their suspicion of Rampolla, whom they rightly regarded as unsympathetic to their attitudes, but whom they wishfully suspected of overstating the liberal intentions of the Pope. At the same time, however, they were never afraid to assume that the Pope might be misinformed. As early as 1893 Picard had taken it upon himself to warn the Pope against the Opportunists. 'They are Freemasons; they will betray you and they will betray us. Méline in particular will let us down – even with a majority. If we do not fight them, we will be handing over our troops to the enemy; and we shan't be able to do a thing.'[9] Since Méline was the premier with whom Lamy hoped to do business, a unified Catholic policy was clearly going to be difficult.

The only concession that *La Croix* was prepared to make was to spare Méline personal attack. But his ministers did not enjoy this immunity; and there were repetitious allusions to the *lois intangibles* which Lamy found embarrassing and obstructive. The situation became so difficult that the Pope warned the Assumptionists that if they did not follow Lamy's lead the campaign would end in disaster.

Faced with Leo's displeasure, Picard's first reaction was to consider dissolving Justice–Egalité altogether. This was the last thing that the Vatican wanted – since the Assumptionist machinery was virtually all that the campaign had. Without it Lamy would be powerless. The result was a series of reassuring messages from Rome, which rapidly restored the Assumptionists' self-confidence and put back the old familiar bounce into *La Croix*'s editorials. The situation was made more difficult by Lamy's patent lack of dynamism. If anything was to be done in time for 1898, it would have to be entrusted to the Assumptionists, since the other groups in the projected federation were too small and impoverished to do much on their own. In desperation, Rampolla entrusted Picard with the task of visiting the French bishops in the latter part of 1897, to explain the Pope's electoral policy. Inevitably, the confirment of the mission was accompanied by protestations of Vatican confidence in *La Croix*, which only served to strengthen the Assumptionists' conviction that they, rather than Lamy, were the true exponents of papal policy.

Lamy was understandably upset by Picard's mission; and it was later to be an important factor in his decision to resign. Nevertheless Rampolla continued to impress on him that he was still the designated leader, with the full confidence of Rome – causing Picard to remark bitterly, 'No one can penetrate the hidden thoughts of Cardinal R[ampolla]. He wines and dines God and the Devil at the same time, and pleases no one.'[10]

To make matters worse, the antisemitic rioting that took place in Algeria and elsewhere in January 1898 convinced Picard and the Bailly brothers that the time was ripe for a Catholic offensive.

Vincent Bailly's younger brother, Emmanuel Bailly, was the order's Procurator-General in Rome. Writing to Vincent, he excitedly told him that 'in France you will find the Dreyfusist ferment pushed to an intolerable level and a deep and widespread feeling against the Jews. What a splendid moment for Catholics, if they were ready and organised to take their place in the sun once more.'[11] What was the point of soft pedalling their demands for Catholic rights. As Picard told Emmanuel Bailly, 'In my opinion the time has come to put Catholic interests in the forefront'.[12]

This was not the view of the Vatican. 'We ask only one thing,' Rampolla said, 'and that is that the Opportunists do not refer to the *lois laiques* as inviolable.'[13] Even this posed problems. Although Lamy and Méline had agreed on some sort of mutual strategy, it was an alliance that encountered many difficulties at grass-roots level. Ralliés deputies found it hard to convince their constituents that times had changed, and that it was no longer appropriate to make Catholic grievances the mainstay of the electoral programme. It was also hard to explain to Catholics in marginal constituencies that it was better to vote for an Opportunist who would get in, rather than a Catholic who might not. Local editions of *La Croix* and their electoral committees often made matters more difficult by claiming that only those Opportunists who favoured a change in the *lois laiques* were eligible for Catholic support. They likewise proposed candidates who in some cases were opponents of the regime. Méline too had his difficulties. Several of his cabinet colleagues still insisted on talking publicly about the inviolability of the *lois laiques*, while some of the prefects and sub-prefects were still instinctively reluctant to support a Catholic candidate against a Radical.

Given these circumstances, it was not surprising that the

newly elected Chamber offered little improvement on the old.[14] What was more serious was the mutual sense of disenchantment. There was renewed Catholic talk of co-operation as a duperie, while a growing number of Opportunists looked back nostalgically to the old days of Republican concentration. On 14 June the new Chamber voted in favour of traditional concentration – 295 to 246 – and Méline, the quintessence of 'the new spirit' overproof, resigned. His successor, Henri Brisson (28 June–1 November 1898) was a Radical, with a largely Radical cabinet; and it seemed that the whole of Lamy's undertaking had collapsed.

THE AFFAIR

If the Dreyfus Affair added nothing fundamentally new to French politics, it highlighted differences at a difficult moment of gestation. Although the future undoubtedly lay with a 'two-grouping' alignment of Parliament, it was too young and sensitive a creature to thrive on traumas of this magnitude. Too many politicians saw the Affair as an opportunity to recreate the old Republican concentration of former years. The Radicals and Socialists had done what they could to inflate the clerical spectre in the 1898 elections; and the vote of the new Chamber in favour of concentration was a short-term victory for their hopes. It was an anachronistic victory, however; and it was the tragedy of the Socialists and Left Wing of the Radical-Socialists to imagine that concentration would eventually produce the reforms that they wanted. Although the 'two-grouping' system revealed their numerical weaknesses, it did at least allow reforms to be debated – as the *procès-verbaux* for the 1890s amply illustrate.

It is tempting to conclude that the 'two-grouping' system was doomed well before the Dreyfus Affair asserted its influence. Yet the system was unquestionably in the logic of the changing preoccupations of parliament; and time was on its side. The Ralliement was only a few years old, and it would have been miraculous if there had not been major setbacks in its early stages. As it turned out, the Brisson ministry was less radical in its intentions than the Léon Bourgeois cabinet three years earlier;

and the increasing strength in parliament of left-wing demands for social reform would almost certainly have re-established the 'two-grouping' pattern fairly rapidly. Even admitting the fact that 'the new spirit' had already engendered its own anticlerical backlash, there is no reason to suppose that it would not have been quickly counterbalanced by the increasing preoccupation with social and economic questions. Concentration on an anti-clerical basis, however, merely created an illusory unity on a limited political front, and postponed debate on the reforms that most interested the Left – as the next seven years were to show. Whenever reforms came up, concentration temporarily gave way to a 'two-grouping' pattern, and the Left was no better off than before. All that concentration did was to assure the government of the temporary support of the Left at little or no expense to the Government. The Left had to live on hope.

It is easy, however, to be wise after the event; and it was understandable that Jaurés and his friends should see the Affair as a chance for the party to come in out of the cold. Nor was their desire to get near the fire without a strong streak of idealism. They genuinely believed that the generous Republican *élan*, engendered by the Affair, would gather a momentum that would carry it into the sphere of social reform.[15]

It was the suicide of Henry that made the Affair a crisis. Until 'the gallant colonel' cut his throat, most Frenchmen assumed that Dreyfus was guilty. It was a time when criminals were still guillotined in public, and onlookers dipped their handkerchiefs in the victim's blood to keep or sell as souvenirs, as they were still to do some forty years later. It was therefore a matter of no particular concern that an officer, convicted of selling military secrets to Germany, should be sent to Devil's Island for life.[16] Great interest and excitement had certainly been engendered by Zola's celebrated accusation that the army had sacrificed individual justice to its own public image;[17] but excitement was not the same as believing that Zola's claims were true. Henry's death, however, cast doubts on the integrity of the army's proceedings – though Henry's crime by no means proved that Dreyfus was innocent.. All that Henry had irrefutably done was to try to 'strengthen' the case against Dreyfus by adding a forged item to the dosier. In the eyes of many, he was guilty of no more than mistaken zeal. Nevertheless it looked bad; and it undoubtedly tarnished the image of a virtuous army defending its honour against a Jewish traitor, supported by 'the Judeo-Masonic sect' – an image which *La Croix* had sedulously polished from the outset.

The Assumptionists feared above all that 'the messy business of Mont Valérien' would check the mounting wave of antisemitic feeling that *La Croix* had been encouraging throughout the year – and which they hoped would prove a political springboard for the Catholic *avant tout*. Since the fall of Méline, *La Croix* had lost its surviving elements of caution. It was among the loudest in claiming that the Republic was falling deeper into the hands of Jews and Freemasons. Only *La Libre Parole* surpassed its obsessive concern with 'the Jewish invasion'. As early as 1892 the Assumptionist press had praised the Tsar for his 'energetic' policy against the Jews, and had urged other countries to close their frontiers to Jewish refugees.[18] Although *La Croix* never specifically commended physical violence against Jews, it portrayed the antisemitic riots of 1898 as the understandable reaction of an exasperated people.

La Croix dismissed Henry's forgery as a foolish act of zeal which changed nothing.[19] A retrial of Dreyfus would mean war with Germany, Vincent Bailly claimed; but anything was possible, now that 'France had fallen into this dreadful sewer', with the Jews everywhere triumphant, and Brisson and his foreign friends in power.[20] A fund, opened by *La Libre Parole* for Henry's widow, obtained subscriptions from some 300 secular priests and thirty regulars – but nothing from the senior clergy. A few subscribers enclosed antisemitic mottoes with their gifts – the Abbé Cros remarking that he would like 'a bedside rug, made of Yid-skin, that I could trample first thing in the morning and last thing at night' [21] – but pastoral sentiments of this order were uncommon.

When the Government reopened the case, *La Croix* lumped its various enemies together as a single target, the Government being clearly allied with the Judeo-Masonic sect. Fear that public opinion would swing in favour of Dreyfus drove the anti-Dreyfusards to feverish activity – now that the army's credit was in question. The jingo poet, Paul Déroulède, had already reformed his Nationalist Ligue des Patriotes (25 September); and

Jules Lemaître's Ligue de la Patrie Française, of right-wing intellectuals, was shortly to make its appearance (31 December).

The climax came with the death of the President of the Republic, Félix Faure, on 16 February 1899. The circumstances of his death have remained obscure, but speculation on them has given so much pleasure to successive generations of Frenchmen that one wonders whether the ubiquity of avenues and impasses bearing his name is not intended as an early-morning pick-me-up for the depressed or lonely. The diplomat Maurice Paléologue noted in his diary:

> I have just learnt the details from Casimir-Périer, who had them from his old butler, Joseph, who has remained in contact with the servants at the Elysée. . . . The President [was found] unconscious, in a fit, in the most significant state of undress, and near him, entirely naked, Mme Steinheil, screaming, hysterical and frantic . . . the President was clutching her hair in his clenched fist . . . Dr. Lannelongue and Dr. Potain . . . diagnosed cerebral haemorrhage.[22]

With devastating if unconscious precision, at least one newspaper made the traditional lament: *'Ainsi est mort un grand président dans la pleine exercice des ses fonctions.'*

Whatever the truth of the matter, his death removed a President who had been opposed to the retrial of Dreyfus, and who had been sympathetically viewed by the Right, including the Assumptionists. His successor, Émile Loubet, was chiefly remembered for his attempts to damp down the emotions caused by the Panama scandal seven years earlier. Such a man could expect a rough ride from the Right, and he got one. In an article entitled 'The Loubet disaster', *La Croix* exultantly reported the jeers and catcalls that had greeted the newly elected President as he drove through the streets – and contrasted them with the ovations for Déroulède, the gallant leader of French patriotism.[23]

Four days later the Déroulède '*coup*' exploded; *coup d'état* or mere *coup de théâtre*, it is hard to know with certainty. Déroulède always maintained that it was an intended *coup d'état* – and it is not easily explained in other terms. It is tempting to dismiss his account as an attempt to give dramatic seriousness to a ludicrous episode; but the preparations and the appeal to the army become pointless, unless the broad outline of the story is accepted. There is also too much confirmation from other sources for it to have been a purely cerebral piece of *quichotisme*.

It gains in plausibility when seen in the context of shifting public sympathies. The Dreyfusards were making converts, and the Nationalists were desperate. There was also the factor of Faure's death. A sympathetic President had disappeared: and the new President was not only uncongenial to the Right, but the boos and whistles in the street showed him unpopular with the general public – or so the Nationalists liked to claim, while ignoring the subsidised nature of these demonstrations. Faure's funeral would bring troops and people into the streets together – in what Déroulède naïvely imagined would be an emotionally charged situation. A vilified army would be paying public homage to a President who had put his trust in their integrity. They had endured months of slander from the Dreyfusards; they had then seen the government feebly capitulate to the demands for a retrial. Surely this was the moment to appeal to the army. How could they refuse the anguished appeals of true patriots to rid them of '*le régime infame*'?

As Déroulède later told Barrès, 'The only way of salvation is a revolution of the people and the army, jointly led by a civilian and a soldier, both loyally determined to keep the Republic.'[24]

If the civil leader was initially to be Déroulède, who was to be the soldier? It would appear that Déroulède had in mind the embittered General de Pellieux, a man who had trusted Henry and had all but resigned from the army on the news of Henry's forgery.[25] Pellieux would be leading part of the funeral cortege on 23 February – and it was Déroulède's plan to confront him near the Place de la Nation and urge him to lead his troops to the Elysée.

Accounts vary on Déroulède's ultimate intentions.[26] Once the coup was established, Déroulède would call a constituent assembly to frame a new constitution, and then step down in favour of a democratically appointed government. His electoral programme of 1898 had favoured a president elected by universal suffrage; and all his sympathies were for a plebiscitary regime. He apparently hoped that Pellieux would consent to be Minister for War, with Cavaignac as Minister of the Interior. Whether Cavaignac was aware of these plans is far from clear, and the reaction of a Pellieux himself has been variously reported. Some say that Pellieux disliked the elective character of Déroulède's proposals, and disapproved of the army being involved in a political coup. Others suggest that he was prepared to offer benevolent neutrality; but in no case would he accept a ministry. A third version attributes him with initial interest but subsequent cold feet.

Déroulède was not a person who easily took 'no' for an answer. And his obstinacy was matched by his courage, as even his bitterest opponents were the first to concede. With a distinguished record in the Franco-Prussian War, not only had he later outfaced the duelling pistols of marksmen like Clemenceau, but more recently he had forced his way into a violently hostile hall of Dreyfusards to harangue them on their lack of patriotism. That he escaped uninjured was something of a miracle. Pellieux, knowing the man he was dealing with, decided to keep clear of trouble. On the day of the funeral he arranged for his contingent to leave the main column before it reached the Place de la Nation. The result was that when Déroulède rushed into the middle of the street to exhort the troops to march on the Elysée, the bridle he seized was not that of the expected General de Pellieux, but General Roget, who, utterly mystified, assumed that Déroulède was an unbalanced spectator, overexcited by the martial scene. Indeed it was only with considerable difficulty that Déroulède got himself taken sufficiently seriously to be arrested.

The Nationalists, however, were not alone in hoping to profit from Déroulède's *bravura*. Supporters of the Duke of Orleans had unsuccessfully tried to persuade Déroulède to subordinate his coup to a royalist restoration. Despite his contemptuous refusal, they hung around like jackals throughout the day, hoping that some hitch or loss of nerve would drive Déroulède into buying their support. After hours of fruitless waiting in the streets around the Elysée, they eventually went home; and the Duke's chief agent, André Buffet, told his master to unpack.

Grotesque though these events were, they were a challenge to the regime; and the leaders were eventually exiled or imprisoned – albeit for modest periods. Sterner sentences might well have been imposed, had these men controlled a more effective network of propaganda, capable of influencing a wider section of public opinion.

Yet it was just an instrument that the Assumptionists possessed. Having built up a readership of half a million, whatever the Assumptionists did or wrote was of immediate concern to the Government. Vincent Bailly's squibs might have passed unheeded in a small confessional weekly, but in one of France's largest newspapers they were literally front-page news, and would have repercussions for the rest of the Church. Apart from their massive labours in the 1898 elections, the Assumptionists' involvement in politics had mainly consisted of blowing raspberries from the touchline. Unsavoury and unchristian though much of their writing was, it had only occasionally outstepped what was legally permissible within the current limits of French press law.

A new dimension to their activities, however, was suddenly suggested, when the Abbé Pierre Dabry publicly accused them of sympathising with the subversive activities of 23 February. The *abbé* belonged to a Republican group of priests, known as the *abbés démocrates*, who had no love for the intransigent *avanttoutisme* of the Assumptionists. His accusation, published on the day after Déroulède's *essai*, indirectly raised the issue of whether the activities of the Assumptionists were compatible with the safety of the State.[27]

In restrospect it would be hard to accuse the Assumptionists of doing more than entertain temptation. And when the voice of prudence eventually triumphed, it spoke loudly and clearly. Even so, the Government was never to know how closely Vincent Bailly allowed temptation to touch him on the eve of Faure's funeral; only with the opening of the Assumptionist archives is this now apparent. All the Government had were Dabry's accusations – despite a massive police raid on *La Croix* in the following November, when 120 men combed the paper's offices, without finding anything of note.[28]

Bailly's own sympathies were vaguely Bonapartist and plebiscitary. But the Bonapartist pretender, Prince Victor, was too prosaic a figure to form a serious focus for insurrectional propaganda, with the result that a significant section of the Napoleonic inheritance passed to the republican Nationalists, notably to Déroulède's Ligue des Patriotes. *La Croix* had consistently given

Déroulède a good press since the reconstitution of his league in September 1898;[29] but *La Croix*'s respect for papal directives had inhibited it making a direct demand for a stronger regime. In a highly ambiguous article of 19 January 1899, it declared, 'On all sides people are demanding a strong-fisted man, determined to devote his life to liberating France from the traitors, *sectaires* and imbeciles who are betraying her to the foreigner.' But it went on to say that the nation's infidelity to God had yet to be expiated; and until that time 'Christ must inflict on the Eldest Daughter of the Church a punishment reminiscent of his own passion. That is why he has allowed her to be betrayed, sold, jeered at, beaten, covered with spittle, and crucified by the Jews.'[30]

Faure's death, however, and the election of Loubet gave immediacy to the issue. With Faure's body still warm from its exertions of the previous day, Picard was already asking Vincent Bailly whether General de Pellieux would make a good President.[31] Given Pellieux's remoteness from the parliamentary world, it suggests that the Assumptionists were well aware of the drift of Déroulède's scheming. Three days later they were secretly asked to give financial help.[32]

The invitation, if direct, was somewhat ambigously wrapped. It was given to Vincent Bailly by Gabriel Ardant, who claimed that the money was for the Jeunesse Antisémite, who were prominent among the rank and file of Déroulède's following. Seeing Bailly's embarrassment, when he started to broach the matter, Ardant sought to overcome his scruples by saying that the youths would be used to provide strong-arm protection for *La Croix*'s offices on the day of the funeral. Bailly was not deceived, however. Since Déroulède had already publicly invited his followers to stand by in readiness on 23 February, a *coup* was clearly on the cards. And it was most unlikely that the Dreyfusards would attack the offices of *La Croix*, when trouble was expected elsewhere. 'Whatever may happen on that night,' Bailly replied, 'I would sooner have nothing to do with an insurrectional movement. I wish to be faithful to the spirit of Leo XIII's directions.' This declaration of loyalty to the Supreme Pontiff was nothing if not impressive – until Bailly added a Gilbertian footnote that if he changed his mind he would let Ardant know by four o'clock that afternoon. Ardant then left Bailly to wrestle with his conscience, while the bright-eyed scions of Antisemitic Youth hung around outside, hoping that patriotism would eventually prevail in the Gethsemane of his tormented soul. When the sun set and the lamps were lit, however, it became clear that Bailly was not going to fork out; and they left in undisguised disappointment, uttering, one imagines, many an unchristian sentiment.

Whatever temptation Bailly may have experienced, his eventual stance was an energetic one. On the day of the funeral, *La Croix*'s leading article was a strong warning against violence. 'This day, zealous men, indignant at the triumph of Jewry in the presidential election, wish to resort to armed force. We reply to them as Christ did to Peter – and the comparison should flatter them – "Whoever lives by the sword shall die by the sword." . . . Only moral force will prevail.'[33] Bailly may well have been influenced by a gentle warning he received from his Superior-General, Picard. 'Be humble and meritorious in the midst of your political activities. I think the Nationalists are on the wrong tack. Let us take a more elevated view and let supernatural considerations guide our work.'[34] Even so, a certain wistfulness may be detected in Bailly's comment, 'Déroulède has spoilt everything by launching the adventure in the rue Reuilly, while [the royalists] were gathered in the Place de la Bastille.'[35]

Given Bailly's mammoth struggle with himself, Dabry's denunciation came as something of a cruel irony. Bailly's main worry was how Rome would take it. He was saved, somewhat improbably, by a fistular cyst on the Pope's left buttock. The day that his brother was to answer to Rampolla for the order's behaviour, the apple-sized growth was surgically removed, without anaesthetic; and Rampolla feared that the shock might prove too much for the eighty-nine-year-old Pontiff. Apart from the deep affection that united the two men, Leo's death would have serious repercussions for Rampolla. He might well be elected Pope himself; and if not, it would be unlikely that the winner would keep him on in his present office. Bailly was therefore spared the searching cross-questioning that he had anticipated, and Rampolla appeared satisfied with *La Croix*'s 'put up thy sword' leader of 23 February.[36]

Having survived this crisis, *La Croix* then spoilt its luck by publishing reports that the Pope had been subject to fits of giddiness in the last ten years. Rampolla feared that readers might assume that this was a euphemism for mental aberration – and might even conclude that the Ralliement was the product of this aberration, with Rampolla exploiting the incapacity of the Pope to push his own policies. The result was a couple of very sharp reprimands.[37] Nor was the Déroulède affair forgotten. 'The Siege of Fort Chabrol' in August found *La Croix* sympathetically reporting the quixotic exploits of Jules Guérin and his royalist colleagues. Their prolonged attempt to defend No. 51, rue de Chabrol, against the besieging forces of order was good copy in a lean month, when the Rennes retrial of Dreyfus was the only big news. Rampolla, remembering the Dabry accusation, asked Vincent Bailly if the Assumptionists were involved in 'the plot',[38] while Leo asked him point-blank if he had been giving money to Guérin.[39] When Bailly rigorously denied the allegation, the Pope then asked him whether the Jesuits had been giving money to the extreme Right – to which Bailly replied that he did not know, but thought it unlikely.

In what must have been a very unnerving audience, Leo took Bailly to task for his severity towards Dreyfus. In common with other European courts, the Vatican had been assured by German visitors that Dreyfus was innocent; but irrespective of the merits of the case, Leo feared the political dangers of *La Croix*'s attitude. It had also embarrased his relations with the Church of England. 'It is arousing great anger against Catholics; and I tell you this in strict confidence: I had prepared a letter to the English on the question of union. Because of *La Croix* I had to stop it. . . . I had a letter from Cardinal Vaughan this morning saying that the anger over Dreyfus has suspended all question of a return to Rome.'

5 *Mémoires d'outre-Combes*

The year 1899 was a sad one in the fortunes of the French Church. The mildly enervating fumes of the *esprit nouveau* had long since been dispersed by the glacial wind of the 1898 elections. But the recipe still existed; and there was still a strong demand for it among the socially conservative Republicans. '*Les événements*', however, of 1899 had given new life to the old democratic cry 'The Republic in danger'; and there was an increasing demand for a new ministry which would keep order and restore public confidence in the integrity of the servants of the State. The man selected for this daunting task was the cold but honest René Waldeck-Rousseau (22 June 1899–7 June 1902), a one-time Gambettist who had gradually moved in a conservative direction, as his legal practice took him into the world of big business and high finance. Untouched by the parliamentary scandals of the last fifteen years, this fishy-eyed man of few enthusiasms inspired a respect that went far beyond the ranks of the Opportunists.[1]

WALDECK–ROUSSEAU

He saw public confidence as the main issue. Confidence in the law had been shaken by procedural irregularities in the handling of the Dreyfus case. Confidence in the stability of public order had been undermined by the quixotic escapades of the Nationalists. A jury had unanimously acquitted Déroulède of plotting against the State, a verdict that made Clemenceau speak of a coming 'civil war', while at the Auteuil races on 4 June the *chevalaresque* Baron Chevreau de Christiani had set a pattern of Nationalist gallantry by smashing President Loubet's hat over his eyes. Le Cid's scruples about hitting older men were not inherited by his spiritual descendants.

Dupuy's cabinet had fallen with the President's hat, and it was clear that only a premier who could ensure order would get the

Chamber's support. Waldeck-Rousseau responded to the challenge by a vigorous campaign against the right-wing leagues, even to the point of manufacturing a false dossier of incriminating evidence – honesty being a relative term where the safety of the regime was concerned.[2] Déroulède, Guérin and André Buffet were arraigned before the Senate in its High Court capacity, and were sentenced, with their colleagues, to varying terms of imprisonment and exile.

There was also the question of confidence in the army. Waldeck-Rousseau had initially been disinclined to see this as a major issue, since the main lesson of the Déroulède affair was the refusal of the army to respond to subversive appeals. The case for a military shake-up largely emenated from the new Minister of War, the Marquis de Gallifet, whose main concern was efficiency.[3] One of the few generals in Europe to ride a bicycle in uniform, sword clanking against the rear wheel, he was determined to emancipate the army from the more restrictive aspects of its structure. The sackings and shiftings which he inflicted on the upper echelons were mostly the result of his administrative reforms, rather than conscious political retribution. As the former 'butcher of the Commune', he was unresponsive to left-wing demands for a political purge; his aim was to improve not jeopardise morale. He displayed a similar rugged practical sense in his private life. When his wife objected to his living with his mistress, he replied that 'being both good Christians we have all eternity to meet again'.[4]

It was his successor, General L. J. N. André, who inaugurated the systematic watch on the private lives and opinions of Catholic and right-wing officers, with a view to stalling their promotion (see pp. 138–9). An impeccable Republican and Mason, who was determined to put the military network of the Grand Orient to good use, André's shabby system of delation was to discredit the Combes's ministry in 1904 (see pp. 138–9). Although it was under Combes that it was to come to full flower, André had already inaugurated it under Waldeck-Rousseau, with the Premier's knowledge. In fairness to Waldeck-Rousseau, André's initial eavesdropping made exclusive use of the Sûreté Générale;[5] and it was only later that the ex-premier learnt of the use he was making of Masons. But an unhealthy precedent had been set, which Waldeck-Rousseau had accepted – even if reluctantly.

The remaining issue of confidence was a more far-reaching one: the State's ability to control the Church. Waldeck-Rousseau saw the Church as a declining force, and considered the Separation of Church and State a long-term probability – but not in the lifetime of the current political generation.[6] He regarded religion as a private affair of the individual that ideally should not impinge on public life; but since in practice it always did, it had to be closely supervised. He accepted the Concordat as an adequate means of controlling the secular clergy, provided that the State fully exercised its legitimate rights.

Rome initially took an optimistic view of Waldeck-Rousseau. Impressed perhaps by his devout childhood and family background – and in ignorance of his personal evolution – Leo even described him as 'religious'.[7] At least he was not a Mason, and he represented sound traditional views on material wealth. The result was that the new Nuncio, Mgr Benedetto Lorenzelli, was instructed to follow a conciliatory policy – a line which accorded with his own favourable impression of Waldeck-Rousseau.[8] In the course of the ministry, Rome accepted at least six episcopal candidates whom it would have rejected in other circumstances[9] – and also gave way over a lateral transfer. Conversely, the Government responded by adopting at least one of Rome's protegés as a candidate – despite his reputation for speaking his mind.[10] At the same time it failed to browbeat the Vatican into forcing two turbulent bishops to resign – a remarkable example of devotion to duty on Rome's part, since these two loud-mouthed prelates were an even greater embarrassment to Rome that to the Government.[11]

Taking all in all, the Concordat continued to function without undue stress, even in the later part of the ministry when the issue of the religious orders put Franco-Papal relations under heavy strain. Indeed the utility of the Concordat made Waldeck-Rousseau wish that he had a parallel – but more stringent – method of controlling the regular clergy, who lay outside the Concordatory regime.

A negotiated agreement with Rome over the religious orders would be legally inappropriate and politically unacceptable in France.[12] And he therefore made the matter part of a general law which he was preparing on the status of associations within the State. While his precise intentions are far from clear, it is evident that he did not envisage a massive closure of Catholic schools. His prime concern was the re-establishment of public confidence; and such a closure would run the risk of creating too great an outcry – as well as straining the absorbent capacities of the state educational system.

The two orders which caused most concern in the country at large were the Jesuits and the Assumptionists. It was common knowledge that a number of the leading private Catholic schools had a very high entry rate into the military college of St Cyr, the Polytechnique and the École Centrale des Arts et Manufactures.[13] In 1896 nearly a quarter of the intake into St Cyr came from Jesuit colleges, a number of which had special preparation classes for St Cyr – notably the École St Geneviève of the Rue des Postes in Paris, and the Jesuit colleges of Lyon and Toulouse.[14] Until the escalation of the Dreyfus issue in 1898, concern about this state of affairs had been largely confined to anticlerical circles. Radical and Socialist newspapers had denounced the 'Jesuitising' of the army, but the general public had tended to accept it as a natural outcome of the Government's exclusion of such men from the civil administration. Apart from the diplomatic corps, the armed services were the only form of public service open to men from traditionalist backgrounds.

The matter was further complicated by the fact that an increasing number of Republican families were sending their boys to the more fashionable Catholic secondary schools. Attracted by the English public-school ethos, they were impressed by the close personal attention which their children received (see pp. 27–8). At the same time the wives of prefects and magistrates enjoyed rubbing shoulders with *marquises* and *comtesses* on prize-day; there was always the chance that Raoul or Guy might be invited to spend the holidays at the château – even if it meant buying him new sets of underwear, and instructing him to forget some of is father's more Republican table-talk. By 1899, 43 per cent of the entire male secondary-school population was taught in schools run by religious orders[15] – despite the fact that many of these were in an illegal situation. Even in the Jesuit colleges, whose existence defied the expulsion decree of 1880, the Government could no longer assume that the clientele were necessarily hostile to Republican principles. For this and for other reasons, the Catholic education of so many French officers would probably have passed uncommented had it not been for the Dreyfus Affair and its aftermath.

It is significant that the first serious signs of disquiet came from men who were closely involved in the Dreyfus Affair. A case in point was Auguste Scheurer-Kestner, vice-president of the Senate. Early in 1898 he noted in his diary. 'There are ninety-six Catholic military circles in France. . . . All the Paris garrisons are clerical. Officers without patrons, or who are anti-clerical, are exiled to distant garrisons The leaders claim that in the event of a *coup d'état* in Paris, all the officers of the Paris region would side with it and would bring their troops with them.'[16]

After's Henry's suicide (see pp. 71–2), talk of this kind ceased to be isolated. November found members of parliament denouncing 'the invasion of the Écoles nationales by pupils of the religious orders';[17] and the Conseil Général of the Seine department urged the *grandes écoles* to refuse anyone who had not passed at least four years in a state school.[18] There were also rumours concerning the civil administration.[19] It was increasingly said that Méline and other imbibers of the *esprit nouveau* had allowed clerical schools to establish bridgeheads in the civil service, so that there was scarcely a junior cloakroom in any ministry where you might not discern the familiar bulge of a missal slyly distending a side-pocket in the serried ranks of black overcoats.

The cry of 'traitors in the camp' could not be lightly ignored by a government of Republican defence. Waldeck-Rousseau sought to appease it by introducing a bill which would exclude from the public service candidates who had not passed their last three school years in a state institution (14 November 1899). Despite the loopholes it left open, the bill had little hope of passing a middle-class parliament whose progeny loomed large among the distinguished products of the Jesuits and Oratorians. In fact it never got beyond the committee stage.

Clerical influence in the army, however, soon became an obsessive theme. Sensational rumours began to circulate about the fashionable Jesuit, Fr Stanislas Du Lac, who had a wide spiritual clientele in senior army circles.[20] His strength of personality had won him a considerable reputation as a confessor; and among his penitents was General Raoul de Boisdeffre, the

French Chief of Staff – who resigned on learning of Henry's forgery. Another penitent was the long-suffering Monsieur Monnier, whose wife was accused of being the celebrated 'veiled lady' in the Dreyfus Affair. It was supposedly Madame Monnier who had given Major Esterhazy the equally celebrated '*ce canaille de D*' letter which had helped to convict Dreyfus. Given the mystery surrounding the case – and given the highly charged atmosphere of the time – it was inevitable that Du Lac should be denounced as an occult influence. Unfortunately for the Church, he was also chairman of the board of governors of the École St Geneviève in the Rue des Postes, which provided more entrants to St Cyr than any other school in France. Needless to say, his spiritual encounters with the army's top brass were popularly seen as a forum for pushing the prospects of the school's choice pupils.

This was but the beginning of the charges levelled against him. Among much else he was reputed to have acquired extensive knowledge of the nation's mobilisation plans. There was even the smell of insurrection about him, since he was accused of being on close terms with General de Pellieux, Déroulède's great white hope for 23 February (see pp. 74–5). Indeed it was to General de Pellieux that Du Lac had supposedly revealed the secret of 'the veiled lady'.

Waldeck-Rousseau treated these rumours with the amused indifference that they deserved. But he could not ignore the collective effect of anti-Jesuit rumours on public opinion. When even Leo XIII suspected the Jesuits of financing insurrection (see p. 79), it was not surprising that there should be widespread unease in France concerning their presence. The new associations bill, however, would give Waldeck-Rousseau the weapon he needed; and until it became law (1 July 1901) he saw no reason to take special measures against them.

The Assumptionists were a different matter. Their chief crime in the premier's eyes was the venom they put into politics – and the fact that it reached half a million readers through the multiple channels of the Assumptionist press. Waldeck-Rousseau disliked antisemitism – some of his best clients were Jews. It was an irrational disruptive force which offended his sense of order; and the fact that the Assumptionists propagated it under the image of Christ crucified gave it an insidious air of quasi-respectability, which it could never acquire in the scurrilous pages of Edouard Drumont's *La Libre Parole*. Not that the Assumptionists despised Drumont's methods. *La Croix* frequently reproduced *La Libre Parole*'s cartoons and verses – some of them mildly obscene. Indeed there was a strong Rabelaisian side to Vincent Bailly which responded sympathetically to Drumont's talents. He would repeat with pleasure a remark by Drumont, 'If you ever get tired in the middle of a speech, shout "Down with the Freemasons!" and that will give you time to spit. Shout "Death to the Jews!" and and that will give you time to go out for a pee.'[21]

Waldeck-Rousseau had further scores to settle with the Assumptionists. As an Opportunist of conservative social views, he had attached a great deal of importance to the Opportunist-Rallié electoral alliance of 1898. He was never to forgive the Assumptionists for their part in wrecking this piece of electoral strategy. In his view, it was their preoccupation with divisive issues that had largely prevented the emergence of a stable conservative bloc that would have prevented the wild men of either extreme getting a hearing in parliament. This was a grievance that the Premier shared with the Pope. Indeed, when the Assumptionists were dissolved as an unauthorised order in January 1900, it was erroneously assumed by many that this had been done with the tacit connivance of Rome.

Once dissolved, the Assumptionists shaved off their beards and attired themselves as 'free' secular priests under the authority of the local bishop.[22] In some towns they felt safe enough to neglect these precautions, and continued life much as before.[23] The bravura of beard and sandals, however, was a short-lived gesture, for February 1904 found them prosecuted once again for living in community;[24] and thereafter they became more circumspect.

The greatest blow to their self-esteem came from Rome. After years of hard-hitting journalism, where they had more than held their own against the bitterest of enemies, they were suddenly ordered by the Pope to withdraw completely from political writing.[25] As Emmanuel Bailly sadly wrote, 'What the Pope has done is far more cruel in its consequences for us than anything the persecuting government has done'.[26] The tempestuous Archbishop Gouthe-Soulard of Aix blamed the Pope for 'cutting off the index-finger of his right hand',[27] while all over France there was alarm and disappointment in right-wing circles. On hearing the news, the Duc des Cars burst into tears;[28] and, if the press is to be believed, there was scarcely a château where *particules nobiliaires* did not shake with rage or sorrow.

La Croix, however, was too valuable a piece of artillery to be dismantled; and it was the Pope's intention that it should be handed over to enterprising laymen. A group of northern manufacturers offered to keep it fully functioning; and under its new editor, Paul Feron-Vrau, it looked as though Rome could now count on more discriminating marksmanship, while losing nothing in fire power. The Assumptionists, however, were loath to lose control. Either on their own suggestion, or that of the new management, an emissary was sent to the Nuncio to ask whether *La Croix* could retain at least two Assumptionist fathers as part of its editorial board.

The new Nuncio, Benedetto Lorenzelli, was not noted for his tact. Nor was he one of those new-fangled diplomats who thought it necessary to acquire proficiency in the language of his hosts. A former philosophy lecturer, he was not a *salon* man; and unlike his secretary, Mgr Carlo Montagnini, he did not enjoy the company of women. As Canon Edmond Renard observed, 'he lived in a state of virtual social disgrace'.[29]

He was not an easy man to talk to at the best of times. And when the emissary of *La Croix*, Alexandre Maupetit, called to see him, he was perspiring in bed, choked to the eyes with influenza.[30] When Maupetit suggested that at least two Assumptionists be kept on the board, Lorenzelli retorted that the proposal was 'a dirty lie'; and, sitting up in bed, he treated the startled Maupetit to a ninety-minute perororaration in his imperfect French, denouncing the Assumptionists for their obstinacy and bad faith. Given its coherence, there can be little doubt that this diatribe represented the sentiments of Rampolla and Leo – only too well in fact, in that the Nuncio's feverish condition almost certainly resulted in his saying far more than was intended. At the same time his '*furibonde*', '*effrayante*' performance – to quote Maupetit – contained none of the paternal reassurances with which Leo usually laced his reprimands.

The Pope, he said, had lost patience with the Assumptionists, having been disobeyed by them for so long. 'They are always making the most eloquent protestations of submission. Their idea of Christian union is a union under the control of the leader of French Orleanism, the Comte d'Haussonville. But only the Republic has an assured future. The Duc d'Orléans has no chance; he has leaders but no army. Prince Victor [Bonaparte] could only come to power by a *coup de force*, which has been out of the question for a long time. And in any case Napoleon signifies the Revolution with a crown on – despotic caesarism, the persecutor of the Church, scheming to enslave it.' And then, with a prophetic indiscretion that he might not have allowed himself in normal health, he went on to say that 'the conduct of the Assumptionists contains a great danger which the Pope fears and which he wants to eliminate immediately. The attitude of *La Croix* in the elections has made Rome anxious. Faced with the many checks and failures which are the result of [*La Croix*'s] equivocal and unfortunate attitude, the Vatican fears that the eventual successor of Leo XIII may be influenced by the poor results of Leo XIII's policies, and be tempted to abandon them.'

His next remarks were unfair as well as hard; but they may well have reflected the views of Rampolla, and possibly the Pope.

> The devil is very strong . . . he batters in the door of humility and takes up residence by means of monastic pride. The Assumptionists regard themselves, with absolute conviction, as a pillar of the Church; and, together with the pious aristocrats, they deplore the vagaries of the only true pillar of the Church, the Pope.... The curse of the Assumptionists has been their aristocratic clientele, which has forced them into all sorts of concessions and compromises and which has prevented them going to the people. Needing money for their various works, [the Assumptionists] have maintained a passive resistance to the Pope's instructions and directives – while always displaying and protesting their entire submission – their aim being to win the support of a rich clientele whose political preferences are well known to them.

To conclude his bedroom disquisition, Lorenzelli denounced 'the tendencies of certain self-styled Catholic papers which favour the abolition of the Concordat. The question of the Concordat is of the utmost gravity, and only the Pope can deal with it.'

The vehemence of Lorenzelli's attack astonished the Assumptionists – as did the unjustified allegations of dependence on the rich and the royalists. But the broad content confirmed their suspicions only too well. As Emmanuel Bailly later told his brother:

> In everything that concerns France, the Vatican's guiding principle is this: every possible sacrifice is to be made rather than lose official diplomatic contact or the Concordat. Consequently, if one has to sacrifice monks, nuns, projects, newspapers and colleges . . . Rome will heave heavy sighs, but will not make it a matter for breaking off diplomatic relations, because none of these victims are essential to the hierarchy. They do not affect the main aspects of the Concordat – to which Rome will sacrifice everything that the government demands.[31]

The prospects offered by the 1902 elections were very different from those of 1898. As a result of the Affair, the Chamber was realigned once more on the issues that had divided it in the eighties – religion and the 'moral' purpose of the state. Consequently the ever pressing needs of social and economic development were pushed yet again under the carpet, and the elections took place amid the old familiar battle cries that had been passed from father to son. Waldeck-Rousseau's appointment in 1899 of a Socialist as Minister of Commerce had been a demonstration of Republican solidarity against right-wing subversion. It was a gesture which had made little difference to the cause of social reform – though it was to make a great deal of difference to the man in question, Alexandre Millerand.

More specifically the elections would decide the fate of the religious orders. In his initial associations bill, Waldeck-Rousseau had created an instrument of great flexibility, which would have made the authorisation of each order a matter for administrative decree. It would have enabled the Government to authorise the schools and establishments of a particular order in one area, while refusing them in another. In this way it would have been open to the state to curtail the influence of Catholic education in areas where Republican sentiment was weak, and tolerate it where it was politically expedient to do so. Ingenious and far-sighted though this provision was, the parliamentary committee guiding the bill felt that authorisations were too important a matter to be settled outside parliament. And so the application of the bill was now entrusted entirely to shifting parliamentary majorities, who in practice would have no time to do more than say 'yes' or 'no' to each order as a whole, irrespective of regional considerations.

The election results of 1902 showed that there would be more 'no' than 'yes' answers. There was a distinct shift to the Left, which guaranteed the Bloc Républication nearly 370 seats out of 588.[32] 'Too many', Waldeck-Rousseau said, and resigned. He had in fact already arrived at this decision before the elections; but the task of shepherding the religious orders through a Chamber full of snarling anticlericals made the prospect of a further spell in office even less congenial. Health was a prime consideration; he was to die of cancer two years later. But he was also grooming himself for the presidential election of 1906; and to retire on his laurels now might do him more good than the uncertain role of trying to control a bloodthirsty Chamber.

It may also have been considerations of this kind which prompted him to suggest Émile Combes as his successor. As already indicated (see p. 49), there was a world of difference between the small-town Radicalism of Combes and the Parisian *grand bourgeois* that Waldeck-Rousseau had become – if only by adoption. Combes's narrow anticlericalism, the fruit of a hard experience, had little in common with the patrician lawyer's system of checks and balances. On the other hand, as chairman of the Senate committee on the associations bill, Combes undoubtedly had a certain competence to implement the bill – even if his manner of envisaging the task was very different from Waldeck-Rousseau's. Yet, according to some suggestions, it may have been precisely these differences which prompted Waldeck-Rousseau to put him forward.[33] With the presidency in mind, anything that could enhance the memory of the great three-year ministry would be welcome. A brief stretch of pettifogging government under an undistinguished Radical might serve as the black velvet choker that would show to advantage the lustrous white neck of the late ministry. It certainly never occurred to him that the Combes ministry would last nearly as long as his own – and that when it eventually fell he himself would have been six months in his coffin. Nor did he foresee the lengths to which Combes was prepared to go in his anticlerical policies. Even so, the motivation seems strangely irresponsible in a man who was so sensitive on matters of public order; and in the absence of decisive evidence for this explanation, one is tempted to give him the benefit of the doubt. Nevertheless it has to be admitted that statesmen often do behave irresponsibly where their own pride is involved; and Waldeck-Rousseau may have been no exception.

COMBES

Combes was a ghost from the Second Empire. His goattee beard and the curve of his nose suggested a spectral evocation of the long-dead Emperor – the Emperor as he might have been, if bladder-stones and the cold exile of Chislehurst had not finished him off. Combes might even have taken a malign pleasure in the simile, since his Republican disapproval of the Second Empire was never in doubt. On the other hand his concept of Concordatory affairs was something of which any Bonaparte might have been proud.

Cartoonists, however, were more conscious of the stooping back, the old-fashioned frock coat and the oversized briefcase which put them in mind of a notary out of Balzac. The malicious glint in his eye and his shaky little laugh completed the effect. In fact Combes had risen, not through the law, but on that other professional ladder of provincial Radicalism – the calling of a country doctor. Indeed his career under the Third Republic had been exemplary of all that was most typical of small-town Radicalism. While acquiring his Masonic grades, he had risen from municipal councillor to mayor, from departmental councillor to chairman of the departmental council, and had then become senator in 1885 at the age of fifty – all within the department of Charente-Inférieure, and most of it in the town of Pons where he lived from 1868 until his death in 1921.

Paris he had known mainly as a student, and it was perhaps characteristic of his austere provincialism that when the cares of the nation obliged him to live there he should choose to live in the rue Vaugelin, next to pedagogic Sparta of the rue d'Ulm. On the other hand his daily walk through the Quartier Latin to the Palais de Luxembourg doubtless helped to keep him young, while the vistas through the park compensated for everything. Indeed the new routine of cab rides to the Place Beauvau was to be one of the trials of office.

However orthodox his Radical development under the Republic, his roots lay in a darker and more tormented past.[34] His outlook was permanently coloured by what he had seen and experienced under the Second Empire. He had seen autocracy at work and he had seen the effects of clerical influence.[35] More intimately he had experienced the conflict of religious belief and intellectual scepticism. Reared in a large family of scant means, he had been steered by a clerical godfather towards holy orders, the 1850s being mainly passed in the successive stages of preparation for a doctorate and ordination. Censured as 'proud', he was prevented from taking final orders – though in the meantime he obtained his doctorate with a thesis on 'the psychology of St Thomas Aquinas', his supplementary thesis being 'The Quarrel of St Bernard and Abélard'. A piquant irony of these years was his employment as a teacher in the Assumptionist college of Nîmes, where the headmaster was none other than François de Cabrières, the future royalist Bishop of Montpellier. Long after Combes had become a Mason and a Radical Senator, Cabrières was to make use of this early acquaintanceship to further the career of an ecclesiastical protégé – for when it came to chasing sees, Cabrières knew the ropes as well as any Republican.[36]

Cabrières still possessed a copy of Combes's thesis on Aquinas; but it was clear that the Angelic Doctor had had little to say to Combes since the mid-1860s, the point at which he had abandoned Catholicism for a curious mixture of 'spiritualism' and the rationalist 'free thought' that was the stock-in-trade of most doctors of the time. 'Spiritualism' merely implied a subjective faith in some sort of after-life, a faith that existed in a separate compartment from the naturalistic concept of man which his intellect and medical training sustained. Unlike Flaubert's Monsieur Homais, to whom he is so often compared, he understood the world of subjective belief. There was also in Combes a strong Romantic streak which had early shown itself in rather indifferent Lamartinian verse, mainly dedicated to young girls he had met in adolescence.

Until his marriage, he suffered from loneliness and a lack of close friends; his letters of those years too often address his various correspondents as 'my only friend'.[37] And even fifty years later, when entrusted with the nation's affairs, he remained isolated from his colleagues and something of a provincial outsider. A visit to a gala performance at a Paris theatre filled him with a terrifying sense of vulnerability before all these sharp-edged ornaments of Paris society.[38] But, conversely, if Paris made him feel insignificant and defenceless, nothing gave him greater consolation that his various ministerial visits to the rural provinces, where the arrival of a notability could always assemble an enthusiastic crowd – as did a circus or a public execution. His memoirs are full of long descriptions of the orations he was given; 'never has a premier been kissed by so many women as I'.[39]

Seeing himself as despised by the fashionable world of right-wing opinion, but adored by the mass of the nation, there was a prickly aggressiveness about his handling of the contentious issues he inherited. His attitude to the religious question was complex enough, without having this additional dimension; but the contrast between the harshness of many of his measures and the basic kindliness of his nature owes something to this context. More than most premiers, he was showered with abusive letters and postcards, most of them anonymous, and most of them dating from his onslaught on the religious orders. None were more obscene than those signed '*une jeune fille de treize ans*' or '*un enfant amoureux de Christ*'. Unlike most politicians he carefully kept them; and where the writer was imprudent enough to sign them, Combes instructed the police to make a report on him.[40] That was as far as the matter generally went; but it illustrates Combes's somewhat literal understanding of the term 'Republican defence'.

The seeming dichotomy between the implacable defender of Republican ideals and the man of sentiment is well illustrated by his friendship with Princess Anne Bibesco, Prioress of a Carmelite convent in Algiers. Daughter of a Romanian noble family, her parents obliged her to take the veil at the age of fifteen to extricate her from an emotional entanglement with one of the household staff. When the drift of Combes's intentions towards the religious orders became clear, Archbishop Oury of Algiers ('*satisfaisant*' – 1st) sent her as an emissary to plead with Combes. The Archbishop was primarily concerned for the future of the missionary White Fathers in North Africa; but with commendable percipience in one of his cloth, he decided that a young attractive noblewoman, vowed to a life of chastity and poverty, might make more impression on the Combes than an old archbishop with nothing to recommend him but his Republican sentiments. He was right; and apart from helping to exempt the White Fathers from Combes's massacre of the innocents, her visit led to a strange quasi-sentimental, but basically platonic, exchange of letters that was to last for many years. There was much to appeal to the Lamartinian in Combes in this noble virgin, who, far from being a Judith or a Charlotte Corday, chose to commune intimately on matters of the spirit with this ageing politician of humble origins. She, for her part, seems to have had a somewhat confused notion of Combes's policies; and her Carmelite flock, sheltered from newspapers and all regular contact with the outside world, were even more confused, imagining him as 'a sacred being', to use her own phrase,[41] who would purge the French Church of its impurities. When a cousin of the princess informed Pius X of her relationship with Combes, 'the Holy Father fell silent for the whole of two minutes, his look transfixed with a stupefied air'.[42]

FREEMASONRY

Pius's predecessor, Leo XIII, would have been equally astonished. He had unhappy memories of Combes's brief innings in the mid-nineties (see p. 49). Combes, moreover, was a Freemason – albeit of the Scottish rite, and not the more militant Grand Orient. His cabinet too was entirely made up of Masons, with the arguable exception of Delcassé who had long ceased to attend his lodge, despite a dreary succession of unanswered invitations.[43]

Leo XIII had always regarded the religious problem in France as primarily political. The nation as a whole he believed to be 'too Christian to want Separation from the Church';[44] and in his opinion the difficulty lay with parliament and government. Until his death he continued to assert that French Catholics had largely themselves to blame for their current state of affairs. Had they united with the Opportunists in the 1898 elections, the bloc that emerged from the events of 1899 would have been deprived of the decisive weight of the Opportunists. At the same time he strongly believed that the bloc was being guided by Masonry. 'France is in the hands of the Freemasons'[45] – a conviction that reflected the outlook of a man of his time and social milieu. While Leo was more conscious than many churchmen of the shortcomings of the Church, he shared the penchant of Latin patrician prelates to discern in current problems the malign influence of occult forces.

Even so, Masonry in France was on the increase. Its total membership grew from some 24,000 in 1903 to 32,000 five years later.[46] It was believed, moreover, that the new Chamber of Deputies of 1902 contained somewhere between 170 and 250 Masons, and the Senate between 90 and 150 – impressive figures, if one takes Masonic membership at its face value. In fact, however, the active membership of most Masons averaged only five years, and generally corresponded to periods when the member was most in need of professional or political advancement. Right-wing politicians made a great deal of the fact that resolutions of the general assembly of the Grand Orient often featured in the following congress of the Radical party. It was easy to infer that the Grand Orient was the brains of the party, and ultimately of the Radical governments that came to office. Combes's predominantly Radical cabinet – Masons to a man – seemed living proof of the accusation. But to condemn the Combes cabinet for its Masonry was to mistake a symptom for a cause. Masonry was a function rather than a factor of the secular movement in French politics. Masonic membership was generally a means to an end: it was a form of solidarity which gave protection and opportunities to men who shared a number of broad democratic and secular assumptions. Its ideology was accepted because its basic content corresponded with what most Radical freethinkers already believed. Its ritual and language were not taken very seriously. They were either tolerated as a small price to pay for the material advantages of membership; or they were regarded as a vaguely satisfying substitute for the more congenial aspects of corporate religion.

It was scarcely surprising that the annual assemblies of the Grand Orient should see a great deal of kiteflying by young ambitious Radicals. And not only Radicals, for by 1905 a third of the Grand Orient's *ateliers* were Socialist. Nor was there anything particularly sinister about the fact that a small selection of these kites were flown at subsequent Radical congresses. The Masonic assemblies were in the happy position of not being governed by political time-tables and were therefore able to give opinions on what was desirable – as distinct from was practically attainable. They had regularly voted for the Separation of Church and State in the secure knowledge that their resolutions obliged no one to do anything rash until the time, if ever, was ripe. It was particularly significant that when Separation entered the realm of possibility in 1903, the great assembly rejected a proposal that Combes be invited to proceed to Separation at once.[47] For it was a broad truth of Masonic gestures that as soon as the assembly's activities touched the fringe of real politics, then the Grand Orient became very careful.

The real power of Masonry lay at the local level.[48] It was there that its favours or animosity could make or break. The provincial lodges generally knew more about local affairs than the prefects or the ministries in Paris, whose life span was generally too short to acquire comparable information on who was who at grass-roots level. It was therefore understandable that civil servants and Radical politicians should use the lodges as additional sources of information. In a country where the *piston* was a central ingredient of the selection system, it was inevitable that Masonic protection should be a major force. But in this, as in so much else, it largely duplicated and extended existing methods and channels of influence. A large part of every politician's time was spent in writing and reading recommendations. Deputies and senators regularly recommended 'good Republicans' for state tobacco kiosks or a sub-post-office and other public concessions; and they likewise did not scruple to recommend the children of 'good Republicans' to the attention of boards of examiners. This was often done in covert form. A deputy might warn a board of examiners that the daughter of a deserving party supporter was 'shy' during oral examinations. It was not unknown for an obliging board to respond by asking the deputy the sort of questions on which she was likely to be least shy.

Such methods shocked English observers. And when practised on a massive scale, as in the Affaire des Fiches (see pp. 138–9), they shocked Frenchmen too. But they were the natural outcome of a situation where political differences were so deeply felt that every area of human activity became a battlefield, to be filled with loyal supporters. What the Radicals and their allies were doing at the turn of the century, the Right had done in 1877. Where the Masons scored was in their organisation and local knowledge; but otherwise they were merely one set of practitioners among many, albeit the most powerful.

THE RELIGIOUS ORDERS

Combes's handling of the religious orders was one of the most depressing episodes in the history of the Third Republic. The just suffered with the guilty – and clearly outnumbered the guilty.

France contained no less than 3216 different orders, totalling nearly 200,000 men and women. Five male orders and 909 female orders had already been authorised by previous governments, and were in principle safe from attack. The male orders were the Frères des Écoles Chrétiennes, who were the backbone of Catholic primary education in France, teaching upward of 203,760 children;[49] the Lazaristes and Sulpiciens who staffed many of the seminaries for the secular clergy; and the Holy Ghost Fathers and the Society for Foreign Missions who were a vital part of the French presence overseas, and could therefore count on the indulgence of successive governments. But in the years following their authorisation, these various orders had gradually established thousands of schools and hospitals for which they had not obtained official sanction. Even so, Waldeck-Rousseau did not regard them as a political danger, and had unofficially told them that they need not bother to submit requests for authorisation, if their existence predated the Associations Law of 1901.[50]

This was far from being Combes's view, however. His purpose was to tear French youth from the clutches of the clergy, and he refused to be bound by the unofficial undertakings of his predecessor, however eminent and urbane a statesman. Despite Waldeck-Rousseau's protests, he ordered them all to be closed. There were, however, 11,000 houses which had thought to play safe by submitting requests for authorisation, despite the premier's smooth assurances. Belonging to authorised orders, the decision on their future would lie not with the moody whims of a parliamentary majority but with the faceless men of the Conseil d'État. A good doctor like Combes, however, was not to be thwarted by a bunch of lawyers; and so he persuaded the council to hand over the right of examination to the Government. Needless to say his sharp knife cut through the orders' requests for tolerance, and these houses too were scheduled for closure.

There remained the vastly greater number of orders which had never been authorised. It had almost certainly been Waldeck-Rousseau's intention to recommend clemency for the bulk of them. The Jesuits would undoubtedly have been axed; but Waldeck-Rousseau had assured the Nuncio in 1899 that 'Never, never, will I renew the error of 1880' – when the Republic had initiated its first programme of expulsion (see p. 24).[51] Combes's succession to office, however, absolved Waldeck-Rousseau from yet another unofficial undertaking. The poet from Pons shovelled the orders' application into parliament like coke into a furnace. Only five were earmarked for sympathetic consideration: the Hospitaliers de St Jean de Dieu, whose services were too useful in a country where secular medical care fell short of national requirements; the Cistercians and Trappists, whose silent ways and concern for the hereafter limited their political significance; and the White Fathers and the Society for African Missions of Lyon who were worth more to France than a fleet of gunboats and a division of Légionnaires. The rest were rejected without hope of appeal, and their property sequestered by the State.

Persecution, however, was nothing new in church history; and the experience of two millennia had not left the Church without resource. Although a large number of clergy took the long road of exile, and transferred their communities to Britain, Belgium, Spain and Italy, many, especially the unordained, stayed behind. Resurrecting their civilian clothes from family wardrobes, they startled the local population by appearing in the fashions of the eighties and earlier, until a timely loan and a visit to the tailors could put things right. The Carmelites especially, who had not seen the outside world for years, occasioned most comment. The much maligned prioress of Laval (see p. 134) appeared '*harnachée comme une mondaine du plus mauvais gout'*, wearing a scarlet mantle and a mauve dress studded with stars.[52] Nevertheless, despite these initial sartorial singularities, the Church could now dispose of a skilled force of teachers and nurses whose presence was unlikely to invite the attention and harassment of over-zealous local authorities. The result was that although Combes's measures closed down over 10,049 primary schools by October 1903, 5839 of them had already reopened, 3858 being staffed by secularised nuns and brothers.[53] Prudence dictated that the key positions of legal responsibility be put in the hands of laymen whose civil status could not be questioned; and the confiscated buildings were largely rebought in their name. But in many cases, apart from these administrative adjustments and the heavy financial outlay, the life of many church schools continued much as before. Combes had vainly tried to counter this situation by prohibiting secularised clergy from teaching in the same municipality as before. This at least would have forced a geographical movement of personnel, with a fair amount of disruptive upheaval. But Clemenceau condemned this as an unjustified interference with individual liberty; and Combes's bill never passed the Senate, despite initial success in the Chamber.

For similar reasons Combes could not create a state monopoly of education. Some of the most fervent anticlericals were equally fervent partisans of individual freedom. The Radicals and Radical-Socialists believed in limiting state control as well as clerical influence; and for many of them, a state monopoly of education would have merely substituted one form of tyranny for another. Even Socialist intellectuals like Francis de Pressensé (see pp. 108–11) were opposed to it. In addition to these ideological considerations, there remained the stark financial fact that no French government dared increase taxation to the level needed to extend state education on such a scale. As in Britain today, the taxpayer with his children at a private school was a golden buttress of the state school system.

Faced with these obstacles, the only area where Combes could still make secular inroads was in the sector of the authorised schools. The outcome was the law of 7 July 1904 prohibiting authorised regular clergy from teaching, and ordering the closure of their schools within ten years. All that they were allowed to retain were their novitiates for the overseas missions and their teacher-training facilities for overseas schools – assets which Combes was persuaded to recognise as in the national interest. Otherwise the authorised schools had to go through the same contortions as their unauthorised brethren, or face closure. Of some 8200 schools, 1843 were closed by 1911, which meant that of all the congregational schools in France, authorised and unauthorised, Combes succeeded in closing one in three.[54] Some 150,000 children were thereby put on the street, of whom less than half were absorbed into the state system. The rest mainly went to other Catholic school – to imbibe the same sort of mixture as before, with the added ingredient of justified hostility to the Government.

The net harvest for the State of 71,000 children was relatively modest. But it was as well for Combes that this was so. The Ministry of Education calculated that the pupils of the Frères des Écoles Chrétiennes alone would have cost the State 60 million francs in new buildings and 6 million francs a year in providing the necessary teachers.[55] Had all the 1,257,000 children taught in congregational schools invaded the state system, the cost would have been at least ten times higher than this. Combes could also take consolation in the fact that most of the others were at least taught in semi-secularised schools, where the ambiance was less overtly that of a religious community. Like many anticlericals, Combes found it abhorrent that children should be daily witnesses of a way of life that was an affront to individual freedom and equally abhorrent that they should be taught by men and women bound by vows of celibacy and obedience. Combes likewise genuinely believed that secularisation was widely welcomed among those clergy who had chosen to pay this price to keep open their schools. The adolescent experience of Princess Bibesco seemed to him but one of many examples of a premature and semi-coerced vocation.

Taking all in all, the disruption of community life was arguably his most sweeping success. A fair number of religious houses had abandoned distinctive dress, but had initially attempted to continue living together under a rule. They soon found themselves subject to prosecution, however.[56] They either had to adopt a much looser form of organisation, little different from that of the laity, or they had to join their brethren across the Channel, teaching well-scrubbed children amid the scent of votive flowers and highly polished yellow woodwork. Of those who stayed in France, the communities most able to preserve their traditional way of life were the secularised clergy in Catholic boarding schools, there being little to choose between the austere life of a *professeur interne* and that of a nun or brother – certainly not enough to enable the State to intervene effectively.

For the Church, a depressing feature of the dissolution of the orders was the relative indifference of the public. There were token demonstrations in the more *bien pensant* regions of the country; and a number of officers and civil servants resigned rather than have a part in the expulsion. But the confiscation of over 200 million francs' worth of property excited little sense of injustice outside specifically Catholic circles, it being argued that the unauthorised nature of these establishments entitled the State to make these depradations. As in all operations of this sort, however, a lot of money never reached the State. Over a third of the proceeds disappeared in 'expenses' – some legitimate, in the form of pensions to elderly and invalided clergy – but others took the shape of inflated administrative and legal costs. One of the principal liquidators was subsequently convicted of fraud and sent to French Guiana. There he could pass his days contemplating the silhouette of Devil's Island, whose former illustrious inmate had been the unwilling *primum mobile* of the whole sordid business.

6 The Separatist Minority

It is one of the great paradoxes of the period that Combes's most durable legacy to France should be the Separation of Church and State.[1] There are still many historians who believe that Combes wanted the Separation. Combes himself sustained this interpretation in his memoirs, posthumously published in 1956;[2] and there is no doubt that in 1904 Combes made an outward show of favouring Separation, even to the point of putting forward a Separation bill in the autumn of that year. The evidence of both his papers and his acquaintances, however, makes it clear that Combes initially used the threat of Separation as a stick to intimidate the Vatican. He wished to bully Rome into accepting his own rigorous interpretation of the State's rights under the Concordat, especially in the matter of episcopal appointments.

Combes was too well acquainted with the religious history of his time ever to believe that the Church could be freed from the spiritual domination of Rome. What he envisaged was a Church whose personnel would be largely if not completely at the Government's disposal, a Church which would thereby be weakened and which would eventually disappear as a significant feature in the social and political life of the country. Slow suffocation seemed the only policy that would not involve a major political upheaval; and whether one wanted to smother or merely imprison the Church, the Concordat seemed the most promising point of departure. It was true that many politicians thought otherwise. But most of them assumed that the Church was a declining force which would not survive the economic hardships of Separation. Perhaps of more importance, these men were not as yet in the sobering position of being called on to resolve the problem. Combes knew the electorate and was scared of it. So it was not surprising that he told President Loubet (2 June) that his new government would keep the Concordat.[3] And when questioned by Jaurès in the Chamber, he declared that the time for Separation had not come (12 June).

Anyone fearing for the Concordat would have been cheered by Combes's cabinet which contained four known opponents of Separation,[4] and no one who was militantly in its favour.[5] The chief danger lay in the new Chamber where Combes would have to find a supporting majority.

Initially the drive for Separation was largely confined to the Socialists and Radical-Socialists, who together accounted for little more than a quarter of the new Chamber. Virtually all the fifty-three Socialists were partisans of Separation.[6] Anticlericalism was their passport into middle-class politics; and for them it was a means to an end, not a way of life. Nevertheless one must distinguish between the bulk of the Socialist group and the Socialistes Révolutionnaires (eleven), who were disciples of Blanqui and represented a more obsessively anticlerical tradition. For them, any Separation bill worthy of the name should be a crippling blow against the Church; and they felt little sympathy for the viewpoint of Jaurès and his friends, who believed that if Separation was to succeed, it must appeal to the moderates of the chief party of the Centre, the Union Démocratique.

This is not to deny the enmity that existed between the Church and other brands of socialism in parliament – a traditional enmity with deep roots in the nineteenth century. Jaurès defined Christian belief as 'the old lullaby which soothed human misery', and most socialists saw the Church as one of the main bastions of social injustice. Leo XIII's encyclical on social obligations, *Rerum novarum* (1891), had little to offer to men who were desperate for practical reform; it seemed too much like a last-minute entry in the race for the allegiance of the masses, a belated clerical reply to the weary appeals of half a century. The Ralliement, moreover, had been presented by churchmen as a papal appeal to French conservatives to join forces against socialism, and was consequently no passport to socialist indulgence.

Even so the Church was regarded as an obstacle, not a lifetime sparring-partner; and, unlike the Radicals, the Socialists were anxious to have done with the clerical issue as soon as possible. As Jaurès was later to say, 'It is time for this great but obsessive problem of the relations of Church and State to be finally settled, so that democracy can devote all its attention to the immense and difficult task of social reform . . . which the Proletariat is demanding.'[7]

The Radical-Socialists (110), despite their name, were no more than the left wing of the Radical party. But while they shared in the full anticlerical tradition of the Radicals, they also had other aims in life, and therefore shared something of the 'have-done-with -it' attitude of the Socialists, as far as Separation was concerned.[8] Their Radical colleagues (77), however, represented a much more varied and complicated range of opinion. While anticlericalism and opposition to strong government made up their principal *raison d'être*, many of them shared Combes's view that the Church would be more dangerous separated than salaried; and most of them feared the reactions that Separation might provoke among the electorate. It was argued that Combes's expulsion of the religious orders was meeting with only limited opposition because it did not directly affect the mass of the electorate, except for the sizeable minority with children at the schools that had been forced to close. The Separation, however, would directly affect social life all over France. Although the vast majority of French adults no longer went to Mass, most of them had their children baptised; and a church wedding was the norm in most families. In the event of Separation, however, only practising Catholics would make a serious financial contribution to the upkeep of the Church; yet other sections of the community might well resent the withdrawal of clergy from poor parishes and the visible deterioration of familiar church buildings. And such resentment could well express itself at the next elections. Few foresaw that the Separation would meet with relative public indifference – a fact that was to come as a surprise to most politicians. Nevertheless political caution of this kind was open to conversion, provided the Separatists could convince the Radicals that their seats would be safe, and provided the Radicals could escape personal responsibility for framing the bill.

These considerations also applied to many members of the newly formed Union Démocratique, who were the left wing of the old Opportunist party. The programme of Republican defence had split the Opportunists in two. On the one hand there were those who regarded the Church as an integral part of the social status quo. These deputies had voted with the Catholics and the Right against Waldeck-Rousseau's programme of Republican defence. In the new chamber they retained the title of Progressistes – by which the Opportunists were generally known in the late 1890s – whereas their colleagues, who accepted the necessity for the anticlerical programme, took the title of Union Démocratique (29 May 1902). Numbering eighty-eight against the Progressistes' ninety-one, the Union Démocratique represented preferences which dated back to Gustave Isambert's modest Union Progressiste of 1894 – a penchant for maintaining contact with the Radicals and a marked nostalgia for Republican concentration, both of which found fulfilment in 1899. Forming the right flank of Combes's working majority, the Union Démocratique held the balance in the Chamber, since without them the Radicals and the groups to their left held only two-fifths of the seats. No Separation bill could pass parliament without the support of at least fifty of them – and in 1902 this seemed most unlikely.

With the Government cherishing the Concordat, and only a minority of the Chamber against it, the odds seemed in its favour. Yet in little more than two years the Separatist minority was to become a majority, dragging a reluctant government in its wake.

The principal danger came from the guerilla sharpshooters of Right and Left who saw the issue as a useful means of harassing Combes. As early as 20 October 1902 a group of Nationalists presented a Separation bill with just this in mind. The manoeuvre was sufficiently transparent for at least one noted Catholic to vote for it, and for a number of genuine Separatists to vote against it. But although it was easily defeated (269 v. 172) it had unfortunate results for Combes. It aired the issue, and provoked a motion that a parliamentary commission be set up to examine future bills on Separation. It was difficult for Combes to oppose this, however much he would have liked to; and in response to his silence a large number of Radicals and nearly all the deputies to their left voted in its favour (280 v. 243). The motion, however, remained without practical effect until the following year; and in the meantime Combes kept the anticlericals happy with the slaughter of the religious orders.

But if Combes hoped to steer clear of the Separation issue in the meantime, he was mistaken. On 26 January 1903 the Socialists proposed that the *budget des cultes* be abolished, and in the ensuing debate they accused the Government of adopting a deliberately ambiguous attitude towards Separation. Combes, completely cornered, felt obliged to explain his position; and, at the risk of alienating a considerable section of the Left, made the following remarkable statement:

> When we took office, although several of us were theoretically partisans of the Separation of Church and State, we said that we would remain on Concordatory ground. Why? Because we believe that at the moment moral ideas such as the churches teach are necessary ideas – and, apart from the primary schools, the churches are the only institutions that teach them. For my part I find it hard to envisage present-day society composed of philosophers like Monsieur Allard.[9] Until such a day should come, you can't transform overnight a society based on religion into a society solidly based on rational principles. I said in the Senate two years ago . . . that I was a *philosophe spiritualiste* and that I considered religion as one of the most powerful moral forces of humanity.

THREE SOCIALISTS

In the spring of 1903 there was very little to give heart to the Separatists; and few of them could have foreseen that the Separation would be a reality before the next election. The Separation campaign owed what impetus it had to the Socialists; and the next few months were to see them give it a number of hard pushes which were to have unexpectedly far-reaching consequences. This was largely the work of three men – Francis de Pressensé, Jean Jaurès and Artistide Briand.

All three were Socialist members of the Délégation des Gauches, the unofficial steering committee of the parties of Republican defence. This body had come into existence as a response to the unexpected resignation of Waldeck-Rousseau. Decapitated, it was feared that the bloc might disintegrate, unless its constituent groups kept close contact. So each group delegated between five and seven members to represent its aims. The Socialists, being a small group, had only five members; and faced with seven members of the Union Démocratique they had to reconcile themselves to the fact that the decisive weight of the Délégation lay with the Radicals and Radical-Socialists.[10]

The decisions of the Délégation were not binding on either the constituent groups or the Government. But it was a useful forum for achieving agreement or testing opinion before matters were put to parliament. Inevitably the unrepresented groups of the Right denounced the Délégation as an occult body that pre-empted parliamentary discussion, and usurped the functions of government. Combes, however, felt no shame in being a Duke of Plazatoro. 'In reply to the Opposition's daily reproach that I follow the majority instead of leading it . . . it matters little to me whether it is the ministry that leads or is led, when it applies to an agreed programme.'[11] As long as the army was marching in the direction he wanted, he felt his own whereabouts in it to be irrelevant. And what was particularly gratifying was its evident reluctance to march in the direction of Separation.

Jaurès has become one of the few canonised saints of French political mythology. Other leading Republican figures were too heavily tattooed with generally conceded defects. In the history books, Gambetta – like Disraeli – was always 'flamboyant', while even Clemenceau's leading admirer mixed his praises by calling the Tiger 'a cunning old sod'. With Jaurès, as with most haloed heads, however, it is often hard to distinguish fact from legend. Jaurès's personality and powers of oratory have led historians to exaggerate his influence both in the Chamber and the Délégation des Gauches. He has been described as 'the veritable master of the situation under the Combes ministry' and 'the heart of this famous Délégation des Gauches'. No one would deny the enormous prestige he had in the Chamber nor the extraordinary personal influence he had on those who shared his political sympathies. But however impressive a speech may be, its impact has to survive the personal and party interests of its listeners; and the legislative record of these years scarcely suggests that Jaurès and the Socialists had the degree of influence that is often ascribed to them.

At the beginning of his ministry Combes undertook to bring

in an income tax, old-age pensions and a reduction in military service from three to two years. But these reforms were also demanded by many non-Socialists; and, for all that, they were to be slow in coming. None of them became law during Combes's three-year ministry, old-age pensions not becoming a reality until 1910. The Socialists were influential as long as they were backing what other parties wanted; and Jaurès was at his most effective when supporting the Government.

It is also highly instructive to follow Jaurès's personal fortunes in this period. Although he was elected in January 1903 as one of the vice-presidents of the Chamber, it was only by a very narrow margin; and in the following year's election he was defeated.

The exaggerated belief of historians in his influence springs from several sources. In the first place, it was the constant cry of the Right that Combes was the tool of Jaurès and the Socialists – a cry which they hoped would detach the less enthusiastic members of the Union Démocratique. It was also an accusation that Combes's rivals in the bloc were to level against him in the later part of 1904, when they were seeking to unseat him. Secondly Jaurès's personality and persuasive powers acquired the proportions of heroic legend, following his assassination in 1914. Nor must one underestimate the effect of that other, and very different, martyr of 1914, Charles Péguy, whose *Notre Jeunesse* (1911) accused Jaurès of being the master spirit behind Combes's anticlerical programme. Péguy wrote with all the bitterness of a disciple who saw his master selling his ideals for short-term gains; and Péguy's lofty incantation has impressed generations of readers from then to this day.

Nevertheless it was the leadership of Jaurès which rallied the bulk of the Socialist group behind a constructive concept of Separation that was politically viable and not a mere gesture of anti-catholic enmity. The concept itself, however, owes most to Francis de Pressensé, who in retrospect comes nearest to being the author of the present ecclesiastical regime in France. It was his draft bill of 7 April 1903 that was to provide the basis of the Separation Law of 1905.

Pressensé was the son of a well-known Protestant liberal, Pastor Edmond de Pressensé, a distinguished Republican critic of

Napoleon III. Francis had a varied and influential career which has yet to find a biographer.[12] His early years alternated between political journalism and the diplomatic service. After being First Secretary in Washington, he eventually became permanent foreign affairs correspondent of *Le Temps* – a position he filled with great distinction from 1888 to 1898. His political views accorded well with those of *Le Temps*. 'Liberal' in a conservatively Republican sense, he despised the Radicals and all that savoured of the Jacobin tradition of 1793 and 1871. A constant sufferer from rheumatism and gout, a more serious illness in the late 1880s led to a period of intense religious preoccupation. After his father's death in 1891, he became increasingly interested in social Catholicism in England and America – an interest that bore fruit in his book, *Le cardinal Manning* (1896).[13] His personal notebook reveals that by January 1896 he was very near to becoming a Catholic. He was already following the Roman liturgy day by day: and it seemed only a matter of months before he would formally enter the Church. He was now on close personal terms with Ferdinand Brunetière, the convert editor of *La Revue des Deux Mondes*, whose assault on 'the bankruptcy of science' made him the spokesman of the fashionable Catholic intelligentsia who had their roots in the neo-Orleanist world of the Académie Française and the genteel erudition of Brunetière's review. It was in these pages that Pressensé wrote in February 1897, 'The Republic will not be secure until it allows the Ralliés to govern it.' It was rumoured, moreover, that Brunetière was grooming him for the Academy.[14]

That same year, however, found him deeply involved in the Dreyfus Affair. Convinced by Mathias Morhadt that a serious injustice had been committed, he thereupon devoted himself to seeking support for a retrial. He assumed that the cause of justice would find a ready response among Catholics, notably from the Comte Albert de Mun. Mun's concern for the poorer sections of society, his unimpeachable record as a war hero, and his gifts as a public speaker designated him as the ideal parliamentary advocate – or so Pressensé hoped. Dreyfus's innocence, however, was far from obvious; and most Catholics disliked the company the Revisionists kept. Pressensé's appeals met with embarrassed silence, and then, when the Affair became a national issue in 1898, open hostility. Pressensé was bitterly disappointed. In the words of his friend, Victor Basch,

> This Church – which he saw as an aspiration towards social justice and alone capable of stirring the conscience of the bourgeoisie – was now fighting truth and justice with all its forces. . . . With a strenuous effort he recreated a new moral life for himself, he built up a new faith. . . . His bible henceforth was the Declaration of the Rights of Man. . . . And he took as his religion the social, anti-egotistical and anti-individualist content of Christianity, stripped of its supernatural elements[15]

One of the first committee members of the newly founded Ligue des Droits de l'Homme et du Citoyen, he began a nation-wide campaign of speeches on behalf of Dreyfus (July 1898). '*Homme de cabinet* . . . he had none of the physical gifts of an orator. He did not look at his audience . . . his eyes were too weak. . . . His voice was not well pitched, his delivery was monotonous and rushed, and he rarely used gestures.'[16] And yet as his fellow Dreyfusard, Joseph Reinach, was later to observe: 'he took and held the attention of his audience . . . he forced the most unwilling to listen to him and stay with him to the end of his argument, which was often violent, sometimes wrong, but always strong, robust and profoundly honest'.[17] With the constant threat of violence from antisemitic gangs, it required great courage to speak at these meetings. On two occasions he was severely beaten up; he was also shot at – narrowly escaping being hit by a bullet. Another meeting saw him arrested by the police.

In May 1899 he formally became a Socialist, thereby setting the seal on his personal evolution. His indignation, moreover, at clerical attitudes during the Affair – notably *La Croix*'s – turned him into a remarkably virulent opponent of the Church – the narrowness of his escape from membership no doubt adding to the bitterness of his feelings. Even so, his anticlericalism was of the constructive Jaurèsian variety, and had little in common with the *mangeur de curé* vindictiveness of the Socialistes Révolutionnaires. He nevertheless supported Combes's campaign against the religious orders – thereby departing from the more liberal attitude of his father, who had denounced what he saw as the undue severity of much of the anticlerical legislation of the 1880s. Yet despite his support for Combes's programme of excluding the orders from teaching, he always remained an opponent of the idea of a state monopoly of education.

Another point of difference with many anticlericals was his firm belief in Separation. As early as January 1901 he was publicly demanding the appointment of a parliamentary committee to prepare a Separation bill;[18] and by the following year he had elaborated a bill of his own. It is at first sight tempting to assume a strong Protestant influence on his thinking and on the Separation campaign in general. His father had been a partisan of Separation, like his mentor, Alexandre Vinet (1797–1847). There undoubtedly existed substantial Separatist feeling among the French Protestant minority, especially among those denominations that were not salaried by the State – such as the Églises Libres de Paris to which Edmond de Pressensé belonged. Even the two subsidised denominations, the Calvinist Église Réformée and the Lutheran Église de la Confession d'Augsbourg contained a considerable number of Separatist pastors, who felt that if state funds were withdrawn from all denominations Protestantism might make substantial converts among Catholics. They argued that even the subsidised Protestant churches had a stronger tradition of self-sufficiency than Catholicism, and that Separation would hit the Catholic Church much harder than themselves.

Francis de Pressensé had an enormous admiration for his father, and was undoubtedly closely acquainted with the whole Protestant canon of Separatist arguments. But there is no evidence of his having propagated them during his 'Protestant period'. Similarly his work on Manning familiarised him with the views of Catholics who held that Separation might inject new life into the Church; yet he did not publicly profess them during the years when he was attracted by Catholicism. When he eventually became an active Separatist after the Dreyfus Affair, it was for totally different reasons, which had little appeal for Catholics or Protestants.

The general principles of Pressensé's bill of April 1903 were probably well established in his mind by 1901, when he publicly launched his campaign, while the details were almost certainly put into their final shape in the course of 1902.[19]

The preamble specifically stated, 'in drafting the bill I have been guided not only by republican doctrines, the traditions of the Revolution and the interests of French democracy, but also by the Socialist programme'.[20] And although his father and Alexandre Vinet were mentioned in the list of eminent Separatists, most of those he included were freethinkers. Similarly, of the fifty-six deputies who signed his bill, twenty-six were Socialists, while the rest were Radical-Socialists. Pressensé's close connections with the Ligue des Droits de l'Homme et du Citoyen won the bill the League's official sponsorship (30 May 1903) – a relationship that was consummated when the League elected Pressensé as its President.

The tone of the preamble was markedly anti-Catholic – so much so that the moderation of the bill itself came as something of a surprise. It denounced 'the sworn enemies of liberty, the disciples of the Syllabus, the heirs of the most dangerous system of intellectual slavery, the accomplices of the most odious attempts at moral and political oppression'. Its ninety-eight articles, however, were remarkable not only for their comprehensiveness and precision, but also for their attempt to dispense an impartial if somewhat austere justice.

The only other bill that could be considered a serious rival from either a political or a legal point of view was that of Eugène Réveillaud (25 June 1903) .Réveillaud was a freethinker turned Protestant. Radical deputy for Combes's own department of Charente-Inférieure, he was also a member of the Conseil de l'Ordre of the Grand Orient. A convinced Separatist for many years, it was he who had proposed the appointment of a commission to examine the question (20 October 1902 – see pp. 105–6) – though it was Pressensé who was to make the Commission a reality by demanding that it be elected without further delay (8 June 1903 – see p. 114). Réveillaud drew up a Separation bill in the early months of 1903, which was discussed step by step by a group of eminent Protestants, with Louis Méjan as *rapporteur*. The preamble laid emphasis on the illogicality of the existing system of state support and pointed out the advantages that the subsidised Churches would gain from Separation. Its tone, like the bill itself, was essentially conciliatory, avoiding the anticlerical outbursts of Pressensé's *exposé*. Although the terms were more generous, they borrowed a number of Pressensé's ideas – as Réveillaud specifically acknowledged.[21]

Despite the bill's liberal character, Réveillaud's motives were not altogether disinterested. As was to be apparent in 1905 (see p. 175), he hoped that the Church in France would fall victim to internal divisions, once its structure was no longer buttressed by the Concordat. These hopes, however, were not reflected in the bill itself, which, unlike Pressensé's, made a specific attempt to guarantee that church property would be given only to *bona fide* Catholics – at least, in the first instance (see p. 175).

These two bills attracted differing clienteles. Pressensé's appealed to the active freethinkers who saw the Church as a positive danger, but who recognised the need for a politically acceptable, non-punitive system. Réveillaud's bill had a more 'liberal' following, with Protestants providing a qualitively important element in its propagation. By contrast Protestant Separatist opinion was bitterly critical of Pressensé's bill, and accused him of betraying the liberal traditions of his family.[22] Pressensé for his part reacted sharply, denouncing 'the virulence and injustice of the Protestant attacks, as well as their personal character'.[23]

The third Socialist who was to make a decisive contribution to the Separation was Aristide Briand. 'A very monster of charm and geniality', he was thrice blessed with a seductive voice, the ability to think on his feet and the gift of transforming his thought into engaging and persuasive speech. Son of a Breton bistro proprietor, there was something almost Irish about his good nature and his willingness to sacrifice strict truthfulness to the maintenance of friendly relations – an easy-going disposition that was nevertheless entwined with an acute grasp of practical realities. Even his rebukes took the form of wistful observations; and his hatred of scenes resulted in his entourage being peppered with a fair number of mildly crooked but devoted assistants, most of whom would have been dismissed long since by a less indulgent master. The indulgence, however, was mutual, for he was one of the few men who could sleep with a friend's wife and keep his friendship.[24]

Even his most loyal admirers admitted that he was 'incorrigibly Bohemian'. Trained as a lawyer, he was obliged to leave the bar of St Nazaire in 1893 for political journalism in Paris, after being convicted '*pour outrage public à la pudeur*'. A *garde-champêtre,* crossing a field, had stumbled on him 'in flagrant delight' (to mistranslate the charge) with a respected married lady of St Nazaire – the field being appropriately named the Pré-de-toutes-Aides.[25] Thereafter he had worked his way through syndicalism and the left-wing press into the confidence of Jaurès – the election of 1902 bringing him a seat in parliament.

Some say that Briand initially doubted the wisdom of Separation, and that it was Jaurès who persuaded him to be a candidate for the Separation Commission.[26] Whatever the truth of the matter, it was Briand's appointment as *rapporteur* of the Commission that brought him into the centre of the Separation issue, and helped to keep it a clean one, open to a non-sectarian solution.

The election to the Commission showed clearly where Separatist enthusiasm lay. Not only was it Pressensé who persuaded the Chamber (8 June 1903) to proceed to an immediate election (11 June), but in the body that emerged the Socialists had seven of the thirty-three seats – double their proportional strengh in the Chamber.[27] They were only exceeded by the Radical-Socialists, who, with nine seats, were the principal Separatist group. Symptomatically the Radicals presented no candidates for election. Those who were sympathetic to Separation preferred to pass the responsibility to the Radical-Socialists and Socialists. The Radicals who were opposed to Separation were prominent among the 150 deputies who suddenly discovered urgent business to call them away; while those who dared show their faces mostly chose to abstain rather than sully their principles by voting for Concordatory candidates. Among other things, their abstention was responsible for the defeat of the two leading Separatist candidates – Pressensé and Hubbard.[28] The Commission in fact would have had a Concordatory majority had not the Nationalists decided to put a spoke in Combes's wheel by securing the election of two Separatist candidates – thereby giving the Separatists a majority of one.[29]

Even so there was still a good chance that the Commission

would prove a burial ground, not a workshop; and that the various bills submitted to it would never see the light of day in parliamentary debate – given the deep divisions within the Commission.

As far as Combes was concerned, the appointment of the Commission was not without advantages. The knowledge that there was a commission discussing a serious draft served to stop the flow of bills into the Chamber and Senate. While there had been six bills in the first year of Combes's ministry, there was to be only one more before Combes was forced into patronising Separation in the autumn of 1904. At the same time Combes felt confident that the work of the Commission, even if completed, would encounter prolonged difficulties in parliament. As he said to Henry Béranger (13 September 1903), 'The Separation, Monsieur Béranger, you're not serious! France could not take it for another twenty years.'[30]

Had Pressensé been elected to the Commission he would have been an obvious choice for *rapporteur*. Whether in fact his Socialist colleagues would have proposed him is less certain in that Pressensé lacked the charm and debating skill of Briand, qualities that would very much be needed in both the Commission and the Chamber if the Separation was ever to be sold to a sceptical majority. As Victor Basch was to comment, Pressensé 'was not a talker, his handshake lacked warmth; he inspired admiration and remained distant'.[31] Even his younger relatives, for all their affection, found his manner 'severe and intimidating'.[32]

Briand by contrast was geniality itself. The inevitable cigarette dangling from his lip, he spent most of his day talking. Verbal discussion was his method of thought; constant company was an essential to him, since he needed to persuade others in order to persuade himself. He likewise preferred to receive verbal rather than written explanations – a trait he attributed to his school days, when being the only pupil in the class, his classics master would take him on long saunters along the river, expounding the lesson as they walked. Briand had not pretensions to either the erudition or the intellectual integrity of Pressensé; they would have impeded his *souplesse*. But he had a remarkable capacity for understanding and retaining what he encountered. As Clemenceau once remarked, 'Briand knows nothing and understands everything'.

With Pressensé excluded from the Commission, the Socialists could propose Briand as *rapporteur* without embarrassment (12 June 1903).[33] The appointment accepted, Briand undertook to prepare a draft bill over the summer vacation; and the document that he took as his working guide was Pressensé's bill of the previous April. In this way the Socialists were able to use the talents of both men.

Briand's conciliatory skill was to show itself in the modifications that he brought to Pressensé's bill. Using Réveillaud's bill as a box of liberal spare parts, he deleted what he saw as the more controversial details of Pressensé's and substituted items based on Réveillaud's. When the Commission met on 28 October, it was this hybrid draft – substantially Pressensé's – which was to be the basis of their discussions during the long sessions that lay ahead.[34]

In the course of the next two years little was to be said about Pressensé's authorship, either inside the Commission or elsewhere. Jaurès and his Socialist colleagues felt it necessary to link together the fortunes of Briand and the Separation. Briand's skill and personal charm were the qualities needed to carry the bill through the Commission and parliament. It would also launch Briand's career; and socialism needed politicians of his calibre – Briand being undoubtedly the most promising orator that the Socialists had found since their capture of Jaurès in the late 1880s. Pressensé generously kept quiet when Briand was publicly accredited with his work. It was a sacrifice he was prepared to make in the tactical interests of both socialism and the Separation. And it was only when Briand abandoned the Socialists in 1906 that Pressensé began to wonder whether his attitude of self-effacement had been, after all, in the best interests of socialism.

7 The New View from Rome

Having outlived all but one of his electors, Leo eventually died on 20 July 1903. Tenacious of life to the end, his last illness prompted an eminent reporter to write: 'My preparations to cover the final illness and death of Leo XIII lasted over ten years. . . . Eventually the day came. Leo was ill for eighteen days, and for eighteen days I never went to bed. I think that if the Pope had lived even a little longer I would have died before him.'[1] Leo would surely have savoured reading these words.

Unlike Leo, his successor, Pius X, did not enjoy being Pope. Leo had wanted to be Supreme Pontiff, and made sure that he was. Joseph Sarto, by contrast, bought a return ticket when he set out for the conclave that made him Pope. And his modesty was nearly justified. Rampolla would certainly have been elected had not the Viennese Government intervened against him. When Rampolla was within thirteen votes of the decisive score – with Sarto a good eight votes behind – the Archbishop of Cracow suddenly announced that 'the Austrian Emperor . . . by virtue of an ancient right and privilege, pronounces the veto of exclusion against my eminent lord, Cardinal Mariano Rampolla del Tindaro'. Although the conclave indignantly rejected the Emperor's claim – and gave Rampolla an extra vote to prove it – Rampolla's chances were finished. To rule the Universal Church effectively, every Pope must have the respect of the major powers; and to have elected the francophile cardinal against the expressed wishes of Austria and the Triple Alliance would have been inviting trouble for years to come. It was a risk that no assembly of elderly cautious men could be expected to take. And so the Church forwent its chance of having a *Léon Quatorze, le Pape Soleil*.

Sarto was a non-political figure with no obvious predelictions among the nations. In so far as his candidature had political significance, it seemed to suggest a *détente* with Italy. As Patriarch of Venice, he had been on good terms with the public authorities and the royal family – a strong recommendation in the eyes of many Italian cardinals. As the Abbé Landrieux noted in his conclave diary. 'They want a Pope who will raise the famous prohibition, *ni eletti ni elettori*! . . . The Holy See, having no longer this bone of contention with the Quirinal, would have less need of the support of other nations, and would consequently risk less in acting towards them in a firmer and more independent fashion.'[2]

The man whom the new pope chose as Secretary of State was the thirty-eight-year-old Mgr Rafael Merry del Val. With neither age nor Italian blood to recommend him, Merry del Val owed his appointment to a peculiar set of circumstances. When Leo XIII lay dying, the secretary of the future conclave dropped dead while waiting with Merry del Val in the papal antechamber. Merry del Val was elected in his place; and it was in this capacity that he was brought into intimate contact with the newly elected Pope. It was Merry del Val who sustained Sarto in the initial agony of his appointment; and it was as secretary of the conclave that he automatically became Pro-Secretary of State, pending the Pope's choice of a permanent chief minister.

There was much to attract Pius in this austere accomplished diplomat.[3] Neither relished his work; and both shared the same Gethsemane-attitude to important office. Pastors by inclination, their strength of character and stern self-discipline had won them rapid and unwanted promotion. They regarded the various stages of their ascendancy as so many Stations of the Cross. And in making difficult decisions they would seek mutual inspiration by contemplating a crucifix together.

Apart from a congeniality of temperament, Pius admired in Merry del Val skills and accomplishments which lay outside his own experience. Son of a parish clerk, Sarto's success as a bishop had sprung from his essentially pastoral concept of the job. Venice for him had been a huge parish, which looked to him for firm direction and an exemplary life. Born and raised in Venetia, he felt he understood its people and their needs. The papacy was a different matter. 'It's all right steering a gondola, but this is like steering a battleship', he told a visitor, shortly after the conclave. He spoke nothing but Italian and Latin; and his knowledge of French was too rudimentary to be a safe channel of communication. Merry del Val, by contrast, belonged to a noble family of Hispano-Irish ancestry. His father had been Spanish ambassador to the Holy See and his brother was private secretary to Alfonso XIII. Brought up in England, he had been entrusted by Leo XIII with various diplomatic missions. He was a fluent speaker of English, French, Spanish and Italian, and had a passable knowledge of German. To Pius he seemed the perfect corrective to his own deficiencies.

The atmosphere of the Vatican changed rapidly. Pius was a stranger to Rome, and Merry del Val disliked its social life. When president of the Academy for Noble Ecclesiastics, he had discouraged his students from frequenting it. If a new recruit asked him for permission to accept an invitation to dinner, he would reply, 'Certainly, if you wish, but I never do it myself' – which effectively drained the propect of any attraction. The student invariably opted for a wistful evening in the lonely seclusion of his college study. Given his age and temperament, Merry del Val did not mix easily with his older Curial colleagues; and the genial Roman tradition of *combinazione* and mutual indulgence towards personal failings held no attractions for him. The continued presence of Rampolla in the Vatican, like the Ghost of Christmas Past, was also a factor that encouraged him to keep himself to himself.

Although both Pius and Merry del Val enjoyed company, they were happiest with people of few pretensions – Sarto with his secretaries and Vatican domestics, Merry del Val with the boys of the Trastevere slums. Pius abandoned the aristocratic seclusion of Leo's mealtimes and had lunch with his secretaries. Merry del Val, for his part, spent much of his afternoons climbing up and down the jungle of steps and stairways in Trastevere taking gifts or words of reassurance to people in difficulty. His Sunday afternoons were always devoted to the Trastevere boys' club, where he played billiards and organised theatrical presentations. It was there that he bestowed the sociability that was lacking in his relations with his colleagues. His face lost for a while its oppressive sense of impending tasks and duties which made him rather depressing company in the Vatican. Photographs mostly show him with a remote abstracted look; and although he possessed charm and humour, there was a chilling seriousness about him. If the Pope was in the room above him, he would occasionally disconcert visitors by suddenly saying, 'Listen, the footfall of a saint!'

His interior life was equally austere. He had a hair shirt of woven wire with protruding points, and a leather discipline of which he made frequent and vigorous use. These facts were known to few; and the cleaners would occasionally be mystified by bloodstains on his floor, apparently not the result of careless shaving.

Pius, for his part, was benign rather than warm. Although at times his manner bordered on the jovial, it could also turn to anger – with loud words and vigorous thumps on the table. As with Merry del Val, his face was perpetually haunted by a heavy sense of responsibility. Given their predilection for pastoral work, it was natural that they should both have a deep devotion to the Curé d'Ars. His statue stood on their desks and although cynical visitors often assumed that they had a selection of statues within easy reach – the one on display being appropriate to the nationality of the caller – it was the *curé*'s image that dominated their working day. Oddly enough neither appears to have been disturbed by the *curé*'s Voltaire-like smile, so strongly reminiscent of Leo XIII.

Even so, it was widely felt in Rome that a lot had disappeared with the malign smirk of Leo XIII. And some of the older aristocratic noses in the Curia did not take kindly to the new odour of sanctity that was drifting through the Vatican. Leo, though remote, had enjoyed his role, and was therefore stimulating to work for. The new rulers, however, inspired an uneasy veneration, which, taken with their concept of work as a crown of thorns, had a cumulatively depressing effect.

As many of his electors had hoped, Sarto's appointment led to a certain *détente* with Italy. He had spent most of his life in Venetia and had none of the Roman nostalgia for the Temporal Power. Merry del Val, for his part, had been brought up in England in a diplomat's entourage, and was well aware that many people considered the Papacy morally strengthened by its loss. Nevertheless the problem of papal independence remained; and until it was solved there was to be no formal renunciation of papal claims.

Even so, Pius once remarked that if Victor Emmanuel offered to restore Rome, his reply would be 'Stay where you are'.[4] Rumour had it that Pius 'would be content with the Trastevere railway station and its surrounding quarter, together with the railway line that leads to the sea'.[5] The papal train, with its chapel on wheels, would no longer be a mere museum piece, but a life line of freedom. Proudly puffing its way from St Peter's to the sea, its plume of smoke would proclaim to the long-legged marsh birds that the Prisoner of the Vatican was a prisoner no more. But it would seem that Vatican thinking was becoming less specifically territorial. The official Vatican newspaper, *L'Osservatore Romano,* commented that if an alternative guarantee of papal independence could be devised, 'the Church would willingly abandon the Temporal Power without regret'.[6] As Merry del Val explained to the Belgian Minister Plenipotentiary, Baron d'Erp, 'The Church does not want the temporal power for its own sake, but as a safeguard of independence. . . . The Holy See would be prepared to negotiate a settlement of the Legations issue, if one were sought.'[7]

In Merry del Val's view the best solution to the problem would be an improvement in the Vatican's international standing. Not only did this method appear more realistic than a territorial guarantee, but once attained, it might prove more effective. It was with this in mind that he sought papal representation on the various international conferences that met in these years, ranging from the Second Hague Conference to sundry discussions on social conditions. It was also a factor that made him move warily in his olive-branch relations with Italy. 'The Pope could compromise his prestige. . . . He is Pope of the Catholic Universe, not just of the Italians.'[8] Pius put it more explicitly. 'I encouraged Catholics in the last [Italian] elections to vote for moderates. That does not mean that I have lifted the *non expedit. I shall never lift it* as long as the Pope is deprived of freedom. I am not the Catholic head of Italy alone; but the head of Catholics throughout the world. If I accepted the present situation, Catholics outside Italy would regard me as a subject of the King of Italy.'[9]

Vatican policy was to be well summed up by the Rome correspondent of *La Corriere della Sera,* who had close Vatican contacts. 'With Pius X, the true formula of Italian-Vatican relations is a tacit understanding under the guise of antagonism. . . . The official antagonism reassures Catholics of other countries, and safeguards the Papacy's international prestige; while the tacit understanding with Italy takes adequate care of the essential religious interests of our country.'[10]

This rapprochement with Italy had certain affinities with Leo's *ralliement* to France, in that both represented a conservative alliance against left-wing forces. Although Pius had inaugurated a new style in papal attitudes by receiving Court personnel at the Vatican, the first major initiative came from Giolitti's Liberal cabinet (November 1903 to March 1905). The general strike of September 1904 focused attention on the activities of the Left; and in response to government overtures, Pius allowed Catholics to vote in the November elections wherever their support was needed to defeat left-wing candidates. This now familiar brand of Catholic strategy was given an open blessing in the following June, when the encyclical *Il Fermo Proposito* authorised bishops to dispense Catholics from the *non expedit* wherever Church interests recommended it. Lest this be seen as a capitulation, however, there was to be no Catholic party as such in parliament – only Catholics sitting as private individuals.

Welcome though this change was, it did not constitute such a break with Leo's policies as is often supposed. As Merry del Val confided to Baron d'Erp, 'When Pius IX proclaimed the *non expedit,* he meant that Catholic participation in Italian political elections was inopportune. It was Leo XIII who later transformed this into an outright prohibition. When I was Leo's Private Chamberlain, His Holiness told me that a day would come when his successor would have to remove this prohibition. Besides, if Pius IX had been able to see that the [post-1870] situation . . . would last so long, he would certainly not have proclaimed the *non expedit.*'[11]

Just as in the case of the Ralliement, however, there were plenty of Jeremiahs who saw the *détente* as a one-sided dupery, in which all the prizes went to the Government. Despite Catholic electoral support, the foreign office still sabotaged papal attempts to find a seat at international conferences. The only change was that it did so more discreetly, and was loud in its denials of anything so base. This two-faced behaviour was less excusable in that Merry del Val had different objectives from Rampolla. He was not seeking an international forum to air the Roman Question; he merely wished to increase the Vatican's influence as an alternative to a territorial solution. And it would have been in Italy's interest to support him – though the sea-change in Vatican policy may not have been fully apparent through the dusty windows of the Quirinal.

The Second Hague Conference was a case in point. It was symptomatic of Merry del Val's clear-eyed intentions that he should first raise the matter with Italy herself – unofficially, through the medium of Cardinal Svampa and Victor Emmanuel.[12] But the Italian cabinet still had doubts, and secretly asked other governments to oppose entry.[13] All the Vatican could do was to take a certain bitter satisfaction in the grotesque contortions of the Government to conceal its opposition.[14]

The sweet smile to Italy had its counterpart in the cold shoulder to France. As Sarto's supporters in the conclave had hoped, a *détente* with Italy would permit a tougher line elsewhere. At the same time the softening of the Roman Question removed the last withered rose from Leo's wreath of francophile hopes. There was no longer any point in pursuing the mirage of French diplomatic support over Rome. That it was a mirage had been apparent for years; but now that it was decided to look for security elsewhere – on an elevated platform of international activity – the pursuit could be forgotten. Yet if this particular gallop could be dismissed as a bizarre expression of Leo's hunting instincts, there was still the problem of making life tolerable for the Church in France. And on this point Leo's policies of appeasement still had their admirers in Rome – but neither Pius nor Merry del Val was among them.

They accepted the Republic, but believed that French Catholics should unite beneath the banner of Church interests and compel respect from the Government. Appeasement in their view had sapped the fighting spirit of French Catholicism. Like the Assumptionists, they felt that Rampolla had demoralised the Catholic electorate and got nothing in return. It was symptomatic of the new spirit in Rome that the Assumptionists should rapidly rise from semi-disgrace to a position of unrivalled esteem in the Pope's confidence. By 1906 the Bailly brothers had become the trusted recipients of papal thinking on France; and both Pope and Secretary of State were regularly to confide in them their doubts and misgivings concerning leading French churchmen. Similar confidences were made to other Assumptionists, with the result that the order came to regard itself as the Pope's conscience on French affairs. After the insults and blows of Rampolla's dark days, it had now been moved to the head of the table.

It was to the Assumptionists that Merry del Val revealed his private thoughts on the policies of Rampolla and Leo XIII. Speaking in December 1906, he was to say:

> 'Ah, if only the policy of resistance had begun twenty years ago! What a splendid situation the Church in France would have today! But too many holes have been made in the dyke, and today the flood is overwhelming us.'
>
> 'Ah, Eminence, how true!'
>
> 'If only the Church had pulled itself together six years ago, when it was apparent that the enemy was preparing its most furious assault.'[15]

He would repeat, with silent incredulity, Rampolla's dictum: 'France is a woman, a lady who must be cajoled and flattered.' Yet although Merry del Val assigned a heavy responsibility to his predecessor for the Church's difficulties in France, he was also distrustful of the Catholic leadership in France. As he said to the Assumptionists in December 1906,

> If only one could persuade the French that their salvation lies in battle. They should oblige us to restrain them, to moderate their ardour. But instead we have to push them. Yet they are on the battlefield and in the front line. Men in that position are generally only too anxious to fight. But *they* just want to surrender. I am thinking particularly of the leaders, the intellectuals who are actively involved.[16]

'*Les intellectuels*', the directing forces, had always been a term of abuse on Assumptionists' lips – especially since the Dreyfus Affair. Merry del Val's suspicion of French intellectuals was more subtle and more selective, but none the less real. There had always existed in Rome a distrust of the French *penchant* to elevate issues on to the level of intellectual principles. Clerical delinquency or unorthodox opinions often passed unchecked in Italy, because their authors did not attempt to give them an intellectual justification; they remained on the level of personal transgressions. In France, however, issues rapidly became matters of principle because their authors chose to defend them on this level – and the Vatican was thereby drawn into passing verdicts on them. An Italian priest 'with a little woman to whom he took off his clothes' would either admit that he was in sin or seek to excuse himself on the grounds of diminished responsibility. The rules of the game were never in doubt. With a French priest, however, one never knew whether he might not treat one to a disquisition on Christ's silence on fornication (as distinct from adultery), or a critical analysis on the Manichaean tendencies of St Paul. Such cases were rare, but had frequent counterparts in the realm of theology and biblical exegesis. The Italian would capitulate and be forgiven, whereas the Frenchman would defend himself and cause trouble.

At the same time the very quantity and prestige of intellectual output in France obliged Rome to keep a close eye on it. Merry del Val's Hispano-British background scarcely disposed him to take an indulgent view. He had been trained at an English seminary where the intellect was firmly subordinated to the will; and while he had the highest respect for the intellect, he feared its vagaries when left undisciplined. Although this distrust was to be most apparent in his handling of the Modernist crisis (see pp. 196–7), it was also evident in his attitude to politico-religious matters. He saw French Catholics as too prone to equate innovation with emergent truth, and to assume that anticlericalism reflected the failings of the Church, rather than the ignorance or malevolence of others. Merry del Val was a strong believer in the forces of evil, and saw Freemasonry as its most obvious manifestation. Leo XIII had likewise had an exaggerated fear of Masonry – but he had also had a much stronger faith in the will and capacity of French Catholics to resist.

The new pessimism in Rome about France did not promise well for the Concordat. Merry del Val undoubtedly wanted to preserve the treaty as a symbol of the Church's international standing; but he was less disposed than Leo to make sacrifices to keep it. Pius was likewise against concessions. 'There are those who fear the rupture of the Concordat. The Concordat is a chain. . . . However, I shall not take on myself the responsibility for such a rupture. But rather than fail in what I believe to be my duty, I shall not prevent it. I shall abandon myself to Providence' (April 1904).[17] Indeed Pius was ready to see positive advantages in Separation. 'Separation will make the *curés* more zealous. They will have to live off the people; they will have to devote themselves to them, and win the people's sympathy by visiting the sick. . . . Just look at the Catholics of the United States, what zeal among the clergy!' (November 1904).[18]

Combes was largely unaware of this change. He had embarked on a policy of making the Concordat a more effective instrument of state control, but failed to realise that threats would no longer work with Rome. Leo's attachment to the Concordat had been a vulnerable point for pressure. In the tussle over episcopal appointments Combes had lugubriously warned Rome that papal obstinacy would make it hard for him to defend the Concordat before parliament.[19] And his wagging forefinger had in fact extorted minor concessions (see pp. 127–8). But Leo's soft spots were buried with his corpse – as Combes was to discover, much too late.

Like the erastian Goliaths of earlier centuries, Combes liked to present his Concordatory policy as a work of restoration. Even he, however, did not expect to restore the regime to its Napoleonic purity in the brief lifetime of a ministry; and he consequently restricted his efforts to the more important issues.

As always, the appointment and control of bishops was the key question. On the level of semantics, he won a minor skirmish over the wording of the papal bulls appointing bishops. Under the Third Republic most bulls stated that the candidate had been nominated 'to Us' by the Government (i.e. to the Pope). The phrase 'to Us' implied that the Government's right of nomination was merely one of designation – and remained subject to the Pope's approval.[20] This was an interpretation that Combes was not prepared to allow – except where the candidate was manifestly unfit to be a bishop (see pp. 49–50). Waldeck-Rousseau had already questioned the propriety of including 'to Us' in the bulls,[21] and Combes was determined to fight and win the issue. No bishop would occupy his see until his bull of appointment was properly worded.

Rome was used to this sort of situation. With his customary practical sense, Rampolla decided to drop the phrase while fully intending to use the veto in practice.[22] As long as the Vatican continued to block unsuitable candidates, the phraseology mattered little to him. He was too good a Sicilian to let the written word stand in his way – that was a failing he left to the French. But before the concession could be made known, Leo died; and it was left to Pius to draw the credit six months later.

If this concession caused Combes to misjudge his man, he was soon to be disillusioned. It was significant that Pius would allow no change in the French letters patent nominating candidates: 'we name him and present him to your Holiness'. This was a sign of things to come. But Combes too came of tenacious peasant stock; and he proposed to match his little victory in semantics with a substantial one in practice. He had no intention of seizing the shadow and losing the substance – as had been said of the German Emperors after the Investiture Contest.

Combes's intentions were clear from the start. Months before Leo departed for the Happy Hunting Ground, Combes set the style of his procedure by curtly presenting Lorenzelli with his first batch of nominations – with no attempt at prior discussion (23 December 1902).[23] Nor were the nominations themselves reassuring. The candidate for the tiny Alpine diocese of St Jean de Maurienne was the Abbé Mazeran, notorious for his ambition and willingness to serve the Government if it would further his career.[24] A protégé of Bishop Fuzet (see p. 57), he reflected the dark side to his master's character. The limestone desolation of Savoy would not have satisfied him long; and his presence there would have prompted uneasy thoughts in the minds of his episcopal colleagues, as they sat moodily in the Paris-Rome express, while it laboriously took on water a stone's throw from his palace.

Turning westward into the stiff Atlantic breezes of Bayonne, Combes's candidate for this pine-clad diocese was Mgr Gazaniol, reigning Bishop of Constantine. This lateral transfer involved an important question of principle which had already divided Combes and Rampolla in the *Sturm und Drang* period of the

Bourgeois cabinet (see pp. 49–50). The matter was made more difficult by the accusations of immorality that had been brought against him; his '*vis de chien*' was even the subject of lengthy verse.[25] Although the Vatican was disinclined to believe these rumours, he was clearly an awkward subject for a trial of strength since refusal might seem to confirm the truth of local gossip.

Subsequent nominations were scarcely better. Casanelli d'Istria had been a Republican candidate for the see of Ajaccio since 1870; and his name regularly came up like a bad joke at the Chat Noir. Nephew of a former Bishop of Ajaccio, he had been notorious in the seventies for packing the chapter with friends and relations. He had also contested his uncle's will with the diocese, and was accused of making off with property earmarked for pious purposes. These purposes included the saying of Masses for his uncle's soul – something which Casanelli had apparently neglected to do, or so it was said.[26] When his principal rival won the see in 1870, Casanelli's chief agent publicly reposted by calling Pius IX 'an old imbecile' – a remark that Pius X was unlikely to forgive. With great forbearance and remarkable tact Merry del Val told Combes that Casanelli was too old for such a large and mountainous diocese.[27]

There being deadlock on these candidates, Combes refused to propose others. Nor would he allow an agreed nomination for Nevers to go forward.[28] In Rome's experience, vacant dioceses were quickly torn apart by local jealousies and scandal; and Merry del Val, sensing stalemate, decided to brave gossip and rescue the much maligned Mgr Gazaniol from African obscurity.[29] It is far from clear, however, whether Lorenzelli conveyed this concession to Combes. Combes later accused Lorenzelli of keeping it from him; [30] and others have suggested that the Nuncio intended to sell this peace-offering to Combes as the fruit of his own persuasions with Rome. Lorenzelli was frequently accused of soliciting bribes – by Catholics as well as anticlericals. And although none of these claims was ever substantiated, there is no doubt that the Direction des Cultes was in complete ignorance of the papal concession. An alternative explanation is that it was Combes who chose to keep his colleagues in the dark – in order to convince them of Rome's insufferable intransigence and the need for tougher action.

Whatever the truth, further vacancies hardened the deadlock. As Pius said in December 1903, the Pope would never resign his right of veto, 'even if all the sees of France were to remain vacant'.[31] It seemed that he was ready to outface Combes indefinitely.

In Combes's view the only alternative to siege warfare was a *coup de théâtre*. If one of his candidates was prepared to stand firm in the face of papal opposition the Vatican might have second thoughts. While Combes never regarded schism as a serious possibility in France, he was perfectly prepared to use the fear of it to intimidate Rome. If just one ambitious priest would consent to have his appointment announced in the *Journal Officiel* – despite papal rejection – the Vatican might be panicked into accepting the other nominations. None of the existing candidates was sufficiently thick-skinned for such an enterprise; and Combes therefore asked Dumay to take his Diogene's lamp and search for such a man. All that Dumay could suggest, however, was Canon Chrestia of Nice.[32] His name had been bandied in the *ententes préalables* of former days, but always without success. Although he had the support of several bishops, his name was wormwood to others; and he was too controversial a candidate for the operation. It says much for the cohesion of the French Church that Dumay could make no alternative suggestions. Combes would clearly have to think of other coups.

In the meantime Combes's campaign to control appointments had its counterpart in his efforts to control the clergy. His suspensions of salary reached an all-time record – 632, as compared with Waldeck-Rousseau's 150 – and the bag included an archbishop and eleven bishops.[33] In most cases the victim had done no more than express sympathy for the hounded religious orders.

Like his predecessors, Combes invoked the Organic Articles only when it suited government policy. Traditions of irregularity had become so deeply rooted that a systematic restoration policy would have been impossible. In so far as it was attempted at all, it was mainly used to restrict episcopal freedom of speech and movement.

8 *Le Festin de Pierre*

It was now clear that Pius X was not open to the traditional forms of French persuasion. The prospect of vacant sees all over France left him saddened but unshaken; and it now seemed to Combes that something more dramatic was needed. Hitherto Combes had used the threat of Separation sparingly and indirectly; he had merely intoned the familiar lament that Rome was making it hard for him to defend the Concordat in parliament. The summer of 1904, however, brought words of a more desperate kind: Combes was threatening to throw his own substantial weight behind Separation.

This portentous change in tactics arose from a controversial if colourful event. In April 1904 President Loubet defied Catholic protocol by paying a state visit to Victor Emmanuel in Rome; and the Vatican responded in unusually provocative terms.[1] The consequent storm of anti-papal feeling emboldened Combes to promise a debate on Separation in the new year – words that would have burnt his lips a few weeks earlier. With moderates puffing with indignation, this seemed to Combes too good an opportunity to miss. The rumbling of French public opinion would at last penetrate the consciousness of the remote dignitaries of the Vatican, and make them listen. They would at last see how serious were the alternatives to accepting Combes's demands. As is so often the case, however, in invoking this particular spectre, Combes gave it a life of its own.

The vehemence of the papal protest has puzzled most historians; and the episode deserves a closer look.[2] Loubet's state visit was the logical outcome of the Franco-Italian rapprochement of 1898 (see pp. 44–5). When the arrangements became known, Rampolla was quick to point out that this would be the first time a Catholic country had disregarded the papal ban on such visits.[3] The fact that it was France added a piquant irony to the situation – France being the country for which Leo had sacrificed so much, in the hope that she would one day restore his independence.

Eminent visitors to Rome were usually given a papal audience; and Loubet hoped to be no exception – even if the Pope would only see him unofficially. Rampolla feared, however, that even an informal audience might strike other countries as a feeble acceptance of what France had done and be seen as a sure sign of the Pope's declining influence. Any semblance of acquiescence in the French state visit might encourage them to bolder action of their own – either against the Vatican diplomatically or against the Church in their own territories. Consequently neither Rampolla nor Merry del Val was prepared to permit an audience. As Pius explained to a French visiting journalist, 'I understand the reasons of policy that motivate Monsieur Loubet's forthcoming visit to Rome; in the same way it ought to be understood in France that for reasons that are equally political I have to follow the line of conduct adopted by my predecessors in comparable circumstances, without that it implies in any way a sign of annoyance or discourtesy towards the French Government.'[4]

This mixture of firmness and conciliation reflected Merry del Val's own attitude. In order to minimise friction, he agreed to meet Delcassé during the course of the visit – a proposal which originated with the French ambassador at the Quirinal, Camille Barrère. Barrère's accomplice in the affair was the Baron Denys Cochin, who undertook to secure Delcassé's agreement to the meeting.[5] Of mildly monarchist sympathies, Cochin was a born conciliator and an able representative of Catholic interests in parliament.[6] All might have passed off with a minimum of bitterness had not *Le Figaro* decided to break the news in its own particular way. In a recent lawsuit Delcassé had given evidence against *Le Figaro*; and its editor, Gaston Calmette, was determined on revenge.[7] The quintessence of sleek urbanity, Calmette was one of the great charmers of society journalism – 'But absolutely, my dear fellow – but certainly, but of course, I shall be only too delighted.' But he had a hard vindictive streak, which he was later to pay for with his life, when Madame Caillaux shot him dead at his desk in 1914. Calmette knew that if Delcassé accepted the proposal he would still have to use some eloquent persuasion with Combes if the battling premier was to agree to it. A premature indiscretion could make things very difficult for Delcassé; judiciously worded, it might even lead to his dismissal. Accordingly, while Cochin was travelling northward on the Rome-Paris express to see Delcassé, *Le Figaro* told its readers that 'Monsieur Delcassé, *putting the interests of the country above ministerial solidarity,* is rightly striving to obtain an audience with the sovereign Pontiff. It has been decided as from now that our Minister of Foreign Affairs will have an interview, probably several, with Cardinal Merry del Val. . . . It is probable that it is through our columns that the Prime Minister . . . will learn of this news.'[8] This distorted report nearly achieved its purpose. Combes sent a furious message to Delcassé, insisting on a public denial within the day; and although Combes affected to assume Delcassé's innocence, he clearly thought him the originator of the scheme.[9] Delcassé complied;[10] and when the breathless Cochin arrived at the Quai d'Orsay he refused to see him. It was 'a trap' was his later verdict.[11]

Delcassé's public denial of the meeting transformed Merry del Val's attitude. His agreement to the interview had been a considerable concession. That this concession should be thrown back in his face was a disaster. The Vatican had already been humiliated by the forthcoming state visit; and this added humiliation could only do further harm to papal prestige. Accordingly, when the state visit was over he sent an acid note of protest to the Catholic nations, denouncing the visit. And to emphasise that Rome would not submit to similar insults, in future, he added, 'if . . . the Papal Nuncio has still remained in Paris, this is due entirely to very serious reasons'. This last remark, with its threat of diplomatic rupture, did not appear in the version that was sent to France; and its main purpose was to deter the King of Portugal from visiting his royal cousin in Rome.[12]

Retribution was not long in coming. The Prince of Monaco sent his copy of the letter to Jaurès, who published it in *L'Humanité* (17 May 1904).[13] It was just what Combes needed. Locked in combat over episcopal appointments, he saw the letter as a splendid opportunity for doubling the pressure on Rome – with the full approval of French public opinion, Catholics included. Few French Catholics knew the real reasons for the Vatican's anger; and the ostensible issue of the Temporal

Power seemed as dead as the Second Empire. By contrast they believed it vital to detach Italy from the Triple Alliance; and the vast majority of Catholic deputies and senators had voted for the credits to send Loubet to Rome. The ever faithful baron, Denys Cochin, had made a speech, supporting the visit – despite his mounting collection of papal blessings. And Rampolla himself, now in retirement, had approved his attitude.[14] This, however, was too much for Merry del Val. The ability of the nimble old Sicilian to ride two horses at once – the thesis and the hypothesis – never ceased to disconcert his young successor. And he told Cochin in no uncertain terms that the deputies' conduct in voting the credits was indefensible.[15] Such reproof, however, left French Catholic opinion unshaken; they never doubted that the visit was essential to their interests.

The result was that the papal protest briefly ranged a fair number of Catholics behind Combes. When he withdrew the French ambassador – after a show of demanding an explanation – only ninety-five deputies opposed the withdrawal. Combes was well aware, however, that anti-papal feeling on this scale was exceptional and bound to be short-lived. It was therefore essential to exploit it to the full while it was still there.

Separation was not a threat Combes liked using. He shared Dumay's view that to give the Church its freedom would be like letting loose a horde of wild beasts in the Place de la Concorde. Even pretending to open the cage might loosen the bolt. But the papal protest was an unusually suitable occasion for such a threat. As Delcassé pointed out to the Chamber, 'As far as defending national interests is concerned, the paradoxical consequence [of the Vatican's ruling] would be to place the head of a Catholic nation in a situation of unmistakable inferiority to that of the heads of nations belonging to another belief' (27 May 1904). The logic was clear and too good to be missed: Combes promised a debate for 1905.

The year 1905, however, was a long way off; and on the law of averages the Combes cabinet would almost certainly be ancient history by then – or so most people calculated. Even Combes was aware that a more immediate gesture was needed if his candidates were to become bishops. So far he had avoided a formal rupture of diplomatic relations, since this would have removed the mechanism for appointing bishops – thereby defeating its purpose. The withdrawal of the French ambassador had been an informal move, which left unimpaired the Nuncio's position in Paris. But his continued presence brought no break in the deadlock over mitres. At what point Combes would have resorted to a formal rupture, it is hard to tell. What brought it about was another but related matter: the control of the existing bishops.

The unfortunate men who occasioned this bizarre episode were Bishops Le Nordez of Dijon and Geay of Laval. Standing third and tenth in the Government's list of loyal bishops, they were intensely disliked by right-wing elements in their dioceses and the subject of lubricious gossip, far surpassing the limits of routine episcopal scandal. The disturbing feature was that much of it was retained by men of eminence and integrity. Before his elevation to the purple, Le Nordez was said to have shared the favours of a pair of ladies with Eugène Spuller, the Minister of Cultes – a singular foretaste of the *esprit nouveau*.[16] By January 1904 Rome was investigating reports of a recent visit to Paris where 'he spent his nights in orgies with his actresses' – thereby outpacing his legendary counterpart in English bar-room mythology.[17] Geay, for his part, had supposedly competed with his secretary for the affections of an eccentric Carmelite prioress. As far as the prefect could ascertain, his relations with the lady amounted to no more than a correspondence 'reminiscent of the Canticle of Canticles'.[18] But the affair had culminated in an attack on the secretary by a gang of youths – allegedly in the bishop's pay – as he was emerging late one night from the convent. A reconciliation between the two men had eventually been effected, in which the secretary agreed to burn his copies of the bishop's sentimental correspondence – in return for the promise of a titular canonry.[19] And there the matter might have rested. But Geay, it was said, had other fish to fry. By 1904 the papal Under-Secretary of State – the future Benedict XV – strongly believed that he 'was living in concubinage and had three children'.[20]

These and other rumours prompted Merry del Val to summon both bishops to Rome under pain of canonical suspension.[21] This was Combes's cue for a formal rupture. He maintained that suspension, like appointment, was a bilateral business, needing his consent.[22] Merry del Val reposted that it was a mere matter

of episcopal obedience, and refused to withdraw the summons – despite Combes's threat of a formal breach.[23] Retreat would have conceded the French claim to monitor relations between Pope and bishops; and Rome would never accept this. The result was a formal break on 30 July.

The episode highlighted a number of contentious aspects of the Concordatory regime. While standing firm on Rome's right to suspend bishops, Merry del Val had tacitly conceded that deposition was a bilateral matter. Prior to summoning Bishop Geay, the Vatican had advised him to resign before action was taken against him (17 May 1904).[24] Combes had challenged this barbed piece of counsel as a breach of the Concordat;[25] whereupon Merry del Val had commuted it to a mere summons – without formally admitting Combes's point. More fundamentally the episode raised the whole issue of the dual loyalty which bishops were supposed to observe. Napoleon regarded them as his 'prefects in purple', and Geay and Le Nordez had come nearer to this concept than most. Geay had regularly sent personal letters to Combes, denouncing the presence and activities of the religious orders in his diocese, including their connections with local royalists.[26] 'Through you, the Church of France will be delivered from those who oppress her', was but one of the many accolades he bestowed on Combes.[27] Le Nordez had likewise been a zealous agent of government policy towards the orders – so much so that his subordinates spread the rumour that he was a Freemason. But in Roman eyes these bishops' greatest crime was their running to Combes at the moment of reckoning. When summoned to Rome, they had thrown themselves under Combes's protection, invoking the Organic Articles to excuse their non-arrival.

A Republican bishop's life was at best a lonely one. Distrusted by his subordinates, and with no wife to confide in, a Lacroix or even a Fuzet led a morose existence of introspection and lengthy letter-writing to unhelpful politicians. Geay and Le Nordez turned this limbo into something approaching a hell. Having opted for the tender care of *le petit père*, they soon discovered that they were no more than pawns in his game. Realising at long last on what side a bishop's bread was buttered, they quickly changed horses and made their way Romeward – Geay more reluctantly, as his pathetic letters to Combes amply indicate.

Resigning their sees, they eventually reconciled themselves to the pensioned life of a bishop *in partibus infidelium*, with nothing but the past problems of long-dead desert hermits to trouble them.

The diplomatic break with Rome did not represent a new direction in Combes's policy. This was but the biggest and best of his detonations to shake the Pope into compliance. And to make the bang still louder he increasingly made Separation a subject for public statements, notably in his Auxerre speech of 4 September. Gustave Hubbard had ably and bitterly summed up Combes's policy in the previous September. Urging the Grand Orient to insist on Separation, he declared. 'The Separation of Church and State ought to be something more than a mere bogey, with which one tells the Church "Be good, or you'll be separated!" '[28]

Anyone who chose to analyse Combes's Auxerre speech would see that even at its face value it promised nothing before 1906. Perhaps more ominous were his remarks to the *Neue Freie Presse* on 10 August, when he spoke of making a few necessary amendments to the Commission's draft bill. He was clearly alarmed by the moderation of the Commission's draft and the speed with which it was being perfected. What is not clear is how high he rated its chances in the Chamber. The events of the previous months – notably the Vatican protest over Loubet's visit – had undoubtedly lessened the reluctance of most deputies to envisage this solution. Whether there was now a majority positively in favour of it was still far from obvious. What was also uncertain was the willingness of Separatists to continue tempering their zeal in the interests of cabinet stability. At the time of the papal protest in May, Jaurès had resisted the temptation to stampede the Délégation des Gauches into demanding Separation at once.. Combes was still too useful to be trampled into the carpet. But the Amsterdam conference of the Second International (14–20 August 1904) found the French parliamentary Socialists under bitter attack for supporting a bourgeois government; and it was uncertain how long Combes could rely on their sympathetic restraint. Similarly no ministry of two years' duration could expect to be without jealous enemies; and Combes had every reason to suppose that the deputies who wanted another spin of the wheel would exploit the Separation issue to unseat him.

In the meantime he had commissioned Dumay to draw up for him a short draft Separation bill which should serve as a basis for discussion. This Dumay sent him on 24 August.[29] Dumay knew his master too well to be unduly put out by this request. As he told a young inquirer, '*La Séparation, cher Monsieur, vous n'y pensez pas! C'est une impossibilité.*'[30] But within the depths of his substantial being he was worried lest Combes's sabre rattling might create a situation that the premier could no longer control.

Although Dumay regarded his task as a purely theoretical exercise, the terms of his bill were remarkably generous. A notable feature was the salarying of the existing clergy throughout their lifetime. The younger clergy would be a charge on the national budget for half a century or more. Having dealt with clerics all his life, Dumay understood their difficulties and thought that generosity was political wisdom. Besides, a salaried clergy would still leave the State with the weapon of salary suspension. The wild beasts, roaming the Place de la Concorde, would still be held by a silver chain – which in turn would require a keeper holding the other end. And who would this keeper be, other than Dumay? His bill, however, was far too openhanded for Combes's liking, and was duly consigned to a bottom drawer.

With the approach of autumn, Combes began to suspect that he was a sorcerer's apprentice, with the water lapping coldly round his knees. His majority was slowly sliding from under his feet, and his bluff was being called on a variety of issues, including Separation. Combes first became aware of the bleak turn events were taking when he encountered cold looks from the president of the Gauche Radicale, Jean Sarrien. As *de facto* leader of the Délégation des Gauches, Sarrien's face was a barometer that could not be ignored. When Combes eventually steered him to a quiet bench and asked him what was wrong, Sarrien replied that the Government was showing too much indulgence towards the Socialists.[31] With other members of the Gauche Radicale, Sarrien was anxious that Briand should not acquire credit for himself and his Socialist supporters by proposing an acceptable scheme of Separation. Consequently, on 19 October, the Gauche Radicale formally decided to invite the Government to present its own Separation bill – on the pretext that a measure of this importance should originate with the Government rather than with the *rapporteur* of the Commission. As Jaurès bitterly remarked, 'It is all because the *rapporteur* of the Commission is a Socialist, and neither Briand nor socialism must be allowed a privileged part in this great reform. . . . That is the level to which the Gauche Radicale has sunk.'[32]

In fact the issue was yet more complex. Combes's ministry had now lasted four times the national average of seven months, and the queue of self-groomed premiers, Sarrien *en tête*, was getting restive. By inviting Combes to present a bill and take direct responsibility for it, they were urging him to mount an unpredictable horse on very rough ground – which might well throw him. This was certainly the hope of the Union Démocratique, when it made a similar request on 24 October. Their aim was threefold. By throwing Combes into the saddle, they would kill Briand's bill and his growing reputation.[33] But given Combes's views on Church-State relations, they assumed that any bill bearing his name would be much more stringent than Briand's, with every chance of a stormy run in parliament. Those who feared Separation hoped that a Combes bill would not only kill Combes, but the Separation as well.

It was hard for Combes to refuse. Indeed such freedom as he had in the matter was snatched from him on 28 October, when the Nationalists raised the *affaire des fiches* in the Chamber. Parliament was told how the Ministry for War had been collecting information on the religious commitment and private opinions of Catholic officers, in order to block their promotion. There was nothing new about French governments making private inquiries into the loyalty of their military and civil employees – it was the *sine qua non* of the Republican reign of virtue. But it was usually done discreetly, and with the knowledge of immediate superiors. It now transpired that the War Ministry was using the Masonic network in the army to obtain the information it desired, and that the whole operation was a jointly conducted enterprise by the ministry and the Grand Orient.[34] The rot in fact had started much earlier, under Waldeck-Rousseau, when the Sureté Générale had been used to spy on Catholic officers (see p. 81). Combes inherited the system with General André, the War Minister; and in many ways it was a logical if more disreputable development of his own inquiry of 1895–6 (see p. 49).

One of Combes's first circulars to his prefects reminded them that 'while you owe justice to everyone . . . you keep your favours for those who have unmistakably proved their fidelity to Republican institutions' (20 June 1902).[35] André pushed the principle much further. Officers who sent their children to private schools or were regularly seen at Mass were put on the 'Carthage' list, which condemned them to passing their service in the same familiar routine on the same familiar rung of the ladder. Only those on the 'Corinth' list of Republican orthodoxy could expect to exchange the dispiriting life of dreary garrison towns for staff work in Paris or interesting assignments abroad.

Even within the *heiligen Hallen* of Masonry, however, there were men who had their price; and the Nationalists knew where to spend money profitably. Armed with an impressive pile of *fiches*, they astonished the deputies, and the readers of *Le Figaro*, with the extent and *mesquinerie* of André's great enterprise. Their main aim was to detach Combes's less fervent supporters; and although Jaurès and Pressensé eloquently reminded the Chamber that it would be playing the Nationalists' game in sacrificing Combes, the ministry was undoubtedly discredited. It was only by a handful of votes that it survived the initial indignation of the house. Further unexpected support came from Gabriel de Syveton's brutal assault on the abject War Minister, André. The spectacle of a Nationalist deputy hitting an older man momentarily swung emotion the other way. And the Nationalist cause was scarcely helped when Syveton gassed himself a few weeks afterwards. Despite stories of an elaborate Masonic contrivance to lethalise the gaslight in his room, few doubted that he had taken his life to avoid legal proceedings; he was faced with the double charge of embezzling the funds of the Ligue de la Patrie Française and of entertaining sexual relations with his daughter-in-law. Versatility was always a strong card with the Nationalists.

Given the ministry's predicament, Combes had no option but to deliver his Separation bill. Besides, there were positive advantages. The Commission would be faced with a new unhewn document, which could only lead to long acrimonious debate. To oblige them to scrap Briand's bill and a year's work was perhaps the best way of ensuring that the Separation would remain a shining star in the Republican firmament – ever leading, still proceeding, never to be attained.

The bill which Combes lobbed into the Commission on 29 October epitomised his dislike of Separation. Owing nothing to Dumay, and differing radically from Briand's, it aimed to keep the Church under the closest state supervision: *'le règne concordataire sans le Concordat'*, as Clemenceau derisively called it. It was symptomatic of its character that it should specifically keep the Direction des Cultes in being – something that even Dumay's bill had not dared to do, except by indirect implication. Its material provisions likewise reflected its tight-fisted nature. Property which the Commission's bill had left in church hands was now to be held only in usufruct, subject to decennial review by the Government. It also doubled the fines and prison sentences listed in the Commission's bill (see p. 166) and reduced the size and number of state pensions for elderly clergy. Its most offensive articles, however, were those governing the *associations cultuelles*. Most Separation bills, including the Commission's, proposed that each parish should form an *association cultuelle* which would be the legal embodiment of the Church in that particular area. It would be these associations that would administer the property left to the Church and provide for the material wants of the parish. It was assumed that in practice Catholics would wish to link them in a hierarchy of unions, corresponding to the national pyramid of episcopal authority. In this way the Church would have a strong overall structure that would guarantee its unity and its material well-being. It was precisely this strength, however, that Combes wished to destroy. His bill therefore restricted unions to the size of a department (i.e. a diocese). Moreover, the reserve funds of the constituent associations were to be strictly limited to the absurdly low level of a third of their annual income – thereby denying them the possibility of any sizeable building project.

As Combes's enemies had hoped, the bill aroused a storm of protest. It notably roused the quiescent ranks of Protestants, many of whom had relished the prospect of Separation as a free-trade existence where their superior products would quickly oust the old-fashioned wares of Rome. Combes's ban on large unions would hit them hard. In areas where they were widely but thinly spread, local resources would be insufficient to maintain sufficient churches. A system of unions would have enabled the richer regions to help the weak; but Combes's bill destroyed this possibility at a blow.

But as the Nationalist press was quick to point out, any lobbyist who was not a Jew could be expected to be a Protestant. And the bill was scarcely public before a Protestant delegation sat itself down at Combes's table and talked away the limitation on Protestant and Jewish unions.[36] The Commission likewise softened a number of other offensive features; but the bill remained highly unpopular, except with the more obsessive *mangeurs de curés*.

As things turned out, its days were numbered. So were Combes's. The *affaire des fiches* had deprived him of his thinner-skinned supporters; and it was now merely a question of choosing the best time to resign. When he threw in his mandate on 18 January he did so with the sour satisfaction that he had never once lost a division and had outlived every previous ministry under the Third Republic, except Waldeck-Rousseau's. Although he was now once more among the svelte fountains and lissom statues of the Luxembourg, his attitude to Separation grew no mellower. A few days after leaving the wrought-iron cage of the Place Beauvau, he was proudly presented with a legal treatise on Separation by the rising young lawyer, Paul Grunebaum-Ballin. Combes's reply was scarcely warm : '*La Séparation, Monsieur, oh, c'est une affaire très difficile, très compliquée, et il faudra beaucoup de prudence et d'habilité pour mener à bien une pareille entreprise.*' [37]

ROUVIER

Combes was succeeded by his own finance minister, Maurice Rouvier. In the minds of many he was a shifty relic of the Panama Scandal. Although in his own words his involvement in the affair had not resulted in 'my fortune having increased abnormally', it had cost him ten years' exile from office. Some thought that this was not enough; but as a distinguished historian has said, 'the Republic, if it had shown in dealing with the Lesseps that it could be just, showed in dealing with Rouvier . . .

that it could be understanding'.[38] In short, he understood the stewardship of wealth in something other than the biblical sense.

Sympathetic to the *esprit nouveau*, he stood for the quiet life in Church-State relations. Anything that divided men of sound conservative views on economics was anathema to him. But the developments of the past year made it impossible to bury the Separation, as he would have wished. The monstrous paradox remained that the Concordatory Combes had more or less committed the Government to Separation; and the relative indifference of the general public to the issue had surprised and reassured the many deputies who had opposed it for fear of an electoral backlash. Although this indifference was nothing new – the deputies' fears being excessive – the thinking public may also have been influenced by the Vatican's recent *maladresses* in the Loubet affair and other matters. Whatever the truth of the matter, Rouvier had to face the sad fact that a Chamber which had been against Separation in 1902 was now displaying an unhealthy interest in it. It was also clear that Combes's bill was far too divisive for any cabinet to pin its future on it. It had been partly intended as an obstacle to Separation; and Rouvier was not prepared to indulge in the kind of contortions to which Combes had committed himself. If the cabinet could not avoid sponsoring Separation, then at least it should be on the straightforward wicket of the Commission's bill. The normal tactics of delay and postponement were still open to him; but if in the end they failed, then at least the Separation should be a viable scheme, however unwelcome. He might even derive some credit from it.

Credit was certainly the aim of the new Minister of Cultes, Jean-Baptiste Bienvenu-Martin. A member of the commission of inquiry into Panama, he knew his master well, and was determined to offset Rouvier's lack of enthusiasm. While Rouvier was hoping to delay the matter until after the 1906 elections, by giving precedence to other distasteful reforms, Bienvenu-Martin was intent on ensuring himself a place in the annals of the Republic. Jaurès was not the only politician to regard the Separation as 'the greatest reform to be attempted in our country since the Revolution'.[39]

Such Fabian tactics as Rouvier had in mind were brusquely blown aside by a Chamber vote on 10 February demanding an early debate. And to the astonishment of all, the great debate began on 21 March: the stone guest had arrived.

It was soon clear from each division that the bill was going to go through parliament with very little alteration – other than the Commission's own amendments. The bill's opponents had to face the fact that they could rely on no more than 230 odd votes in a house of 588. And although amendments were coming from all sides, a solid core of some 160 deputies – mainly Radical-Socialists and Radicals – were systematically voting the articles as the Commission presented them. Beyond this bloc there were sixty-nine *mangeurs de curé* who were trying to give the bill a more punitive twist; but however numerous their amendments and explosions of wrath, they could be relied on to vote for the ensemble of the law when the final division took place.

Apart from the Catholics and right-wing opponents of the Government, the main hope of the *concordataires* lay with the Progressistes. Although their leader, Alexandre Ribot, believed in a bilateral Separation *à l'aimable* as a long-term objective, he and many of his following were opposed to the method and content of the current proposal. With most Progressistes against the bill, the balance that would decide its fate lay with some ninety deputies, mainly 'moderates' of the Left Centre. Fifty belonged to the Union Démocratique and twenty-two to the Gauche Radicale. Their vote would depend largely on considerations of political expediency. Only six of them were declared partisans of Separation; and Briand and Jaurès were firmly convinced that if the rest were to be captured the bill must remain moderate and non-punitive. It was to this group that Catholics looked when trying to soften the bill. Those deputies who obliged did so for a variety of reasons, mainly political. In the case of George Leygues, Louis Barthou and their colleagues of the Union Démocratique, a predominant motive was the desire to humiliate Briand by effacing his stamp from the bill. It was their revenge for failing to destroy his bill in the previous October, when they forced Combes to present an alternative.

To get them to join the ranks of the militant *concordataires* would be much more difficult. Leygues's erastian views made him a *concordataire* at heart; and the fact that he had debts led some Catholics to consider offering him material encouragement to display his sentiments less shyly. The papal *chargé d'affaires* in Paris, Mgr Carlo Montagnini, kept Merry del Val regularly informed of these and other propositions.[40] Son of a Piedmontese baker, Montagnini seems to have judged French politicians by the standards of the market place – though in fairness to him he passed on most of this information without indicating his own views on its propriety. Merry del Val, for his part, appears to have ignored these wistful hints as to what a little money might do, his surviving replies containing no reference to them. The withdrawal of the Nuncio in the previous summer left the Vatican with no other official in Paris except Montagnini, and Merry del Val was obliged to use him, despite the little regard he had for him. Entertaining but frivolous, it was unfortunate that circumstances had placed Montagnini in such a responsible position at so critical a time. '*Leger* – a complete muff!' was Merry del Val's private verdict on him, summed up by a friend.

Montagnini often cited Jacques Piou, the leader of Action Libérale, as his source of information on the potential venality of various parliamentary figures. But it is conceivable that Montagnini was concealing personal suggestions under cover of a respected French name. One such letter was to have an unexpected subsequent career. Montagnini told Merry del Val that 'according to Piou, one could buy Clemenceau's consent to a complete hand-over of the churches to the Catholics, and that he would oppose the associations cultuelles as outlined in the law; but Piou said that it would need a very large sum of money'.[41] When Montagnini was subsequently expelled from France and his papers confiscated, this letter was published in several newspapers. Piou denied all knowledge of the affair,[42] and Clemenceau also wrote a typically barbed disclaimer. He confessed to having no recollection of Piou making such an offer, but felt it outside his competence to say whether Piou had indeed received money for this purpose and had merely trousered it.[43]

Fortunately for the Catholic cause, these various proposals seem to have gone no further than the realm of wistful speculation. If they did, one can only comment that the money was ill-spent, for the returns were nil.[44] The most difficult part of the bill, Article 4 (see pp. 176–7) was voted before the Easter vacation, while the whole debate came to an end on 3 July. The result was a surprise to no one – the bill was through by 341 votes to 233. Its moderate character had won over all but six of the Union Démocratique and all but two of the cautious wing of the Radicals.

Its passage through the Senate was a foregone conclusion. Although hostile petitions gathered nearly four million votes, the country saw few demonstrations of any note; and the Senate's main concern was to finish with the bill before the January senatorial elections. It consequently passed the Senate unamended in under a month (9 November–6 December) by 179 votes to 103.

The hero of the parliamentary battle was undoubtedly Briand. For three months he had steered the bill through the Chamber, reconciling what was workable with what the majority would accept. His skilful resistance to attempts to give the bill a punitive character earned him the admiration and confidence of many members of the Catholic opposition; and his defence of Article 4 in particular prompted Albert de Mun to shake him publicly by the hand. Even so, the roots of the bill lay in the preparatory work of Pressensé. Not only had he provided Briand for most of the material for his first draft (see pp. 111–16), but some of the most far-reaching of its later features were the result of Pressensé's amendments. It was his crucial amendment to Article 4 (see pp. 175–7) that allayed the fears of many Catholics and enabled Jaurès to declare, '*La Séparation est faite* !' when the Article was voted.

Yet the credit for both the bill and these amendments was largely attributed to Briand – 'inspired by Jaurès', as journalists and historians have usually added. Amid the banquets that the Socialists held in Briand's honour, only the Ligue des Droits de l'Homme thought of fêting Pressensé; and, perhaps symbolically, the banquet never took place. Even when Briand deserted socialism in 1906, the Socialists chose not to acknowledge the true authorship of the bill; to have done so might have seemed an act of pique; and their earlier tactical silence on Pressensé's role (see p. 116) would have required too much explaining. When Pressensé died of a stroke in 1914, some of his friends publicly recalled his contribution to the Separation. But this passed largely unnoticed outside the Socialist and Ligue press. There was vague talk of the need for some sort of biography; but the outbreak of war put an end to this in a matter of months.

9 Catholics and the Separation

More than most statesmen, Popes lead a schizophrenic existence, straddling life as it ought to be and life as it is. Leo XIII had rephrased this dual existence as the thesis and the hypothesis. The thesis was the ideal, while the hypothesis was the melancholy approximation with which the Church had to be content at any particular given point in history. Indeed the fanciful visitor to St Peter's may choose to see the difference symbolised in the two clocks that face him as he crosses the great disc of the piazza, the one always ten minutes faster than the other. After absently readjusting his watch a number of times, he may experience a sense of fellow feeling with the Faithful, as he wonders which of the two should guide his life for the present.

On the level of 'the thesis', the Separation was undoubtedly a tragedy in Rome's view. Pius made this abundantly clear in his reverberant encyclical of 11 February 1906, where he deployed the whole regiment of Leo's anti-Separatist arguments. When it came to 'the hypothesis', however, there was arguably room for doubt. Pius had been conscious of the invigorating effect it might have on the clergy, forced to fend for themselves; and he did not share Leo's view that it would be an overwhelming disaster. But as a deeply humane man, with a lifetime of pastoral experience, he realised the hardship that would face the French clergy; and as head of the Church he was acutely conscious of the humiliating way in which the Concordat was being unilaterally abolished. It was this aspect above all which troubled Merry del Val – as will be shown in a later chapter. And so, even on the level of 'the hypothesis', Rome concluded that the Separation was a misfortune – to be actively averted, if this could be done with dignity.

A FORLORN VENTURE

Dignity, however, was precisely the missing ingredient in a proposal made to Rome to save the Concordat in January 1905. The initiative came from Dumay, desperate to save his life's work and his livelihood. With the cold winds blowing about him, he hoped that if he could rekindle the damp ashes of the dialogue on vacant sees, he might prod the Concordatory machinery into some sort of life.[1] He had to move warily, however. It was unlikely that his new master, Bienvenu-Martin, would renounce the historic role so nearly in his grasp, for the meagre satisfaction of a hole-and-corner transaction on vacant sees. And although Rouvier detested Separation, its scent was so strong in parliament that it would be extremely difficult to call off the majority. Nevertheless if Rome were prepared to make the first move, Dumay felt that there was just a slim chance of success.

He baited his hook attractively. Not only would he engineer the sacrifice of one of the candidates who had caused most trouble, Casanelli d'Istria (see p. 127), but he also hinted that if the Vatican revealed its real reasons for rejecting Mazeran, he would try to persuade the government to drop Mazeran as well.[2] This ambitious pair of priests being the main obstacle to agreement, Merry del Val was prepared to make this bargain.[3] The leader of the Progressistes, Alexandre Ribot, recommended that the ever obliging Denys Cochin be used as a post box between Merry del Val and Rouvier.[4] This would minimise the risk of parliament getting wind of the scheme, as well as keeping Bienvenu-Martin in happy ignorance for the time being. It was the method of inception that posed problems. Dumay wanted Rome to initiate contact by announcing its formal acceptance of Gazaniol for Bayonne (see pp. 127–8), without waiting for the official nomination from the Government. This was far too blatant a breach with normal procedure for Merry del Val to consider.[5] It would have put Rome in the posture of a begging petitioner, as well as providing Separatists with the sort of ammunition they needed. It was ironic that the nomination in question was that of the much calumnied Gazaniol. Unknown to Dumay, the Vatican had already resolved to accept him; but either Lorenzelli or Combes had chosen to sit on this particular sprig of olive, instead of passing it on (see p. 128).

The delicate chances of the scheme were soon stamped into the ground when Rouvier revealed his presence and brought down his boot. He told Cochin that with the Government publicly committed to Separation, such a scheme would be political suicide.[6] And there the matter ended. For those who knew, its main interest lay in the evident readiness of Rome to rescue the Concordat if it could be done with any decency.

PRINCIPLES AND PRACTICE

Given the relative consistency of Rome's view, it is scarcely surprising that the vast majority of the French clergy either said nothing or merely adopted what they took to be the official standpoint of the Church. This was not mere intellectual subservience; the majority sincerely shared Rome's view, both on the practice and principle of retaining the Concordat. The same could be said of most of the thinking laity – though they displayed a greater readiness to chance their arm in criticising the drawbacks of the system; their careers were not at stake.

Taking an overall view of the years 1890 to 1905, opinion had two phases. Before 1904 Separation seemed only a remote possibility, and was discussed mainly on the general level of what would disappear with the Concordat. In 1904 and 1905, however, Separation slowly changed from a possibility to a certitude, to be discussed in the detailed terms of the available proposals.[7]

Debate during the first period had the intellectual advantage of not being subordinated to defensive strategy. The drawbacks of the Concordat were more openly criticised, and the hypothetical nature of Separation entailed a certain imagination in its treatment. Opinions in these years make rather less tedious reading than much of what was said during the Separation crisis itself – even if they lack the clarity of thought that can only come with the smell of powder in the air. Even so the material is sparse, and unremarkable for its originality or felicity of expression. Given the history of the past decade, no one in the 1890s could seriously imagine that parliament would offer the Church a favourable system of Separation, or indeed a concordat that was preferable to the old. There was no place for a Catholic Separatist group of the eloquence of Lacordaire, Lamennais or

Montalembert. In so far as such sentiment existed, it was largely linked with anti-Republican feeling. It was symptomatic that Separatists who accepted the Ralliement in 1892 generally dropped their former criticism of the Concordat.[8] Conversely those who remained anti-Republican often provided the most outspoken Separatists – until the Government officially adopted Separation in 1904, when they transformed themselves into impeccably loyal supporters of the Concordat.

The Cassagnac family and their blustering paper, *L'Autorité*, were a case in point. Tracing their ancestry to the First Crusade, they combined a staunch Catholicism with a sturdy contempt for Leo XIII's conciliatory policies. Bonapartist by conviction, Paul Adolphe de Cassagnac preached what he called '*N'importe-quisme*': '*n'importe qui ou n'importe quoi sont préférables à la République*'. During the period when Combes openly opposed Separation, *L'Autorité* spoke of it as 'the supreme deliverance', and condemned the Concordat for 'strangling and gagging the Church in France'.[9] But when Combes was forced to give Separation an encouraging pat in 1904, the whole weight of *L'Autorité*'s invective was turned against the barbarity of such a proposal. A few days after Combes presented his bill, Cassagnac suddenly died on his return from a hunting party on the family estates in Solange. Scarcely had his last breath mingled with the *trompes de chasse* in the autumnal woods, when his son Paul-Julien took up the cause with all the family gusto. Throughout 1905 he kept *L'Autorité* in the forefront of the attack on the Government's bill; and he was also unsparing in his onslaught on those Catholic deputies, such as the Abbé Hippolyte Gayraud who were not afraid to point out the advantages of Separation.[10]

As far at the Nationalist deputies were concerned, their changing attitudes were inextricably tangled with their anti-ministerial tactics. Among them, Edouard Archdeacon and the immaculate Comte Boni de Castellane were popularly regarded as leading spokesmen of Catholic interests – as well as those of the turf. Archdeacon had been at Déroulède's side during his ill-fated attempt in 1899 to deflect the army against the Elysée (see pp. 74–5); and he subsequently slid into parliament with the Nationalist landslide in the Paris elections of 1902. When Réveillaud proposed a parliamentary commission on Separation (see p. 105), Archdeacon was one of the few Catholic deputies to vote for it – anything to cause Combes trouble. He was also the only Catholic since 1871 to present a Separation bill (10 April 1905). But once again his aim was to harass the Government, which was already committed to the Commission's bill. The Church, however, was soon to lose the services of this sturdy freebooter. Within a few weeks of the bill becoming law he died of a stroke while following the fortunes of one of his horses at Auteuil.

His fellow patron of the turf, Boni de Castellane, had likewise pursued a devious course on the Separation issue. Following Archdeacon's tactics he had startled Catholics by not opposing Réveillaud's demand for a Separation commission. But he later won the unstinted praise of Merry del Val for his vigorous attack on Loubet's visit to Rome;[11] and when the Government eventually had to sponsor Separation, he became one of the Concordat's principal champions in the Chamber debates of 1905. The result was that he was popularly if undiscerningly viewed as one of the leaders of the Catholic cause in France – especially by foreigners. The Catholics *avant-tout* were only too glad to have support from anywhere, and were consequently happy to let the illusion stand. The price was paid the following year, when Castellane's divorce from the American heiress, Anna Gould, scandalised foreign opinion, especially in America.[12] Having spent his wife's fortune on sumptuous building and Venetian carnivals, he had allowed his discerning eye to rove too openly. American Catholics had been lavish in their promises of financial aid to the French Church; and the news of the count's marital infidelities came at a singularly inauspicious moment.[13]

The *volte-face* of these Nationalist 'Separatists' regarding Separation had its counterpart among Catholics *avant-tout* – but for different reasons. The small minority with Separatist inclinations before 1903 were antagonised by the ungenerous spirit of the various bills under discussion, and were quickly driven into a defensive posture. The subtlest mind among the French bishops, the liberal Archbishop Mignot of Albi, believed that 'Separation is more compatible with the spirit of modern democracy'; but he was forced to admit that 'as much as I would favour a Separation that was honourable for all concerned, I am just as much opposed to the Separation that is being prepared for us'.[14] His fellow intellectual, the abrasive Bishop Le Camus of La

Rochelle, saw the Concordat as a hangman's rope and ridiculed his colleagues' attachment to it: 'They suffer from the same illusion as Aristobule when he let Herod drown him on the pretext of teaching him to swim'.[15] But even he kept quiet during the Separation crisis – though out of prudence rather than conviction. The same was true, if for different reasons, of the royalist Bishop de Cabrières of Montpellier. A life-long opponent of Republican control over church affairs, he remained a vocal Separatist until the decisive events of 1904 – when he rallied with the rest of his colleagues to the defence of the Concordat.

The only section of the clergy who were to retain a marked *penchant* for Separation were the more militant members of the religious orders, notably those that had been dispersed. Given their precarious position, however, they rarely committed their views to print; and it is mainly in private correspondence that they survive. Having always been proudly independent of state finance, they had often experienced a mild contempt for the secular clergy who had sold their freedom for a pittance. 'Come on in, the water's lovely' was their advice in 1905, many of them believing that the morale of the secular clergy would be vastly strengthened once they had tasted freedom. At the same time there were the deeper and more complex feelings of those regular clergy who believed that Leo and Rampolla had sacrificed the orders to the Concordat (see p. 89). They hoped that once the Concordat was abolished, no future Pope would be tempted to indulge in the sycophantic antics of the nineties. For the Bailly brothers the Separation was 'the end of slavery',[16] the breaking of 'the golden chain'.[17] No doubt they also experienced a certain bitter satisfaction in the evident ruin of Rampolla's calculations – exile having deepened their hostility to the Government. Anyone who came to terms with the regime was suspect in their eyes – including the religious orders who had accepted authorisation. 'If the authorised orders stay on peaceful terms with such a government it will be a proof that they are unworthy priests, incapable of doing good.'[18]

POVERTY

As every nervous deputy knew, the most explosive features of the bill were the expropriation of the churches and the abolition of clerical salaries. Both could affect the great indifferent masses. Despite their *s'en fout-isme*, the vast majority of people were married and mourned in their local church, even if they rarely set foot there at other times; and, within a fortnight of birth, each of their successive babies was held, red-faced and indignant, over the grey baptismal font. The legislator was on very sensitive ground. Similarly the end of state stipends would mean the withdrawal of priests from many small parishes and an end to a traditional feature of rural life. To lose 'Monsieur le curé' would be like losing the golden weather vane and its attendant jackdaws from the village steeple.

The bill assumed that churches and cathedrals built before the Concordat belonged to the local authorities or the State.[19] The arguments for this assumption had a respectable lineage in French legal tradition (see p. 271), even if they were hotly contested by Catholics.[20] The ownership of more recent buildings, however, depended on who built them and where. Those built entirely from private funds on private land would be given to the Church, as represented by the Catholic *associations cultuelles* (see p. 140). But the rest, including those built only partly with private money, would return to the local authorities. Until the bill was amended in June 1905, it proposed that the local authorities should rent their churches to the *associations cultuelles* for a fairly modest proportion of their income.[21]

Modest or not, Catholics objected strongly to the idea of renting churches which they regarded as theirs They were not impressed by the argument that the church-builders of the *ancien régime* would have been the freethinkers of 1905 (see note 20). Even if this point were granted, the fact remained that the churches were built by Catholics for Catholics. They therefore thought it unjust that they should be denied ownership of all churches built before 1801, particularly those built by a single pious benefactor. It likewise struck them as unfair that only churches *wholly* built with private funds since 1801 should be regarded as theirs. In La Sarthe, for instance, more than 90 per cent of church building since 1801 had been undertaken with private money; yet, according to these criteria, all the churches belonged to the communes and none to the Catholic population as such.[22] What it meant on a national scale can be seen from Table 3.

TABLE 3

The Ownership of Places of Worship

	Parish Churches	Chapels of Ease	Cathedrals
Belonging to the commune	33,872	5,107	2
the department	1	1	
the state	878	338	85
Undecided	132	147	
Belonging to private individuals	222	466	
Attributable as outright property to the *associations cultuelles*	1,477	841	
Total	36,582	6,900	87

(Compiled from information in A.N., F^{19} 1986^{3})

Many bishops were in favour of refusing to rent these buildings. 'We will abandon our churches, not willingly but thrown out by the gendarmes; and we will go into the woods and caves to say Mass'; Bishop Delamaire's diocese of Périgueux was well provided with such natural alternatives.[23] But the ironic Bishop Briey of Meaux had more comfortable plans. He and his clergy would throw themselves on the mercy of Messieurs Rothschild, Ephrusi and Cohen d'Anvers, who had never let the church want for anything in the diocese.[24] Even the timid Archbishop of Paris, Cardinal Richard, was inclined to favour a boycott of the bill's proposals.[25] Indignation was often tempered with policy. Cardinal Langénieux's secretary, the sharp-witted Abbé Landrieux, put the issue squarely to the Pope. 'If we rented the churches, we would lose at one blow the entire fruit of our sacrifices, for the public, seeing no outward change, would feel its normal life unaffected, and would easily fall in with the new state of affairs. Whereas if we are locked out of our churches, if we are literally forced to say Mass in improvised shelters, then there can be no mistake: the fact of persecution will be clear to everyone.' Pius conceded that this advice was 'the worthiest and wisest attitude' to take, but prudently added that no decision could be taken until the circumstances of each diocese had been assessed.[26] Although Pius and Merry del Val were shortly to show a flair for firm uncomfortable decisions, they were perplexed by the conflicting comment that was coming their way. Montagnini had passed on rumours that if the Church refused to rent the buildings rich Anglo-Saxon Protestants would rent them, to put at the disposal of their French co-religionists – whose number, they hoped, would be increased by the Separation crisis.[27] More plausibly, Catholic liberals feared that the Church would be thrown into the arms of rich anti-Republicans, who would be only too willing to buy its affection with offers of alternative accommodation.

For this and other reasons liberals on both sides of parliament wanted to drop the idea of charging a rent in favour of allowing Catholics the free use of the churches. The Abbé Gayraud even chanced his arm by saying that he could vote for Separation on these lines.[28] It also had appeal for the cautious elements in the Union Démocratique. The parliamentary elections were only a year away, and anything that would reduce potential ill-feeling in the electorate was welcome. For men like Georges Leygues, moreover, there was the added attraction of putting a spoke in Briand's wheel (see p. 138). The Union Démocratique was particularly well placed to act. Holding the balance in the Chamber, it was easy for Leygues to persuade the Commission to accept the change (9 June 1905);[29] and Briand may well have recognised the latent good sense of the proposal. It was he, after all, who was later to develop the principle in 1906 and 1907 (see p. 209).

The change was not without problems for Catholics. The *associations cultuelles* would now be responsible for major repairs as well as normal maintenance; and this would impose heavy burdens on the smaller parishes. Nevertheless the benefits to both sides were so patent that it passed the Chamber by 523 votes to 37.

Catholics tried hard to win a similar solution for the presbyteries, episcopal palaces and seminaries. But being less emotive items than the churches, these buildings were unlikely to be an electoral issue; and parliament could afford to be stern about them. The bill gave local authorities the option of renting or selling them to the *associations cultuelles* – or, alternatively, of putting them to some other use. The question of ownership rested on the same criteria as the churches, and gave rise to the same potential injustice. In La Sarthe alone, private benefactors had given the communes at least seventy presbyteries. But because they had technically been given as outright gifts to the communes – and not to the parish councils – they were regarded as communal property, which could now be only rented or sold to the *associations cultuelles*, not given to them.[30] The national situation is indicated in Table 4, from which it will be seen that only 2233 of the country's 32,531 presbyteries could be given outright to the *associations cultuelles*.

TABLE 4

The Ownership of Presbyteries, Episcopal Palaces and Seminaries

	Presby-teries	*Archi-episcopal Palaces*	*Episcopal Palaces*	*Grands Séminaires*	*Petits Séminaires*
Belonging to					
the commune	29,303		2		7
the department		2	10	2	1
the state	320	15	54	66	13
Undecided	94				2
Belonging to private individuals	581			1	20
Attributable as outright property to the *associations cultuelles*	2,233		3	17	95
Total	32,531	17	69	86	138

(Compiled from information in A.N., F^{19} 1986^{3})

The Vatican was faced with the same problem as with the rental of the churches – should it allow it or not? The issue was not an immediate one, in that the bill allowed the status quo to run for a transitional period of five years – or two years in the case of the palaces. But Rome chose not to wait; it issued a prohibition in January 1906. Only in cases of unusual hardship were the buildings to be rented – and then on terms which few communes were likely to concede.[31] A change of heart was to come two years later (see p. 210), but by then the situation was to be infinitely more complicated.

Fewer problems were posed by the residue of church property. The bill assigned most of it to the *associations cultuelles* – nearly half a milliard francs' worth – while the portion allotted to the public authorities was worth well under 20 million.[32] Even here, however, there were sensitive items. Some of the gifts predating 1801 had religious duties attached to them – such as the saying of Masses for the soul of the donor – and Briand was in favour of giving them outright to the *associations cultuelles*. His colleagues, however, objected that this would undermine the bill's basic distinction between pre- and post-Concordatory property (see p. 152); and so the concession was squashed.[33]

The issue that engendered most heat was the suppression of clerical salaries. For many this was the culmination of the great work of achieving religious neutrality in France. For the Church it ultimately meant a complete reappraisal of its functions and methods.

Whatever their views on Separation, nearly all Catholic writers regarded these salaries as a permanent obligation on the State – for the reasons rehearsed in Chapter Three (see pp. 53–4). They were an indemnity for the church property confiscated at the Revolution, and could not be stopped without equivalent material compensation. Catholics were largely alone in this view, however, in that even their parliamentary allies, the Progressistes, preferred to regard the salaries as a remuneration for a public service rather than the repayment of a debt. When the State no longer required the service, the salary should cease with it. The result was that constructive debate was limited to the terms on which state payment would be brought to an end – notably the details of the phasing-out period and the special arrangements for elderly priests.

The pensions eventually offered to the elderly and middle-aged looked quite generous on paper (see Table 5). But when priests came to tot up their entitlement, a lot of them found themselves excluded by a barbed proviso in the tail of the concession. The bill insisted that pensioners must have twenty or thirty years' *state-paid* service; and this effectively killed the claims of the many priests who had spent their early careers in the hungry role of supernumerary *vicaires*, unpaid by the State.

The terms in fact would have been harsher had not the Union Démocratique made one of its periodic raids on the Commission. Not only did they twist Briand's arm to make him improve the pensions (6 June 1905), but they also obtained concessions on the phasing-out period for other priests.[34] Priests living in poor parishes of under a thousand were to receive transitional benefits over eight instead of four years (see Table 5) – but on condition

TABLE 5

Clerical Pensions and Transitional Benefits Accorded by the Law of Separation

Age	*State-paid Service*	*Pensions as % of Salary*	*Transitional Benefits as % of Salary*			
			1st yr	*2nd*	*3rd*	*4th*
60 plus	30 plus	75%				
45 plus	20 plus	50%				
Others		None	100%	66%	50%	33%

that they stayed put. The condition was an important one, since one of the great fears of the Union Démocratique had been that Separation would see the withdrawal of priests from poor parishes. Deputies might well have to pay the price for this at the next election. If, on the other hand, priests could be held down for eight years by the silver thread of a dwindling allowance, this would allow time for the Separation issue to lose its heat and gain gradual acceptance in the country at large. With luck, no one need lose his seat – either in 1906 or 1910, let alone 1914.

This last flicker of state generosity enraged the leaders of the *politique du pire*. It threatened to take France through the 1906 elections without the explosion of public feeling which was the only hope of the extreme Right. In desperation they urged the clergy to refuse the pensions and benefits – and a fair number needed no urging. Several bishops, not particularly noted for their intransigence, felt that refusal was the only effective means of protest. Of those, moreover, whose ill-will was never in doubt, Bishop Douais of Beauvais ('*mauvais*' – 41st) categorically forbad his priests to apply for their benefits – under pain of suspension. This piece of forcible enthusiasm caused Rome considerable embarrassment. When Merry del Val had sought Cardinal Richard's opinion on the matter in 1904, Richard had been in favour of acceptance[35] – a view which Rome was prepared to endorse. Merry del Val therefore entrusted the smooth-tongued Montagnini with the delicate task of cooling Douais's ardour.[36]

By the time the May elections were over, over 30,000 priests had submitted their claims for entitlement; and most of the rest did so in the next few months.[37] A few wrote to their prefects, formally renouncing their rights; and the text of their letters was splashed across the pages of the local right-wing press. But try as they might, the Right had to admit that this was a poor harvest for their efforts.

So indeed were the elections themselves. The last forlorn card in the hand of the *réfractaires*, they were a bitter disappointment. The Chamber that emerged was, if anything, slightly worse than the last; and the elections, in so far as they had a religious significance, seemed to endorse the Chamber's anticlerical record.[38] There was not even the dubious consolation of blaming it on the electoral campaign. The Church, far from idle, had been unsparing in its support of Jacques Piou and Action Libérale Populaire. Not only did it dissuade Catholics from supporting anti-Republican candidates, but it had also managed to re-route funds that had been collected for these candidates. When the Ligue des Femmes Françaises collected money for the Right, Rome wrote to the Archbishop of Lyon, commenting that their collection was 'worthy of praise' but that its distribution among candidates of their choice 'cannot be approved'. The archbishop should persuade the ladies 'that it is good to collect money, but that it should then be given to Your Eminence in full confidence'. The archbishop was then to confer with Piou on the choice of candidates and the precise allocation of the money.[39]

While Rome had shown a healthy respect for the power of money, the Assumptionists had not neglected the forces of divine aid. Vincent Bailly told his brother that Henri Groussau's flagging chances in Lille had been transformed by a massive demonstration of public piety; the churches had been full of people making the Stations of the Cross, with the result that Groussau's majority surpassed all expectation. The same was true in the department of Tarn where the Stations of the Cross began at six in the morning. The Catholic Reille brothers consequently obtained 'stupefying majorities' – 'despite the fact that this happened in the archdiocese of Mgr Mignot' – where miracles were presumably taboo. Elsewhere, however, Catholics had not prayed 'with the faith that works miracles. Too often hope was based on alliances with the devil, and such alliances do not bring grace.'[40]

The election results turned a cold harsh light on gestures of clerical protest. It became apparent to most French priests that spectacular sacrifices such as the spurning of pensions, would harm no one but the Church. And attention now turned to the practical question of replacing the *budget des cultes* with voluntary funds.

Hopeful eyes were turned to America – not only for money but for experience. Under the Concordat, a number of French priests had looked with envy across the Atlantic, and had attributed the vigour of the American clergy to the fact that the Church in the United States had had to fend for itself without the financial support of governments. The late 1890s had seen a minor clerical craze for *l'Américanisme*. The Abbé Félix Klein had produced a French edition of Walter Elliott's *The Life of Father Hecker* (New York, 1891) – *Le Père Hecker, fondateur des Paulistes américains, 1819–1888* (Paris, 1897) – a book which introduced its French readers to a refreshing frontiersman approach in religious thinking, unlike anything they had hitherto encountered in Catholic writing. 'The Church may still be the old Ark of Noah, but we've got to propel her by steam' was not the sort of thing French churchmen said; and the book quickly aroused among the more liberal clergy an enthusiasm for Hecker's ideas – which many assumed were characteristic of American Catholicism as a whole. On a wider front, a less intellectual interest was shown in the periodic appearances in France of sturdy prelates like Archbishop Ireland of St. Paul, who wore trousers and travelled by tram. Nevertheless, while many French priests believed that the American Church owed part of its vigour to Separation, Americans themselves were often dubious about their relevance to France. The Primate of the United States, Cardinal Gibbons, warned them that it would require many years of Separation before the French would realise their personal responsibility towards the upkeep of the clergy. In America nearly all the ambitious projects the Church had undertaken had been done with money contributed by people of Irish, English or Polish origin. 'The Italians and the French never give to the Church because they know that in their countries the priest is paid by the government; they think of him as a civil servant; and it takes at least a generation to teach these immigrants the duties they owe to the American clergy.'[41]

None doubted that the rich would rally round; but this itself could bring its dangers. As a priest had said fifteen years earlier, 'Instead of being dependents of the government, we will be dependents of the *château*. Instead of having a master a hundred leagues away, we will have him right next to us, every day, at every hour, with his demands and fancies.'[42] The activities of the Duchesse d'Uzès were a warning sign. Since the collapse of Boulangism, she had been relatively discreet in her political activities; but in September 1904 she had launched a campaign to provide for the needs of impoverished priests.[43] What was begun in the gay spirit of a charity bazaar could easily become a connection of the most compromising kind. Despite her genuine concern for the Church, her name was a symbol that could only alienate committed Republicans.

The sort of situation they feared was clearly foreshadowed in the diocese of Angoulême. The ingenuous Mgr Ricard had naïvely disclosed that 'a noble soul' had said to him: 'If the Concordat is abolished, I will support all the *curés* of the canton, Monseigneur – and, if you will allow it, you yourself.'[44]

Reliance on the rich had further dangers. It could enslave Catholic energies to a traditionalist routine of preserving and restoring the Church's existing methods and structure. Marc Sangnier – of Sillon fame – was particularly worried by this aspect of the Separation. The temptation to concentrate all efforts on replacing what had been lost would deflect the Church from its evangelical work among the working classes. 'Millions will be found to adapt huge halls [as places of worship] and fill them with flowers, so that elegant ladies and gentlemen will find there all the comfort to which they are accustomed. Great trouble will be taken to set up learned committees of lawyers to teach us how to get round awkward laws. But no one will give a sou or a day's work to help found a people's institute.'[45]

While the events of the immediate future were to prove this indictment only too true, there were many Catholics who did not share his pessimism. They saw Separation as precisely the opportunity for making Catholics conscious of the vast sections of society that lay outside the Church. The hazards of the new regime would attract seminarists of a more adventurous spirit, and the Church would have to find new methods and a more effective form of organisation.

Priests like the Abbé Gayraud were quick to point out the sort of considerations examined in Chapter 3 (see pp. 60–1). The telephone and new forms of transport would enable country priests to cover several parishes. They might also enjoy the advantages of living in community, with the opportunity of reading periodicals and keeping abreast of current developments, as well as giving each other moral support.[46] Gayraud's colleague in parliament, however, the Abbé Jules Lemire, was strongly opposed to this method of 'fanning out across the countryside in cars and on bicycles'. The only way a priest could serve his people was to live with them, 'to become incrusted' in the parish.[47] This was also the view of the Supreme Pastor himself, a Pope whose whole understanding of his role was that of the traditional parish priest. His feelings on the matter were made abundantly clear in June 1907, when Merry del Val wrote to the French bishops warning them against a restructuring of the parochial system. There must be no withdrawal of priests from poor parishes except 'in exceptional and extraordinary circumstances where there is a moral certitude that it will have good results. Otherwise it would be disastrous to the moral well-being of the Faithful. . . . The Holy Father wishes it to be understood that in no matter what circumstances there should always be in each parish at least one priest on immediate call to exercise his ministry.'[48] This was to destroy at a blow the hopes of those who saw in the Separation a unique opportunity for adapting the Church to the religious requirements of a changing France.

In foreshadowing the papal view, tthe Abbé Lemire had not neglected the economic problems of keeping priests in existing parishes. 'As for finding the wherewithal to live, let us do what St Paul did, *ministraverunt manus istae*. . . . The people will see intellectuals, educated in the humanities and theology, earning a living from the hard labour of the fields. . . . The priest's training will make him the most intelligent, the most perceptive and the most knowledgable of the tillers of the soil, the man of good counsel and increasing influence.'[49]

The concept of the priest engaged in manual toil had much

to appeal to the imagination. Archbishop Servonnet of Bourges thought of providing his seminaries with technical courses in various trades, though few of these – jewellery, watchmaking and sculpture – would have appealed to the ideals of the Abbé Lemire.[50] There was clearly a danger that the liqueur-making image of the great abbeys might find a secular counterpart in the art-and-crafty parish priest, selling cruciform jewellery and breeding pedigree kittens. The peppery Baron de Mandat-Grancey was particularly opposed to priests engaged in 'fancy work'; he cited the case of a priest who had made a small fortune in embroidering skirts and blouses, but had completely lost the respect of his parishioners. In the Baron's view the clergy should stick to religious activities and economise by living in groups.[51] On the other hand, the idea of the priest with a *métier* found eloquent spokesmen in the fourteenth *arrondissement* of Paris, where the Abbés Soulange-Boudin and Jean Viollet were making a name for themselves with their experimental social work in the parish of Notre-Dame de Plaisance. Soulange-Boudin looked forward to the day when the priest would 'work in the daytime in overalls and blouse, and spend the evenings preaching the word of God in bars and cafés, like the socialists preaching revolution'.[52] His *vicaire*, Jean Viollet, one of the few active Dreyfusards among the clergy, saw an impoverished clergy as the surest means of regaining the confidence of the people. 'This Separation Law is worth far more than Napoleon's Concordat. It will make the priests poor – an excellent thing!'[53]

Few ideas have made more appeal to the modern secular imagination than 'the worker-priest'. He ranks with the guerilla leader, grenades at his belt, as one of the cult figures of youth in revolt, a challenge to the bourgeois complacency of the older generation. Opposition from Rome has added the further attraction of martyrdom; and, whatever mistakes its individual exponents may have made, it is clear that 'the worker-priest' is a concept that will continue to excite interest far beyond the confines of orthodox Christianity. Although its roots can be traced to earlier centuries, it acquired recognisable shape during the high tide of anticlerical activity under Waldeck-Rousseau and Combes. With the threat of Separation becoming more plausible, certain priests began to examine the alternatives to the state-paid full-time pastor.[54]

The idea of the industrial scene as a mission field was already well established among progressive clergy, if insufficiently appreciated by the hierarchy as a whole. Its most cogent expression came from Mgr Boeglin, writing in 1905.

> There stretches around Paris an immense China where the parish apparatus has not changed since 1820: the same personnel, the same church, the same resources. When they were founded, they numbered 10,000 souls; today they number 50,000. The withering away of the parish, its excessive conservatism, its routine, and the over-rigid application of the Concordat have resulted in the complete neglect of these recently opened areas where a genuinely pagan untamed people is growing, deprived of any possibility of sustaining its religion through contact with the *curé* and the Church. It is not the people who have let down the parish; it is the parish that has let down the people.[55]

In 1892 the Comte Albert de Mun had told a meeting of *La Croix* committees,

> I would like to see in every French diocese a group of hand-picked priests, young and tough, with courage and initiative, who would study social issues and train themselves to talk about them to working-class audiences. Those studying agricultural problems would explain them to the peasantry, while those studying economic problems would found credit societies, workers' banks and workers' associations. Being neither *curés* nor *vicaires*, and having no state salary, they would be able to appeal directly to the people, so as to reconcile them with the Church.[56]

The priest as counsellor, however, was still a long way short of the worker-priest; and it required a considerable effort of the imagination to make the intervening stride. It was therefore not surprising that it should first be made – in an unambiguously modern form – in a work of fiction. This was *Moine d'Après-Demain. Journal intime*, written by the Abbé Charles Calippe and published in *La Démocratie chrétienne* between February 1902 and March 1903.[57] A friend of the Abbé Lemire, Calippe had deeply interested himself in social issues during the 1890s; and he said of his novel, 'it is neither a prophecy nor a recommendation, but a hypothesis for discussion. The problem is to know how the Church and French clergy would live, if socialism came to power.'

The priest who provides the central character takes up work in a factory as a result of the Separation of Church and State and the cessation of his salary. A Socialist government subsequently obliges all priests to take up secular employment, leaving them only the evenings and Sunday to fulfil their pastoral duties. Although the situation proves to be short-lived, the friendship and mutual respect which it has engendered decides the hero to make factory work a permanent feature of his ministry.[58]

Shortly after the novel appeared, the Abbé Paul Naudet painted a dramatic picture of what Separation would probably entail for the clergy.

> The time is near when only those who have gained their bread by the sweat of their brow shall eat, when only those who can get the attention of ordinary men and speak their language, shall preach. . . . The dream of a quiet life in the shadow of a country steeple will be nothing more than a dream for our generation. . . . Our place is in the *avant-garde*, amidst those priests who already see their parishes as a mission field and who are organising them as such.[59]

If these invigorating words, like a stiffening breeze, shook the branches of traditional attitudes, the leaves were still slow to fall. The first year of Separation gave birth to the Alliance des Prêtres Ouvriers, which soon had a membership of over 400. But their activities were far removed from the prophecies of the Abbés Calippe and Naudet. To be a member it was sufficient to work manually for five hours a week; and in most cases the practical purpose of the work was money-raising rather than apostolic. Although the organisers made a mystique of manual work, it largely took the form of home-crafts, there being no suggestion that members might work in the secular environment of a factory.[60] Such an idea, even if it had been put forward, would have required episcopal authorisation – which would almost certainly have been refused. Apart from the disturbing novelty of the proposal, it would have foundered on the material worries of the bishops. With state salaries a thing of the past, their main preoccupation was finding priests to man existing parishes and fulfil their normal functions. And with these immediate problems on their desks, few thought to ask themselves whether these traditional functions were still adequate or appropriate to the industrialised regions of France. Given the supposed shortage of priests, they would have regarded a full week's secular work as a waste of the priest's precious time: an extravagant expenditure on bait which would leave nothing to provide a hook.

Despite the experience and experiments of seventy years, this attitude still prevails.

The difficulties of finding money after the Separation was one problem; whether the Church would be allowed to keep it was another. The Separation took place in an atmosphere of deep mutual suspicion, and it was natural that even committed Separatists should hesitate before giving the Church unlimited freedom to amass large funds.

The Concordatory system had kept Church resources under close supervision; but anticlericals feared that the new *associations cultuelles* could easily become electoral committees if left to their own devices. They might slip into the gap left by the more militant regular orders that had been driven underground. Even so Briand considered some of these fears exaggerated. Although he had every reason to respect the power of money – he suffered its lack more than many of his colleagues – his bill was more generous to the Church than Pressensé's.[61] Catholics had to admit that the associations were considerably better off than they would have been under French common law – which the Right was always invoking. As *associations déclarées* under the law of 1 July 1901 their sources of revenue would have been limited to members' subscriptions; and since only a small number of parishioners were expected to take out formal membership of the associations, this would have been a serious restriction. The Separation Law, on the other hand, afforded them a fair range of fund-raising methods,[62] and also allowed them to keep a ready reserve of money, as long as it did not exceed six times their average annual expenditure. Any surplus could be placed in the Caisse des Dépots et Consignations to provide for the purchase or repair of property – and there was no limit to the money that could be amassed there. The same facilities were accorded to the diocesan and national unions, which meant that large central funds could be accumulated for long-term projects without being the war-chest that the anticlericals had prophesied.

The good behaviour of the associations was also ensured by other means. There was notably a special scale of fines and prison sentences for priests who used the pulpit as a political platform. Although this distinction between priests and other Frenchmen was arguably at variance with the principle of Separation, it was too ingrained in the French legal tradition to arouse much comment. The scale of punishments was in fact a substitute for certain articles of the Penal Code which disappeared with the Concordat.[63]

LIBERTY

When the Jeremiahs of the Church spoke of poverty, the optimists spoke of liberty. And the liberty they had most in mind was freedom to choose bishops. They wrote about it less often than they thought about it, since it was hard to discuss without implying that the existing bishops were not all that they might be. Few of the lower clergy dare run the risk of seeming to criticise their superiors, while the bishops themselves were chary about condemning a system to which they owed their own promotion. It needed an outspoken layman like the Baron de Mandat-Grancey to state, and overstate, the case against government nomination. He came from a class that regretted the days when bishops were gentlemen and thought like gentlemen; and although he was sufficiently emancipated from his background to welcome the ascendancy of intellect over family he gave a macabre account of the depths to which he believed the episcopate had descended through the influence of Dumay. Nevertheless allegations of political servility need to be seen against the fact that he was writing for *L'Action Française*;[64] and the attitude of most bishops scarcely endorsed his more sweeping accusations. He might also have reflected that only a state-supported Church could afford the luxury of bishops who were remarkable for their intellect rather than their financial acumen.

Whatever their shortcomings, France was spared the droves of Neanderthal-browed businessmen who filled the Catholic sees of the New World and the British Empire. Even so, much of the Baron's criticism echoed what many Catholics were thinking; and, as that flitting socialite, the loquacious Montagnini, reported to Merry del Val, people felt that 'episcopal action has diminished over the last twenty years. It is doubtless the result of the government choosing bishops who are honest but incapable of exercising a sufficient influence over the clergy.'[65]

The new austerity in Rome, however, made some liberal Catholics wonder whether the new-found freedom in France would be such a blessing after all. It would all depend on whether the Vatican was prepared to consult the French clergy in choosing bishops. One of those with cause to worry was Bishop Lacroix of Tarentaise. An intellectual and a liberal, his Republican sympathies had earned him the title of 'the Harlot's trainbearer' from Paul de Cassagnac. His tiny Alpine diocese had afforded few flints for his intellectual fire; and he had periodically asked Dumay to remember 'your little mountain flower' when providing candidates for more important sees[66] – Versailles being his ideal.[67] He personally favoured the formation of electoral colleges within the dioceses and provinces which would provide the Pope with a short list of suitable candidates when a vacancy occurred. And on the principle that wishing might make it so, he made a point of telling newspapers that this was what would probably happen. He also publicly expressed astonishment that the Government had not insisted on some sort of *exequatur* that would guarantee it against firebrands.[68] As he suspected, however, his own chances of promotion were to disappear with the Concordat.

Lacroix was not the only prelate to marvel at the Government's neglect of an *exequatur*. The future Secretary of State, Mgr Gasparri, apparently told a visiting abbé, 'If the Separation Law does not stipulate an *exequatur* for the bishops and principal *curés*, you can tell your ministers that they are *fichues bêtes*.'[69] The idea had not escaped the Government. According to his own testimony – which was admittedly subject to mood and convivial euphoria – Briand later suggested an *exequatur* to Clemenceau, when the two were in office in 1906. But Clemenceau apparently replied, 'We must remain in the logic of Separation. . . . That is none of our business.'[70]

Such a view, however, was incomprehensible to Dumay, who throughout 1905 had fought a remarkable rearguard action in favour of state control. The disconsolate director had even sponsored a press campaign to sow sensational rumours about Vatican intentions. Using the Abbé Charles Denis in the *Giornale d'Italia*[71] and Bonnefon de Puyverdier in *Le Journal*, he had claimed that Rome intended to classify France as a *pays de mission*, in which the episcopal sees would be handed over to the Assumptionists, the Jesuits, the Capuchins, and the Dominicans.[72] Bonnefon de Puyverdier ('Jean de Bonnefon') belonged to the demimonde of fashionable journalists who specialised in backstairs ecclesiastical gossip. Believing that reality rarely lived up to the dramatic possibilities of a given situation, and finding that fiction paid better than fact, his reports were usually liberally laced with fantasy – a tendency which was reflected in the decor of his dimly-lighted apartment, where ecclesiastical bric-à-brac was mixed with a motley collection of Orientalia to create an atmosphere of *fin de siècle* mystery. A close acquaintance of Dumay, he was only too happy to launch the director's *canard*, in the hope that its vociferous quacking might cause the Separatists to think twice before delivering France to the clerical lions.[73]

It caused amusement rather than alarm, however, and, despite talk in other papers of a drastic Roman purge of the episcopate, the regime continued to slide into the abyss. When the Separation bill passed the Chamber and went to the Senate, the incorrigible Dumay made one last effort. He tried to persuade Bienvenu-Martin to fill some of the vacant sees before the passage of the bill gave Rome complete freedom in the matter. Needless to say, Bienvenu-Martin was 'furious and showed him the door'.[74]

Dumay's misgivings were not without foundation. Montagnini had spent September collecting suggestions for the vacant sees; and although he consulted moderates as well as intransigents, his final list of recommendations was scarcely a triumph for moderation. His proposals for archdioceses included Luçon of Belley ('*mauvais*' – 53rd), Cabrières of Montpellier ('*mauvais*' – 63rd), Bonnet of Viviers ('*mauvais*' – 65th and last), and Dubillard of

Quimper, whose public statements had become steadily more violent. Montagnini suggested that the Pope should rapidly fill the existing vacancies himself, without a formal system of consultation, lest the Government introduce an *exequatur* in the forthcoming *règlement administratif* implementing the law.[75] This congenial piece of advice was readily accepted in Rome; but in order to counter accusations of authoritarianism, Cardinal Mathieu was asked to devise a system for consulting the French bishops on future appointments.[76]

The subsequent trend in nominations was to cause many to regret the days of state control. The method of consultation proved to be little more than a gesture (see pp. 214–15); and the new bishops were to be principally chosen for their conformity to the new style in papal politics.

The bishops were not even allowed to speak with a corporate voice. Most Catholics had looked forward to the abolition of the Organic Articles and the freedom to hold episcopal assemblies (see pp. 56–7); 'there are bishops, but no episcopate'. But this was not what the Vatican had in mind. Three assemblies were held to discuss the material problems posed by Separation (see p. 214); but thereafter the bishops were not allowed to meet again until 1951. In the words of one of the better-known back-seat drivers of the Church, Julien de Narfon, 'There used to be bishops, but no episcopate. Now there are not even bishops.' Liberals asked if the Church in France had merely exchanged one form of bondage for another.

10 Some More Principles

United in their opposition to Separation, the Vatican and the French clergy were dramatically divided over the *associations cultuelles*. On 10 August 1906 the sombre encyclical, *Gravissimo officii*, solemnly ordered Catholics not to form these associations. The French Church was thereby stripped of the only embodiment that the State would recognise. This act of legal suicide not only obliged the Church to sacrifice nearly half a million francs' worth of property (see p. 272, n.32); but it also deprived it of the means of rebuilding new material resources on a basis of legal security. It was only when the prohibition was lifted much later, in 1924, that the French Church was able to regularise its position vis-à-vis the law, and undertake new building programmes without risk of legal complication. The property lost in 1906, however, was beyond recovery. It was to take half a century of dreary appeals and collections – and less dreary bazaars and tombolas – to replace the resources that had been so spectacularly discarded.

This enormous sacrifice ran counter to the wishes of most French Catholics. Faced with the problem of maintaining 42,000 clergy[1] and buying or renting the appropriate accommodation, they were not in a mood to add to these difficulties by accepting self-imposed burdens that would further weaken the Church still further.

There were many arguments against the prohibition; and the case in its favour is not easily understandable – least of all in the encyclical's terms. Most historians have confined their attentions to the situation in France. They have therefore assumed that the papal ban stemmed from either a misreading of the French situation, or a determination to enjoy the political fruits of martyrdom. While there is some truth in both these verdicts, available evidence shows that the Vatican was primarily concerned with the wider international implications of the Separation Law. These will be looked at in the next chapter.[2]

When wolves invoke principles, sheep, who have read Aesop, suspect their arguments. It was understandable that churchmen should regard the legal scruples of the Separation Law as so much *chinoiserie,* designed to ease the way to further theft. Yet the principles involved were both logical and honest, however harsh the impact. Even so, it required a certain effort of the imagination to enter into this lawyer's world of abstract possibilities. It was an astrologer's ball where politicians and jurists tried to foresee every eventuality that the future might hold – both for Church and State.

The proposed system of *associations cultuelles* reflected the legal principle that, after Separation, the State could recognise the Church only as a group of French citizens engaged in a certain activity, namely worship: an activity that was legally no different from pigeon-racing or philately. For this reason the Separation bill made no mention of Pope or bishops, since it was not the law's business to give definitions of the Church. To have done so would have been to remove the right of French Catholics to change their concept of the Church. For the same reason, the bill did not stipulate the inclusion of an orthodox Catholic priest in each association. Similarly French law was equally silent on the officers and constitution of rifle-clubs and dramatic societies – despite the wealth of legislation that affected them. It had no desire to bind enthusiasts to a form of organisation that they might later wish to discard.

This legal prudery, however, was beyond the comprehension of many of the clergy. Few Catholics could conceive of the Church without Pope or bishops; and it was pointed out that the silence of the bill on the distinguishing marks of the Church would deprive tribunals of the means of judging whether these associations were truly Catholic. Schismatics might form *associations cultuelles* to contest the ownership of church property; and there would be no legal provision for distinguishing between the schismatical and the orthodox. In the words of one official, '*toute la bohème ecclésiastique*' of unfrocked theological eccentrics would seize the opportunity to create a net-work of self-styled 'Liberal Catholic' parishes.

But when it came to invoking principles, the Church could outdo the State any day. Pius X fired his first official salvo on the Law in his encyclical *Vehementer nos* (11 February 1906), a document which fully lived up to its titular opening. After condemning the unilateral abolition of the Concordat, the document denounced the system of *associations cultuelles* as an attempt to impose a constitution on the Church without reference to it and clearly against its wishes. The State was not competent to frame a constitution for the Church; Christ had given the Church its constitution, and it was for the State to accept it. The Law, moreover, proposed a constitution which was directly contradictory to the principles of the Church's organisation as established by Christ. The Church was essentially a hierarchical body, consisting of a priesthood with divine authority to teach and govern, and a laity, 'the obedient flock', whose duty was merely 'to follow its pastors'. The Law, moreover, ignored the pastors and gave authority in all matters that concerned the State to the obedient flock – by whom the *associations cultuelles* were to be formed and maintained.

Modern enthusiasts for the Apostolate of the Laity would be unlikely to find much inspiration in this document. Nor is Pius X a Pope to appeal to the proponents of Women's Liberation. Amid his cares and tribulations, one of the few subjects that would provoke him to prolonged jocularity was the pretension of women to political rights. When Madame André de la Gorce offered herself to serve the Catholic cause in France, Pius told her ' "Women should devote themselves to their families. . . . There are some who not only want to vote", added the Pope, *en riant de bon coeur*, "but who think they should be entitled to enter parliament and have a place in the cabinet of ministers in order to take part in government! None of that is suitable for women." '[3] It was perhaps no accident that his *Motu proprio*, purifying Church music, should also banish women-choristers to cooking the Sunday roast. They – together with two centuries of Church music – were now to give tongue only in the concert hall.

Vehementer nos went on to condemn the law for its silence on the bishops. This, it claimed, was a highly dangerous omission. It was true that the law insisted that the associations should correspond to the '*règles d'organisation générale du culte*'; but it contained no criteria by which the courts could settle conflicting claims. Rival associations might compete for Church property in the same parish. Only the bishop could competently say which association represented the Church; but the Law refused to recognise his competence in explicit terms. The supreme judge of the issue was to be the Conseil d'Etat; and the Church had no guarantee that parish property would remain in the hands of orthodox Catholics.

The architects of the bill could reply that Article 8 of the bill obliged the Conseil d'État to take account of '*all* the factual circumstances' in giving its judgement, and that these circumstances would necessarily include the bishop's opinion. But, as Catholics pointed out, there was no legal guarantee that the bishop's opinion would prevail against all the other 'factual circumstances' presented to the court.

Rome's objections were developed and put in their decisive form in the momentous encyclical of the following August, *Gravissimo officii*. Since the bill failed to provide adequate safeguards, Catholics were solemnly forbidden to form *associations cultuelles*; and the issue was guillotined, not to be resurrected for another eighteen years.

The blast of these organ-like encyclicals initially numbed most ears to other sounds. But there remained a sharp discordant question which had troubled thinking Catholics months before the encyclicals appeared, and which became increasingly obsessive as the impact of these documents died away. If there really was a danger of church property getting into the wrong hands, the refusal of the Church to form associations would encourage rather than prevent this danger.[4] Insubordinate Catholics who formed an association could claim both the property and the use of the parish churches. If no orthodox association hove in sight, the authorities might well entrust the church to the only claimant, without worrying overmuch whether this association conformed to the Catholic '*organisation générale du culte*', invoked by the bill (see pp. 175–7). The religious loyalty of most peasants was directed to the parish church rather than to any abstract idea of 'the One True Church, Holy, Roman and Apostolic'; and any association that got legal occupation of the building was in a strong position to attract the bulk of parish-churchgoers. If, like Rome, you believed in the Government's malevolence, you could not expect the authorities to leave the church in the personal care of the orthodox *curé*, with no association to represent him. Not even the most optimistic Catholic could have foreseen that this was precisely what the government was later to do in 1907 (see p. 209).

In short, Rome seemed to be inviting the very dangers it claimed to be avoiding. With no associations, the Church could only acquire property in the name of private individuals; and this scarcely promised security for a body which seemingly doubted the loyalty of its members. If a priest thumbed his nose at his bishop, no one could deprive him of the church or presbytery built in his name. Moreover, with the Church increasingly dependent on rich benefactors, a lot of property would remain in the hands of strong-minded *châtelains* and manufacturers – with equally strong-minded heirs, not necessarily sharing their fathers' enthusiasms. It was potentially a lawyer's paradise, full of hazards for the future.

Episcopal control was the key issue in both encyclicals. Yet the law allowed the Church complete freedom to secure this control by imposing its own rules on Catholic associations. The Church could make obedience to the hierarchy a formal condition of membership – as the framers of the law were quick to point out. Briand told parliament, in his smoothest tones of reassurance, that 'the Church can give these associations a uniform set of statutes throughout France . . . and in the case of competing associations, these statutes will be he main piece of evidence on which the tribunal will make its award'.[5] The inventive Archbishop of Besançon, Mgr Fulbert-Petit, took up this point and drew up the specimen code of statutes which was to win the approval of fifty-nine of his colleagues at a plenary assembly of French bishops in May 1906 (see pp. 199–200). His code ensured the orthodoxy of the associations by an impressive array of conditions. No association could be formed without the bishop's consent, and the founder had to be a priest approved by the bishop. The association not only had to be a member of the bishop's diocesan union, but all its important decisions were subject to his consent. Each member of the association had to make a declaration of allegiance to the hierarchy, as well as satisfy the bishop that he was a practising Catholic. Its functions, moreover, were specifically limited to financial and administrative matters, thereby leaving the clergy's spiritual authority intact.[6]

It was as well for Rome that its formal reasons for rejecting the associations were not its real reasons. Otherwise one might have suspected a crisis of lucidity. Yet for an important minority in France the official case was not only real; it had its origins in their own attitudes and apprehensions.

The atmosphere of the previous four years had conditioned them to distrust anything that came from parliament. At the same time anti-Republicans were enthusiastically using it to turn politically indifferent Catholics against the regime. Symptomatically the hunting-pack of *L'Autorité*, *Le Soleil*, *La Libre Parole* and *Le Gaulois* were all for spurning the associations. Their talk of schism moreover had its counterpart in the anticlerical press; and when friend and foe alike spoke of the imminent destruction of the Church in France, it was understandable that the innocent *bien pensant* should think the bill as bad as people said it was. To make matters worse, the president of the Separation commission, Ferdinand Buisson, was rash enough to join the anticlerical chorus, prophesying schism.[7] In his private capacity as President of the Association Nationale des Libres Penseurs de France, he was perfectly entitled to do this; but given his parliamentary position, it destroyed the trust of many in the integrity of the bill's designers. It was these articles that first started the bishops talking seriously about schism, the main outcry being led by the bustling Bishop of Quimper, Mgr Dubillard, who told *Le Gaulois* on 1 March 1905 that he expected the Pope to forbid the associations.[8] His statement received wide publicity, the culmination coming on 28 March, when five French cardinals denounced the associations as 'a formally schismatic enterprise'. The last straw came a week later when the Separatists' apostle of sweetness and light, Eugène Réveillaud, threw off his sheep's clothing and publicly welcomed the schismatical possibilities of the law (4 April).[9] This was the man whose bill of 1903 would have made the bishop's word the test of orthodoxy (see p. 113). If even he was a Judas, what could be expected from the rest?

A further cause of anxiety was the initial absence in the bill of the famous phrase, '*en se conformant aux règles d'organisa-*

tion générale du culte'. At the time Pressensé framed his bill, he had not foreseen these problems; nor had Briand when he adopted Pressensé's system of associations. This, however, had been one of the first targets of the Catholic minority on the Commission. They wanted the bill to designate the bishop as the arbiter of orthodoxy; but both Briand and Pressensé felt that this would be an improper solution (see p. 171.) A near-convert like Pressensé, however, could well appreciate Catholic qualms on this score; the unitary nature of the Church had, after all, been one of Rome's attractions for him in the middle-nineties. With characteristic energy he set himself to the task of finding a solution that would satisfy both sides; and the eventual outcome was the saving phrase that did so much to lubricate the passage of the bill. As he explained to the Commission, he arrived at this formula 'through examining the legislation of certain American states' and the 'Wee Free' case in Scotland.[10] He proposed that the courts should adjudicate between competing associations '*en se conformant aux règles d'organisation générale du culte dont se réclament les associations en constatation*'. Had his proposal been accepted in this form, the issue would have been solved. But when he put it to the Commission on 10 April 1905, the double-headed – if not two-faced Buisson – objected to it being made to that particular part of the bill (the future Article 8 – see pp. 177–8).[11] He would only allow it in the section that defined the role of the associations – a close-fisted attitude that was to cause trouble in the future (see pp. 177–8). Accordingly Article 4 was amended on 19 April: the associations were to be formed '*en se conformant aux règles d'organisation générale du culte dont elles proposent d'assurer l'exercice*'. Coming at a critical moment, the amendment did much to subdue for a while the chorus of bishops predicting schism and indiscipline; and a majority of the Catholic deputies voted for it in the Chamber debate of 22 April.

This debate did much to reassure uneasy minds. As a result of Ribot's prodding, Briand asserted that only those associations that were in communion with their local bishop could benefit by the law – an affirmation that he had not wished to make in so many words. When Réveillaud pleaded that the law leave room for schismatics to claim their fair share of Church property (see p. 175), Briand replied that schismatics had freely chosen to leave the Church. 'They are quitting the home; you can't give them the right to carry off the furniture as well!' Even the circumspect Merry del Val allowed himself to say, somewhat prematurely: 'After the vote of Article 4, Church property will effectively be given to the diocesan bishop.' He then added, reverting to type, 'It is essential that the Catholic press does not admit to this success. That would be impolitic.'[12]

Another reassuring feature of the debate was the indifference of most anticlericals to the question of schism. As their fiercest spokesman, Maurice Allard, commented, 'Monsieur Réveillaud wants us to bring about a religious change. But we don't want either Catholicism *or* Protestantism.' Like most *mangeurs de curés*, his object was a different one. He wanted Church property to be confiscated and put to secular social purposes. His main hope was that in many parishes the Catholic association would be unable to recruit enough members to be able to claim Church property.[13] In such cases Allard wanted the property to be given to works of public assistance – as envisaged in the final draft of the bill (Article 9). What he was determined to prevent was the award of the property to '*cultuelles de fantaisie*', set up by dissident religious groups. '*Il n'y a pas de catholiques en dehors du pape*', he later asserted – to which his Catholic opponents gladly replied 'Amen!'[14]

The issue seemed no sooner settled, when it was suddenly and violently reopened by the debate on Article 8. All might have been well but for a minor amendment to the article. Cases of rival associations were now to be settled by the Conseil d'État '*statuant au contentieux*' (i.e. in its juridical role), not by the civil courts, as earlier. Catholics strongly opposed this change, because of the proximity of the Conseil d'État to the Government. Memories were fresh of the part played by the Conseil d'État in the wholesale slaughter of the religious orders by Combes; and it was alleged, somewhat simplistically, that the Conseil d'État was merely the government's hangman. If the government wished to split the Church, the Conseil d'État could be expected to behave once more as its compliant tool – especially since Article 8 contained no guarantee of orthodoxy similar to that in Article 4. (This point was eventually given prominence in the encyclical *Vehementer nos*.) The replacement was immediately labelled as the revenge of the anticlericals for Pressensé's amendment to Article 4; and since the real reasons for the replacement were not generally known, these claims could not easily be squashed. In reality the replacement was the result of a joint manoeuvre between Georges Leygues of the Union Démocratique and Jean Sarrien of the Gauche Radicale, a manoeuvre aimed at checking once more the ascendancy of Briand, whose prestige had been further increased by his recent handling of the Article 4 debate. Sarrien was still the recognised leader of the Délégation des Gauches; and the Government, not daring to resist such a powerful coalition of its principal supporters, bullied the Commission into accepting Leygues's and Sarrien's amendment – the amendment which replaced the civil courts with the Conseil d'État.[15]

The bulk of intelligent Catholics, with a knowledge of the courts, were relatively undisturbed by the change. They believed that the Conseil d'État would almost certainly prove a more impartial arbiter than local bodies. But the wider effect of the amendment was to reawaken many of the fears that Pressensé's clause had snuffed. Had the Pressensé formula been added to Article 8, as he had wanted (see p. 176), a lot of anxiety and ill-feeling could have been avoided. What was even more unfortunate was that Catholics let slip two later opportunities of realising Pressensé's aim. On 12 April and 26 May Briand and a colleague more or less renewed Pressensé's initial proposal – with slight differences of wording. But on each occasion an independent Nationalist deputy, the vociferous Georges Grosjean, threw it aside as too imprecise; and his Catholic colleagues on the Commission were unfortunately too afraid of loosing face to pick it up.[16] Such a chance, twice lost, was not to return.

Once it became clear that the bill was going to pass without further concessions, debate focused on the simple question of whether the Church should accept or reject the system. Faced with the practical aspects of the problem, many saw acceptance as the only course. A number of priests positively welcomed the associations as a means of vitalising parish life; the laity would have a stronger role to play. Lay control of finance would also increase respect for the clergy by sparing them the invidious duty of collecting for themselves. The Church would likewise profit from secular expertise in the planning and financing of building projects. There were too many cases of enthusiastic but inexperienced priests embarking on ruinous schemes that cost the Church dearly in labour, money and prestige. Even the compulsory state supervision of Church finances (see Art. 21) would have its advantages, since it would put an end to the dark speculation about clerical war-chests. Several priests thought that the Holy See could well profit from this example and make its own accounts public. There might then be less talk of the accumulated loot of millennia salted away in the vaults of London and Zurich.

11 A Negotiated Settlement?

By the beginning of 1906 a majority of the influential clergy in France were in favour of giving the associations a trial. Yet the Vatican was already inclined to the opposing view, and eight months later was to condemn them outright.

Despite the loyalty of the French Church to Rome's decision, the passage of seventy years has not erased a deep underlying bitterness. There was rapidly to grow a widespread belief that Merry del Val was hostile to France, and that Pius X was content to follow his lead. The view was sufficiently current for Jules Romains, thirty years later, to base one of his most popular novels on the theme – *Mission à Rome* (Paris, 1937) – and it was perhaps fortunate for the Church's diplomatic interests that papal government was to change hands shortly after the outbreak of war in 1914. As late as 1972 a French Catholic diplomat, who has studied the period, remarked, 'Basically I have always felt that Pius X and Merry del Val were against us.'

The truth is much more complex than this; and it would be unfair to both prelates to see them as motivated by specifically anti-French feeling. The very complexity of the subject, however, and the emotion it still arouses, demands a close stage-by-stage examination if an overall assessment is to be made. The result may be painful reading, but it cannot easily be summarised without leaving important questions unanswered.

January 1906 found both sides in the debate sending emissaries to the Vatican. The case for accepting the associations was ably put by several of the most distinguished minds among the French archbishops. But it was the hawks and pessimists who winged their way to Rome who received the most attentive hearing.

Nearly all these prophets of doom were genuinely moved by concern for the Church; in many cases their loyalty to the Republic was never in doubt – a notable example being Henri Groussau, an arch-pessimist but a sincere *Rallié*.[1] The same, however, could not be said of everyone who found a ready ear in Rome. Pius X had already instructed the Catholic press to drop the word '*réfractaire*'.[2] Not that he wished to reverse or modify the Ralliement; he merely found that monarchists and ex-monarchists made congenial informants. They had a sounder sense of hierarchy and traditional religious values. They respected the Church without wishing to change it, and could be relied on not to confuse the defence of religion with democratic and social propaganda.

Now that royalism was no longer a working proposition in papal calculations, many Catholic royalists were devoting themselves more or less exclusively to furthering Church interests. Unwilling to accept the label of Republican, they remained outside the parties that were most effective in parliament, including the Nationalists, and stood for the most part as independents of the Right. Religious defence and preservation of the social order were all that they could respectably represent in open politics; and this gave their activity a certain purity in the eyes of Rome. It was not mixed up with a political package of aims and ideals that the Vatican could endorse only selectively. Even the *bien pensant* party in parliament had lumbered itself with the title of Action Libérale; and although everyone knew that '*libéral*' was the most conservative epithet that any self-respecting Frenchman could adopt, it jarred slightly on the ears of the new masters in Rome. The royalists had the added attraction that, being without hope politically, they pulled no punches in their defence of religion. Unlike Action Libérale they were not inhibited by fears of alienating the Centre.

Even so, the Vatican never departed from its formal acceptance of the Republic. As Merry del Val said in 1910, 'When I I meet monarchists, I respect their opinion which is sincere, but I say to them: "You are deluding yourselves. One cannot go against currents of opinion like the one that dominates France." '[3] What is also certain is that in the elections of 1906, the Vatican threw its weight behind Action Libérale Populaire as the only party that had a serious hope of furthering the Catholic cause in parliament (see p. 158).

Another group who enjoyed increasing favour with Rome were the Assumptionists, who were among the most fervent opponents of the associations. Their spirit accorded well with the current outlook in the Vatican; and Emmanuel Bailly and his colleagues became frequent visitors to the papal apartments. Pius would make jokes about Bailly's beard, and their relationship rapidly acquired an informal intimacy which was helped by Bailly's fluency in Italian.

The Assumptionists' claim to martyrdom in France was also a passport to the Pope's affection. Both Pius X and Merry del Val were great believers in suffering as a good counsellor. They were never tired of pointing to the crucifix when delivering unpopular decisions, especially to each other; and the French court verdict expelling the Assumptionists was a strong recommendation to their favour. Whereas the perception of the French secular clergy had supposedly been distorted by their monetary links with the Republic, the Assumptionists had the clearness of vision that is only enjoyed by someone who has looked death – or at least dissolution – in the face. As always, no one expressed it better than the Assumptionists themselves. Speaking of the bishops' desire to accept the *associations cultuelles*, Vincent Bailly remarked '*la soumission* is growing in France, which is natural enough, given that the worthy bishops themselves have all been chosen from among the non-combatants'.[4]

The Assumptionists became contact-men between Rome and the intransigent wing of the French clergy. It was the Assumptionists, moreover, who worked out a secret code by which Merry del Val could send confidential instructions to the French clergy without the contents being known by the Government.[5] Vincent Bailly had been a cipher clerk under Napoleon III, and his skills had long been part of the Assumptionist armoury. The Assumptionists may also have had hopes of becoming the Vatican's hot-line with Paris; but Merry del Val made it clear that he intended to use the Archbishop of Paris as his main intermediary.[6]

It would be a mistake, however, to regard the Assumptionists – or any other group of *réfractaires* – as an occult influence, inclining the Pope towards a rejection of the associations. They obtained a ready hearing because their views were congenial and increased the Pope's confidence in his own inclinations. Nor did the legal arguments of Groussau and his learned colleagues play a major role in the papal decision. Although Merry del Val had the highest regard for the opinion and 'soundness' of Groussau, he listened to him mainly because his arguments provided him with ostensible motives for a decision he already favoured for other reasons. Ostensible motives, moreover, that were more likely to command sympathy in France than the real ones.

For Rome, the least forgivable feature of the Separation was that the government was attempting to impose a new legal constitution on the Church in France, without having made the least effort to secure the Vatican's consent. Combes had broken off diplomatic relations with the Vatican in July 1904; and then, in the following year, France had unilaterally abolished Napoleon's Concordat with Pius VII without any show of attempted negotiation with Rome. The Separation Law, moreover, was now proposing, quite independently, a legal framework for the Church in France, as though the Vatican no longer existed. This was clearly a crushing blow to the Vatican's prestige; and, as already shown (pp. 33–6), international respect was all the secular power it had. Rome feared above all that if it were to accept the Law and the proposed *associations cultuelles*, other nations might conclude that the Vatican no longer had the determination to defend church interests, and might be tempted to embark on similar anticlerical programmes themselves. As Merry del Val explained to Emmanuel Bailly:

> It is not only the French Church and its well-being that is at stake; it is the good of the whole Church. If the system of *cultuelles* is allowed to take root in France – a system which implies pillage on one hand, laicisation on the other, and ultimately state control – we will be responsible for the spread of this disastrous system to all the other Catholic countries. Imitation will be inevitable, and Freemasonry is everywhere preparing to insist that governments follow similar policies.
>
> It is a disguised form of secularisation, where the hierarchy is subjected to the opinions of the laity, be it private individuals, the courts, or the state. The western churches will

undergo the fate of the eastern churches, tightly reined-in by *laiques* who interfere in church administration.

It will be a clear belittling of the Holy See, whose authority and control are rejected both in theory and practice.[7]

Emmanuel Bailly was to hear the Pope use identical arguments a few days later.[8]

The prevailing mood in Rome was gloomily assessed by Bishop Lacroix as follows:

1. Rome has had enough. Pope Leo XIII took appeasement to its ultimate limits.
2. Rome intends to be fooled no longer, nor to be subject to a new set of organic articles.
3. The papal court is the laughing stock of Europe. People compare it with the Sultan's court, compelled to give way to every demand of the Powers.
4. The French example is contagious. In ten years' time there won't be a concordat left in any of the surviving Catholic states. The Church must therefore fight back; and France, as eldest daughter of the Church, must devote herself to defending the future of the papacy.[9]

Although the Vatican was primarily concerned with the long-term implications of the issue. Merry del Val may had had Spain particularly in mind.[10] His father had been an eminent Spanish diplomat and his brother was Alfonso XIII's private secretary. While he always had the affairs of Spain close at heart, this was a time for particular concern.

Church-State relations in Spain had reached a crucial stage. The loss of Spain's overseas empire in 1898 and the dissolution of religious orders in France had resulted in a massive influx of regular clergy into the country, nearly doubling the number of friars and monks.[11] This sudden increase focused Liberal attention on the inadequacy of existing state control. At the same time the granting of universal male suffrage to a half-illiterate nation in 1890 had made education a prime concern to both major parties. And the Church's entrenched position in this field made reform a complicated matter. The Liberal Minister of Public Instruction, the Count of Romanones, had established tighter control over the Church schools in 1902; but his Conservative successor had neglected to enforce it. The Conservatives had likewise come to an amicable arrangement with the Vatican on the regulation of religious orders. But before it could be implemented, the Liberals were back in office (June 1905).

The summer of 1905 found the Liberals in a markedly anticlerical mood. Not only was there lost ground to be recovered, but their own disunity on other issues made anticlericalism an obvious area for advance. Anticlericalism would likewise appeal to left-wing labour leaders who were alarmed by the attempts of Catholic organisations to filch their membership.

Rome drew hope from the very instability of Spanish politics which might well bring a speedy end to Liberal rule and a return of the Conservatives. A difficulty here was the young King, Alfonso XIII, who did not share the admirable piety of his mother, the former Regent. Unfortunately for Rome, the King was on bad terms with the Conservative leader, Antonio Maura, who objected to his passion for motoring at speed. Although a royal smash would have filled Maura with no great sense of personal loss, he felt that the monarchy was insufficiently secure to stand the test of a sudden vacancy.[12]

The Vatican was also disappointed by the failure of papal policy to prevent Alfonso paying a state visit to Paris in May 1905.[13] On Maura's instructions the French Government had taken elaborate precautions to keep a safe distance between Alfonso and the *corps de ballet* at the Opéra – precautions that were more successful than its attempts to ward off would-be assassins – and everything indicated an unhealthy friendliness between the two nations. What was also disquieting was Spain's decision to saddle Alfonso with a Protestant wife, Victoria Eugénie, granddaughter of Queen Victoria. Her readiness to become a Catholic eased the way to a papal blessing, but from the Vatican's point of view the match was far from ideal.[14]

In sum, the Vatican had to face the sad fact that Alfonso could not be relied on to get rid of his Liberal ministers at the first opportunity. And the longer the Liberals remained in office, the tougher would be the terms of their new law for the religious orders. Pressures were also coming from the Left. The Republican elements in Spain had been greatly impressed by the relative ease with which the Separation had been effected in France, without massive public protest. As Merry del Val knew all too well, the main deterrent against anticlerical activity by Liberal governments was the fear of alienating an important section of the electorate. Many Spaniards still thought of France as 'a Catholic country', and consequently felt that if France could expel the orders and separate Church and State without massive public discontent, there was no reason why Spain should not do likewise. A congress of Spanish republican municipalities, meeting in February 1906, adopted a resolution in favour of Separation; and pessimists in Rome felt that the contagion could spread in time to the Liberals.

To prevent a general lowering of Vatican prestige and a possible outbreak of anticlerical activity in other countries, there seemed to be two courses of action open to the Vatican. The first would be to try to open negotiations with the French Government, and attempt to establish some sort of bilateral agreement, abolishing the Concordat by mutual consent. Coming after the Separation Law, this would scarcely deceive anyone into believing that the French Government was acting through fear of Vatican influence and what it could do. But at least it would show the world that even a government with the anticlerical record of France still observed the courtesies that were customary between sovereign powers in its dealings with the Vatican. The alternative course of action would be to refuse to accept the Law. This might salvage papal prestige by the enormity of the sacrifice involved: an institution which was prepared to forgo nearly half a milliard francs' worth of property in defence of its principles could scarcely fail to make some impression on secular governments. Refusal of the Law might also have useful political results. Public feeling might be moved by the Church's voluntary poverty and turn against the anticlericals who were thought responsible. Other governments could be expected to take warning.

Of these two courses of action, the first would seem the more attractive, but also the one with less chance of fruition. If a bilateral abolition of the Concordat was to be of any diplomatic value to the Vatican, it would have to be open and official. But it was precisely this that Rouvier's Government dared not do. Rouvier, Delcassé and President Loubet all favoured a negotiated settlement and listened sympathetically to the advances of Denys Cochin and Archbishop Mignot of Albi.[15] But, as Delcassé pointed out, if Clemenceau got to hear of it the ministry would not last a day; all that he could offer was to send an unofficial French representative to Rome.[16] This was no good to Merry del Val; the representative had to be official, or the project abandoned.[17] He suspected, moreover, that Delcassé was merely trying to buy the Vatican's silence during the passage of the bill.

The situation was made more difficult by Merry del Val's profound mistrust of Delcassé. One of Merry del Val's principal faults was his tendency to assume the worst of people with whom he found himself in disagreement, or whose connections put in an opposing camp. He wrongly attributed the rupture of diplomatic relations in 1904 to a supposed failure by Delcassé to give the cabinet the full correspondence between Rome and the Quai d'Orsay.[18] Delcassé was undoubtedly sly and egocentric, but his policies required a tolerably good relationship with the Vatican, and Merry del Val would have been well advised to cultivate this fact. The main difficulty was that Delcassé was a lone worker who was in no position to impose his conciliatory views on his colleagues, let alone on parliament. And what Delcassé could not do, Merry del Val tended to attribute to ill-will. It was symptomatic that when Delcassé was pushed from office by Germany, Merry del Val tartly remarked, 'The duplicity of Monsieur Delcassé has received its just reward.'[19]

Whether Merry del Val ever considered a negotiated settlement a serious possibility is open to doubt. Admittedly in January 1906 he told the Abbé Birot that the Holy See was prepared to consider renewing its relations with France – though added significantly that it could in no wise run the risk of lowering its own prestige.[20] But if the Vatican were known to be soliciting such an agreement, and its advances were openly rebuffed, the added humiliation would destroy what vestiges of dignity were left to it, and the likelihood of other governments pursuing anticlerical policies would be correspondingly increased.

The fact that Montagnini considered the attempt worth renewing did not necessarily reflect the opinion of Merry del Val. In January 1906 Montagnini commissioned Denys Cochin to see if the Government would consider negotiating a mutual recognition of the new regime. There appears to be no clear evidence, however, that Montagnini took this initiative either on Merry del Val's recommendation or even with his approval.[21] It is true that Denys Cochin assumed both then and thereafter that he was acting as the Vatican's unofficial emissary, and that his mission had the full support of Merry del Val. But it would not have been uncharacteristic of Montagnini to have undertaken this project on his own account.[22] If the French Government accepted the principle of negotiation, Montagnini would be in the enviable position of being able to offer his master an important diplomatic opportunity, to take or refuse, which was largely of his own creation. If his project failed, there was no need for anyone in Rome to know anything about it. Had Montagnini initially told Merry del Val of his project, Merry del Val might have poured cold water on it – which would have been disheartening for a young diplomat anxious to make a name for himself.

Whether acting independently or not, Montagnini employed Cochin to this end continuously until August 1906. With the Separation hard and fast in law, he hoped that parliament might be less hostile to the idea. Another encouragement was the promise of help from the leader of the Progressistes, Alexandre Ribot.[23] His optimism, moreover, was shared by other wearers of the purple, including a cardinal and several bishops, who were mostly members of a working party that had been set up to arrange the forthcoming episcopal assembly (see pp. 191–2). It seems that these bishops met Ribot at about the end of February to discuss the tactics of approaching Rouvier; and in the course of this interview they apparently hinted that the assembly would probably favour the acceptance of the *associations cultuelles*. Hoping that this sanguine line would encourage the Government to be conciliatory, they then addressed themselves to sweetening Catholic opinion. Given its circulation, *La Croix* was the obvious point of departure; and so the paper was gently but firmly warned to be less strident in its comments on the Separation Law.[24]

If Merry del Val had so far been ignorant of these negotiations, he was to know them now, for *La Croix* immediately sent a representative to Rome to find out whether the Vatican's approval lay with the bishops or *La Croix*.[25] The paper's emissary, Canon Masquelier, at once informed Merry del Val of the bishops' negotiations with Ribot; and a grim-faced Emmanuel Bailly, beard bristling, led him off to reveal all to the Pope. Pius

X was furious. 'Who has entrusted the preparatory commission with such negotiations? Neither Rouvier nor Ribot are they part of it. They have no right to deal with such matters. What is the meaning of unauthorised negotiations of this sort!'[26]

Merry del Val's role in this embarrassing episode is far from clear. If he was already *au courant* of what the working party were doing, his task was presumably limited to pacifying the Pope, to whom the whole episode was clearly a surprise. Such a task was well within the capacity of a man who was later to win the plaudits of Italian journalists by climbing Mount Vesuvious in eruption and photographing the seething cauldron from above. If, on the other hand, he was equally surprised, he may have decided to do nothing for the moment, in view of the recent fall of the Rouvier Government (7 March).[27] In any case, until the attitude of the new ministry should become clear the bishops' enterprise was in abeyance; and a wholesale issuing of reprimands at that stage would merely have jangled nerves at an anxious time for the Church in France.

It is not even clear whether he said anything to Montagnini, for the *chargé d'affaires* continued to encourage the venture as though nothing had happened. When Sarrien formed the new French cabinet, the inclusion of Briand gave Montagnini new optimism, for Briand had spoken in private many times of the desirability that the new ecclesiastical organisation in France be approved by the Pope. Briand was the first to realise that the refusal of Catholics to form *associations cultuelles* might well be the ruin of the law upon whose success he had pinned his hopes of a brilliant future.[28] When approached independently by the Abbé Gayraud he made it clear that he personally favoured a resumption of relations.[29] A difficulty lay in the opposition of his Socialist friends, Jaurès and Gabriel Deville. Both had caught wind of Cochin's mission in its early stages, and would do their best to prevent it bearing fruit.[30] On the other hand, Briand was already drifting away from his Socialist mentors, and might be able to outmanoeuvre them. Montagnini therefore felt fully justified in inviting Cochin to resume his advances.

Cochin realised that the most important elements to secure were the foreign minister, Léon Bourgeois, and Clemenceau, who was the effective head of Sarrien's cabinet. Cochin decided to approach Bourgeois directly: 'Send a diplomat who will take a week to dismantle the old agreement. . . . Give him another week to negotiate acceptance of the new state of affairs.' Bourgeois's reply was emphatic: 'No, you want to trap my finger in the works, and then my arm.' [31]

The ultimate decision, however, would lie with Clemenceau. Cochin, conscious that here depended the failure or success of the scheme, put the proposition to him. Clemenceau was vastly amused by it, and equally amused that Cochin should have to come – silk hat in hand – to make it to him. A Catholic monarchist proposing a gentleman's agreement to the scourge of the clericals was not without piquancy: 'Let's face it,' Clemenceau replied, rubbing his hands, 'we're behaving like cads.' [32] And that was that.

Even if Clemenceau had been personally amenable to the scheme, it is very doubtful whether he could have persuaded parliament to sanction it. The elections of May 1906 had strengthened rather than weakened the bloc; and with the fear of an electoral backlash effectively exorcised, there was even less reason than before for the anticlericals to favour conciliatory gestures of this sort. Nevertheless Cochin did not give up; nor did Montagnini. It was only when Montagnini learnt in early August that *Gravissimo officii* was ready for launching that he reluctantly told Cochin to drop the scheme.[33]

12 *Éminences Grises et Cardinaux Verts*

Whatever the extent of Merry del Val's knowledge of the negotiations, he seems from the first to have favoured the alternative course – rejection of the associations. It is here that his handling of the French bishops provides the most controversial aspect of a controversial question. It has made him the subject of charges of dishonesty, and it has indirectly caused critics to question the integrity of his master, Pius X. When the canonisation of Pius X was first discussed in the Vatican, the papal Secretary of State, Cardinal Pietro Gasparri, saw this as a serious and possibly decisive obstacle. The historian is therefore treading on egg-shells; and at the risk of trying the reader's patience still further, he can only move slowly.

Rome's view on the associations was already well established by December 1905, if not earlier. Within three days of the Separation becoming law Merry del Val wearily exclaimed to one of Bishop de Cabrières's priests: 'If only the bishops were all like yours, the Pope wouldn't hesitate to order resistance and the rejection of the law and its slavery.'[1] The main difficulty would be the economic sacrifice imposed on the French clergy. It might also create the unfortunate impression that the Vatican was forcing it on them for some remote Roman *raison d'église*. The Pope was admittedly ready to shoulder some of the cost by forgoing Peter's Pence on the one hand, and making a world-wide appeal for funds on the other.[2] But despite much talk of 'the generous Catholic sons of Uncle Sam', this would cover only a fraction of the loss. Clearly, if the Vatican was to avoid appearing in an invidious role, it was essential that the crew should give an enthusiastic cheer as the ship went down. If the bishops could be persuaded to reject the associations themselves, the

Vatican could prohibit them with much less embarrassment. For Merry del Val this was the main purpose of the plenary episcopal assembly.

Although it was not until the end of May that it eventually met, the project was launched at the end of January.[3] Even then, however, it was already becoming apparent that many bishops wanted to cut the corners of the *via dolorosa* and give the associations a try. If the assembly endorsed this view, what Merry del Val intended as a buttress to his policy could well turn out to be a bomb. The choice soon lay between dropping the assembly altogether or gently steering the bishops towards the right decision. To drop it might afterwards seem like moral cowardice, when the papal ban was eventually published; and it would in any case be a defeatist step to throw away the possibility, however slight, of an impressive episcopal backing. On the other hand, reliance on being able to steer the bishops was risky. Infiltrated by intellectuals and a Gallic respect for material considerations, they were a shifty bunch who could not be counted on to make chivalrous gestures of uncertain utility. If the attempt failed, the papal ban would clearly appear as unpopular. But, as Merry del Val later explained to Emmanuel Bailly, the repercussions of this could be forestalled by imposing secrecy on the assembly.[4] Only the French bishops would know what the assembly's recommendations had been; and only they would know that the papal ban, when it came, ran counter to it. Since their mouths would be sealed under pain of canonical suspension, their knowledge would remain a matter for internal consumption. The price would be some very disgruntled bishops; but two thousand years had taught Rome that nothing came free. And the alternatives, in Merry del Val's view, were even less palatable. If, however, the assembly voted the right way, then its recommendation could be publicised by Rome and its advantages fully enjoyed.

If the bishops were in any doubt as to what was expected of them, the path of virtue was dramatically flood-lit by the encyclical of 11 February formally condemning the Separation Law (see pp. 172–3). Although *Vehementer nos* had much wider aims than influencing the bishops, it seemed for the moment to leave only one solution open. Paradoxically enough, its appearance was largely due to initiatives at the opposite end of the Church's chain of command – initiatives by the 'obedient flock', whose obedience was such a central issue in the encyclical.

The form they took were demonstrations against the Government's inventory of church property. These disturbances were in fact a mixture of spontaneous indignation and political calculation. It was a sad irony that they were ignited by a well-intended amendment to the bill, made by Francis de Pressensé. He prescribed an inventory of property held by the *fabriques*, in order to ensure that it was honestly distributed after the Separation. The *associations cultuelles* would be among the first to benefit from a well-conducted transfer of the property. The proposal was a mere administrative safeguard which need not have featured in the law itself – but which was quickly heralded by militants as an act of desecration in which the forces of iniquity would lay hands on relics and chalices, perhaps on the Eucharist itself. When the issue was first put to the Chamber in April 1905, Henri Groussau had brought all the weight of his legal pedantry to justify a boycott by the *fabriques*, thereby encouraging the more militant bishops to make plans for resistance.[5] The Nationalists for their part saw the inventories as a heaven-sent opportunity for provoking anti-government demonstrations before the elections. They had been cheated of most of the explosive possibilities of the Separation bill by its method of phasing the process of deprivation over several years – most of it to come well after the 1906 elections.

But if the demonstrations were to be sufficiently large and widespread to affect the elections, they would have to be well organised. And it was precisely this organisation that was lacking. Although Jules Delahaye had proclaimed a campaign of resistance as early as June 1905,[6] the intervening six months were wasted. When the inventories began in February, it was only in areas where Nationalism was strong, notably Paris, that the demonstrations showed signs of careful organisation. One reluctant *curé* in Paris was cheerfully offered the services of 500 men by a Nationalist deputy;[7] while others spoke of the 'pious apaches' who took over their churches. Elsewhere it was left to local initiative and the indignation of pious parishioners – many of whom were rightly dubious of the value of demonstrating.

In areas of traditional fidelity, however, local feeling could produce impressive results.[8] Peasants with pitchforks obliged the police to retreat in several parishes; and in Monistrol in the Massif Central the gendarmerie fired on the demonstrators, wounding a number of them. In the Pyrenees bears were chained in the church porches to discourage officialdom from entering, while in Courcité in the Department of Mayenne, resistance was even more *soigné*. Some forty men and women, well wined and dined, shut themselves in the church all night and, when the battle began next day, emptied their *pots de chambre* on the gendarmerie who came to effect the inventory.[9] In most parishes, however, divine retribution did not descend from the skies in so spectacular a fashion. Over a third of the inventories were completed by the end of February – the vast majority without incident – and, by the end of May, only 7 per cent remained to be done.[10]

The demonstrations received the commendation of very few bishops, Turinaz being the only one to favour them publicly. A number of bishops roundly condemned them, while many made pleas for moderation. The Archbishop of Toulouse enraged the more militant of his flock by departing to Monte Carlo at the time of the inventories. While few imagined him at the gaming tables, casting lots while the Redeemer's garments were being divided on his home pitch, enough of them were sufficiently incensed to affix a placard to his palace, 'Lost, one archbishop. Good reward to finder.'[11]

Rome was greatly excited by the demonstrations. They had the unfortunate effect of convincing the Pope that the mass of French Catholics would be prepared to resist the law. Here at last was the proof that France was still a Catholic country – despite the defeatist attitude of bishops and intellectuals. This was what the Assumptionists had always held. To find the heart of Catholic France one had to go to the people – not to the bishops who were the nominees of an anticlerical government, nor to the intellectuals whose learning had sapped the vitality of their faith. As the Pope told Emmanuel Bailly, 'These Catholics who have defended their churches have brought us consolatioin, and we love them. They have shown a fine example of faith and courage. *There is a time for action*, and when that time comes, one must act.'[12]

Merry del Val was no less pleased, in his usual circumspect way. He disliked violence and asked Cardinal Richard to make it clear to certain bishops that the Pope fully approved Richard's request for moderation.[13] Yet it was highly gratifying to see French Catholics prepared to fight. Speaking in a different context at the end of the year,[14] he was to tell two Assumptionist visitors:

> It would seem in effect that French Catholics are not interested in religious liberty, and that they wearily take up a defensive posture only when Rome demands it. It is, on the contrary, the duty of Catholics to push intransigence to its ultimate limits, to reject utterly the laws that the government formulates against them, to go much further than Rome in resisting them, to be so militant that we need to restrain them. . . . If our role was limited to being a moderating influence, you would have the situation that existed in Germany. There, resistance was vigorous, with no quarter given; the Catholics were admirably intransigent; Rome had to moderate them, and it was by no means easy to hold them back. . . . *But what a splendid position for the Papacy which thereby became the arbiter of the situation.*[15] In France, unfortunately it's just the other way round. . . . Is it because *le sens catholique* no longer exists there?[16]

The *inventaires* gave a brief glimpse of the Catholic fighting spirit that Merry del Val had sought in vain among the French. But symptomatically he found it in the common people, not the intellectuals. All that the intellectuals and the priests in parliament did was to pour cold water on it.[17] When the Abbé Gayraud denounced the demonstrations in *L'Univers*, the cardinal wryly remarked, 'I don't understand a priest who fires on his own troops'.[18]

The most important result of the *inventaires*, however, was to strengthen Merry del Val's attitude towards the *associations cultuelles*. As he told Emmanuel Bailly, 'to accept the associations, after what the faithful have admirably done to defend their churches, would be tantamount to saying: "You were wrong to defend your churches, which should be handed over." It would be a disavowal that would throw Catholics into hopeless discouragement, and perhaps provoke an exasperated reaction against the Pope, the bishops and the clergy.'[19]

The Pope had intended to reserve *Vehementer nos* until after the publication of the *règlement administratif*, implementing the law. The substance of the encyclical, however, had been ready since the previous December, if not earlier;[20] and this outbreak of demonstrations was too tempting an opportunity to miss.

The encyclical clearly condemned the *associations cultuelles*; but whether it ruled out their information was not quite so clear. Most Catholics assumed that it did, and thought the debate now over. Merry del Val, however, was still set on getting a sturdy episcopal springboard for the final death-blow; and, to the surprise of many, announced that the issue was still open for discussion by the assembly.[21]

Lest there be any doubt about the outcome, however, he asked Montagnini to tell Cardinal Richard that there were very serious reasons why the associations should not be accepted, even in practice.

> I am very anxious, because I clearly see that we are at a turning-point in history for the Universal Church. All the forces of evil and international freemasonry are ranged against the Church; and it is France which is in the front line of this struggle at this present moment. What happens in France will serve as an example to everyone else, and that is why the decision [whether to form *associations cultuelles* or not] is of the greatest importance.[22]

He made it clear that, whilst it would be embarrassing for the Pope to prohibit the associations if a majority of the French bishops were in their favour, he was nevertheless ready to do it if he was supported by 'a good number of bishops'. And by a 'good number' he meant twenty or thirty – a third of the total – as he later explained to Emmanuel Bailly.[23]

It was to Bailly that he further elucidated these points. The Pope, he said, would be justified in subtracting eight or so votes from the *soumissioniste* total, since these corresponded to the dyed-in-the-wool concessionists whose votes would carry no moral weight. Only if the bishops and the French Church as a whole were virtually unanimous in favouring the associations would the Pope permit their formation – 'regretfully'.[24]

Nor were the 'forces of evil' which Merry del Val saw threatening the Church confined to liberalism and Freemasonry. These external enemies had their internal counterparts in theological Modernism and Christian Democracy. He confided to Bailly that to accept the *associations cultuelles* would be 'a victory for all these young priests and Catholics who have been won over to the freedom of the critical school, the advanced democratic school and all those who dream of reforms and novelties where the human and lay elements attempt to hold in check the divine and supernatural, and where the time-honoured structure of the Church would be turned upside down, in favour of the new Church of their dreams, adapted to the ideas of modern lay society'.[25]

He had an unusual capacity for lumping together those he saw as enemies. People and groups who had little in common would suddenly find themselves thrown together in the cold embrace of one of his anathemas. In yet another of his heart-to-heart talks with Bailly, in which they grimly swapped names of *bêtes noirs*, he fired an unusually wide-ranging charge of shot at the journals that favoured forming associations.

> I'm thinking of *La Paix Sociale*, *Demain*, *La Revue du Clergé*, *La Quinzaine*, etc. . . . that is to say all the papers, bulletins, and reviews of the Protestant, rationalist and semi-Catholic clan which speak the same language as *Le Siècle*, *Le Temps* and other papers of that type. The very nature of the ideas and customary outlook of those who favour the *cultuelles* should put us on our guard against them, for we are dealing here with the whole troup of writers who are less Catholic, and less Roman. They are the accomplices of the critical school and undisciplined democracy, the accomplices of those who are most active in opposing the work of the Holy See.[26]

Other beasts in his menagerie of dangerous animals were the well-heeled neo-Orleanist intelligentsia of the Académie Française and the *Revue des Deux Mondes*. Socially and intellectually superior to most bishops, they had been generous with unwanted advice; and since their money and talents were undoubtedly useful to the Church, it was hard to know how to deal with them. A particular thorn in Merry del Val's flesh was the convert editor of the *Revue des Deux Mondes*, Ferdinand Brunetière, 'this new Father of the Church' as he sourly called him.[27] His latest crime was to have drafted a letter in favour of the *associations cultuelles*, which was sent to the French bishops, over the signatures of Denys Cochin, Haussonville and twenty others of their milieu. More seriously for Merry del Val, it found its way into *Le Figaro* (26 March), thanks to the calculated indiscretion of Mgrs Fuzet and Lacroix. Never slow to seize upon the peccadillos of his adversaries, Merry del Val pointed out that three of these '*cardinaux verts*'[28] had recently attended and publicly applauded a lecture by a well-known Italian atheist. And then, *o culpa maxima*, despite the fact that it was Friday, they had gone to wallow in a sumptuous dinner, meat courses and all. 'The Vatican can do without the advice of Catholics of *that* sort,' he added.[29]

In the meantime the Pope had added his own awesome weight to the pressure bearing on the French bishops. The new bishops, consecrated in Rome on 25 February, had been left in no doubt as to where his inclinations lay.[30] And shortly afterwards the Pope wrote to Cardinal Richard (4 March), outlining the considerations that were to be put to the episcopal assembly before it voted. Let the bishops remember that 'we are born for war: *non veni pacem mittere, sed gladium*', and let them be conscious not only of 'the judgement of God but also that of the world which is watching to see whether they will fall short of what their dignity and its duties demand'. The bishops should then make a formal protest on the principle of the *associations cultuelles*, after which they should vote on whether a 'conditional trial' of the associations was permissible. In taking this second vote, however, they must satisfy themselves on three scores. First, that 'we would not be open to blame in trusting a government which resorts to trickery when it cannot use violence'. Secondly, that the acceptance of 'the miserable advantages' afforded by the Law would not appear as a renunciation of sacred rights. Thirdly, that this acceptance would not encourage the Government to further depredations.[31]

It would take a lot of conviction to resist language of this sort, coming from so eminent a source. Yet it was precisely conviction of this magnitude that was being increasingly provided by events in France. On Cardinal Richard's recommendation, the assembly had been postponed until after the May elections;[32] but these brought little joy (see pp. 158–9). They revealed all too clearly the indifference of most electors to the situation of the Church. Given this perspective, the case for rejecting the associations seemed even less convincing than before; and by the time the assembly opened on 30 May it was rumoured that nearly all the archbishops and some two-thirds of the bishops were in favour of acceptance. Only a minority would have subscribed to Merry del Val's reading of the elections. 'The worse the elections, the greater the necessity to take a firm line on the law and the *cultuelles*. . . . The worse the government, the less justification we have to put trust in its honesty. The straightforward situation of a clearly hostile Chamber is preferable to that of a Chamber with an Opportunist majority, looking for false compromises, where the Church would be exposed to greater dangers.'[33]

The assembly opened in the Archevêché of Paris in an atmosphere of considerable excitement.[34] The votes were secret, each bishop submitting an unsigned bulletin signifying 'Yes' or 'No'. The first question put to the vote was, 'Can one in practice accept the *associations cultuelles, telles qu'elles ont été établies par la loi de Séparation*?' This was purely a formal question, intended to provoke a resounding 'No' which would represent a formal condemnation of the Law's proposals – thereby demonstrating the solidarity of the French bishops with the Pope. It got the required answer from everyone except Mgrs Lacroix and de Briey of Meaux ('*douteux*' – 36th), who did not take it in this sense and voted 'Yes'.[35] The nature of the question was admittedly far from self-evident; but the phrase '*telles qu'elles ont été établies par la loi de Séparation*' presumably meant associations stripped to the essentials specifically mentioned in the law, and without any safeguard of orthodoxy contained in their statutes. Otherwise there would have been no point in going on to the second question, 'Is it possible to institute *associations cultuelles à la fois canoniques et légales*?'

This second question was the crucial one. Mgrs Mignot, Fulbert-Petit and Amette spoke eloquently in favour of 'Yes' – and the verdict went their way – 48 to 26. They then voted to call the associations '*associations fabriciennes*', by 49 votes to 25 – thereby seeking to establish their continuity with the concordatory *fabriques*. This done, they concluded the main business of the assembly by overwhelmingly approving Fulbert-Petit's statutes (see pp. 174–5) by 59 votes to 17.

These decisions shattered Merry del Val's few remaining hopes of a handsome episcopal backing for the papal prohibition. The only consolation was that the second ballot provided the Pope with the respectable minority he wanted – though even this had been somewhat weakened by the final vote.[36]

The issue now passed from the cool elegance of the main archiepiscopal *salon* in the rue de Grenelle to the sweltering heat of mid-summer Rome. There the Holy Congregation for Extraordinary Ecclesiastical Affairs appointed a no less extraordinary subcommittee to deal with it. While the swifts screamed past the windows, like the lost souls of the *prêtres-jureurs* of 1791, this unfortunate gathering of cardinals debated the matter on two very hot mid-July days. According to Canon Edmond Renard, it ultimately rejected the associations by five votes to four.[37] Another ecclesiastical source maintains that it was evenly split four against four, with the ninth member abstaining, despite a personal inclination towards acceptance.[38] Renard's account of their meeting, if authentic, gives further evidence on where the Vatican's preoccupations lay. Rampolla, defending the associations, admitted (in Renard's words) that 'to reject the law would satisfy feelings and safeguard the principles involved, as well as safeguard the dignity of the Holy See. It would also be a warning to those nations who might be tempted to imitate France.' His short sharp reply to this particular argument was that the Vatican had already accepted the law in the matter of pensions and allowances (see pp. 157–8). He then made a rather curious comparison between the current situation in France and that of Europe in the sixteenth century. With considerable audacity he declared that Clement VII had lost England through his excessive intransigence towards Henry VIII, whereas Sixtus V had saved France through his indulgence towards Henri of Navarre, despite the contrary advice of most of his counsellors.

It was arguments of this sort that made Merry del Val bless

the fact that Rampolla was no longer Secretary of State – and, even more, that he had been cheated of the tiara by the Austrian veto. If Merry del Val's face increasingly had an abstracted look, as he played billiards of a Sunday afternoon with the boys of Trastevere, he may well have been reflecting that the ways of God were strange.

Other thoughts that must have occupied his mind, as the ivories rolled across the green baize, were the current developments in Spain. On 6 July a new Liberal cabinet came into office – that of the elderly general, José López-Domínguez, whose grey hairs were offset by the reforming zeal of his minister in charge of religious affairs, the Count of Romanones. This was the man who had tried to take church schools in hand in 1902; and his prime objective in the new ministry was to strengthen state control over the religious orders. The Conservative associations bill of 1904 would clearly be replaced with something much tougher. At the same time he proposed to rescind the royal decree of 1900 which obliged Catholics to be married canonically. Easy-going Catholics could now resort to civil marriage and thereby avoid the penance and almsgiving that the sterner type of celebrant had often inflicted for pre-marital misdemeanours. Not only had the bride been expected to be a virgin, but the happy pair had been obliged to produce Easter Communion certificates. On an earthier level, Romanones also challenged the Church's control over cemeteries, with all its fertile financial advantages. It seemed to Rome that this was but the beginning of a fully orchestrated onslaught on the Church's privileged position in the peninsula.

López-Domínguez was later to deny any intention of separating Church and State;[39] and given the Concordat's erastian advantages, Merry del Val confidently judged that Separation was unlikely. But the position of the religious orders was undoubtedly under active review; and the following months were to see the elaboration of a stricter associations bill which Merry del Val was to declare totally unacceptable.[40] The Conservative leader, Antonio Maura, accused the Liberals of risking a rupture with the Holy See. 'For us the rupture constitutes war and you are the prologue of the civil war.'[41] Only the fall of the Liberals in the following year kept the bill from the statute book.

Nor was the canker likely to stop at the Spanish border. As the Italian ambassador in Lisbon noted, 'Portugal suffers from an acute illness: imitation of whatever is happening in Spain. Having seen the Count of Romanones's objectives . . . the Portuguese government thinks the moment ripe for similar demands here.'[42] The Portuguese King, moreover, was bombarded with complaints about the power of the higher clergy; and as Merry del Val dryly remarked, 'the King of Portugal is no friend of the Vatican'. In the opinion of the Italian ambassador, there were severe difficulties ahead in papal-Portuguese relations – the fortunes of which would partly depend on what happened in Spain.

Pius made no secret of the fact that Spain and France were his main preoccupations in the summer of 1906. He said as much to the Spanish ambassador on 7 August; and, according to the *Figaro*, it was widely held in the Vatican that his main concern was the potential influence of the French example on Spain.[43] Whatever the truth of this, the encyclical *Gravissimo officii* appeared only three days later, firmly slamming down the shutters on the divisive issue of the *associations cultuelles*.

In the final analysis, these latest *contretemps* with Spain could do little more than confirm a decision which the Pope had favoured since the previous December, if not earlier (see p. 191). Even so, Merry del Val emphatically denied any connection between this decision and affairs in Spain. He would not even admit concern for the Spanish situation; to show alarm would let the anticlericals smell blood, and the hunt would be up – not only in Spain.

The encyclical said little of the Vatican's real reasons for rejecting the associations. To have spoken of the dangers of the French example, and of the need to safeguard the Vatican's international standing, would have destroyed much of the document's purpose. To betray such fears might have provoked the onslaught that the encyclical was designed to prevent. Moreover, it would have been embarrassingly obvious that it was the Church in France, not the Vatican, that was paying the price of this salvage operation. For these reasons the encyclical laid emphasis on the dangers to the French Church allegedly inherent in the associations. Hence its stress on the threat to hierarchical discipline in France.

It was therefore particularly unfortunate for Rome that the best judges of this threat – the French bishops – had recommended a trial of the system. Faced with this obstacle, the encyclical made what capital it could from the somewhat byzantine wording of the questions put to the Assembly (see pp. 199–200). It exploited to the full the academic distinction between '*associations cultuelles, telles qu'elles ont été établies par la loi de Séparation*' (i.e. associations without statutes safeguarding their orthodoxy) and '*associations cultuelles à la fois canoniques et légales*' (i.e. associations with safeguarding statutes, such as those proposed by Fulbert-Petit).

> We see that we must fully confirm with our apostolic authority *la déliberation presque unanime* of your assembly.
>
> That is why, concerning the *associations cultuelles, telles que la loi les impose,* we decree that they cannot be formed without violating the sacred rights which are inseparable from the very life of the Church.
>
> Setting aside these associations . . . there could appear some other kind of association, *à la fois légal et canonique*. . . .
>
> . . . We declare that the trial of this other kind of association cannot be permitted.

Most readers would be impressed by the concord between Rome and the episcopate on the first point, and would not be in a position to appreciate that this papal concept of associations '*telles que la loi les impose*' was a purely academic one, designed to elicit a formal rejection, from the assembly. They would not know that the bishops' '*délibération presque unanime*', rejecting these imaginary unguaranteed associations, was merely a statement of principle and did not necessarily exclude the practical adoption of some system of associations. The encyclical did not indicate whether the bishops had even been consulted on the real question of the acceptability of associations '*à la fois légal et canonique*' (the *only* associations at issue, practically speaking) – let alone indicate what their recommendation had been. Conversely, the majority of readers could be expected to assume that the papal prohibition of the associations '*à la fois légal et canonique*' was a mere confirmation of the '*délibération presque unanime*' of the bishops, as in the case of the unguaranteed associations.

It is true that a close examination of the wording would not give positive support to this assumption. But there can be no doubt that this assumption was what Merry del Val wished to encourage people to make – as was evident from his replies to later questions. And as long as the bishops kept their mouths shut – as they were canonically obliged to do – there was no reason why it should not be generally accepted as the truth. Even his closest friends were induced to believe it – one of them was to believe it for fifty years. The same was true of respected confidants like the Baron d'Erp, the most trusted of the foreign representatives in Rome. On 24 August Merry del Val told him: 'All the French bishops except two – and I'm still not sure about these two – declared their opposition to the *associations cultuelles*. To accept these associations would be equivalent to allowing them to nominate the *curés*. The bishop would count for nothing.'[44]

Even while he spoke, however, the cock crew. Mgr Lacroix, incensed by what he called the encyclical's 'lies of heavy calibre', commissioned the freelance Abbé Albert Houtin to help him prepare an account of the assembly for publication in *Le Temps*.[45] Lacroix and Houtin were a curious pair – a clerical Faust and Mephistopheles, each semi-despising his relationship with the other. The summer of 1906 found them concocting a number of revelatory articles, primarily designed to demonstrate the pernicious effect on the French Church of Vatican diplomacy and the activities of the *réfractaires*. Lacroix still walked, with mitre and crosier, in the rectitude of his communion with Rome, and his aims were primarily constructive. Houtin on the other hand had broken with his diocesan bishop in 1901, and although still nominally a member of the priesthood, he was drifting steadily away from the Church. His activities were shortly to be directed to convincing those angels who had not followed Lucifer that heaven was too malodorous a place to be worth staying in. As a friend of Lacroix later remarked, Houtin was one of those priests 'who get their own back, for being exiled from the altar, by peeing in the sacristy'.[46] His mingled contempt and envy for Lacroix's established position in the Church occasionally drove him to writing abusive notes about Lacroix for his own consolation: 'childish vanity', 'scientifically worthless', '*amour-*

eux des femmes', etc. In a more tender moment he once added, 'in spite of his selfishness and *arrivisme*, human'; but that was as far as the relationship went.[47]

Their account of the assembly burst forth from *Le Temps*'s front-page spread on 24 and 25 August, causing many a cassock to be splashed with breakfast coffee.[48] Merry del Val stuck to his guns. Given the encyclical, any alternative action would have bene too humiliating. He wrote to Montagnini instructing him to refute the article.

> It is absurd to claim that the bishops have only voted against the fundamental principal of the law. The Pope condemned the law with his encyclical, *Vehementer*, and did not ask the bishops their opinion on this matter. The question put to the bishops was a *practical* one, to know whether one could set up *associations cultuelles, telles que les voulait la loi* without violating the essential rights of the Church. The reply was 'No', with virtual unanimity. The minutes are clear. Naturally one cannot give all the details to the press. But one could say that all the bishops – *fere ad unum*, as the Pope said – proclaimed that it was impossible.[49]

Like the encyclical itself, this statement made what use it could of the literal meaning of phrases; and if it accorded uneasily with the truth, its transgressions were in the spirit rather than the letter.

Even so, the historian is left asking why a man of the moral awareness of Merry del Val should resort to this sort of procedure, and why Pius X, a future saint of the Church, should have put his signature to an encyclical of such ambiguous veracity. If the Vatican was not prepared to admit a difference of appreciation with the French bishops, it would clearly have been better if the encyclical had said nothing about the assembly at all. Any charitable explanation of the Vatican's behaviour must assume one of two possibilities: first, that available accounts of what happened at the assembly are erroneous; or, secondly, that the Vatican misunderstood or was misled by the official secret minutes that were sent to it. Neither hypothesis, however, bears close examination.

What happened at the assembly was never in serious doubt. The various first-hand accounts of its proceedings show a remarkable agreement on the main points; and it is significant that the Vatican was never to deny the accuracy of these accounts – only the significance of the votes taken. Even if the minutes sent to the Vatican were ambiguous – and there is no reason to suppose that they were – there was no ambiguity about the explanatory letter which followed them. Cardinal Richard specifically told Merry del Val, 'According to the votes cast on the second question, two-thirds of the bishops are favourable to acceptance within the canonical limits allowed by the Holy Father, and a third desire an absolute rejection of the law.'[50] It is conceivable that Pius X did not see this letter and relied on Merry del Val for the interpretation of the minutes. But it is hard to see how any misunderstanding on Merry del Val's part could have been anything but intentional.

It is tempting to be censorious about the deceptions of churchmen, especially when they claim to be the guardians of truth. Historians, however – unlike moralists – are more likely to blame Merry del Val for his misjudgements rather than his mendacity. He had, after all, eminent predecessors in the second field. As a future Secretary of State, Cardinal Tardini, was fond of saying, 'Vatican diplomacy really began with Peter's denial of Christ.'

Less forgivable were the unnecessary burdens that Merry del Val placed on the French Church, through his rejection of the associations. To call these burdens 'unnecessary' is perhaps to be wise after the event. But the situation in other countries gave little reason to suppose that self-mutilation would act as a deterrent to anticlericalism. Indeed the next few years in Europe and Latin America were to shatter such hopes all too thoroughly.

Postscript: Divorce and Cohabitation – a Brief Synopsis

The rest of Pius X's pontificate was a time of ill-feeling. Ill-feeling between Rome and Paris, and ill-feeling between Catholic liberals and intransigents, each of whom accused the other of betrayal. The liberals blamed the intransigents for the financial difficulties of the Church, while the intransigents accused the liberals of wanting to sell 'the divine constitution of the Church, bought with the blood of Christ' for 'the miserable material advantages of the law of Separation'.[1]

It was a sad gathering of bishops that met in the second plenary assembly of September 1906 to consider the bleak future that confronted them. Lest any bishop be tempted to take an independent line, Rome insisted that voting be open by raised hands in full view of the meeting, instead of by anonymous voting slips. Despite wistful talk of an accommodation with the law, the assembly passed off safely. Having wryly thanked the Pope for 'the most illuminating instructions contained in the encyclical', it formally warned French Catholics against joining *associations cultuelles*, and then proceeded to the pressing task of organising diocesan funds for supporting the clergy. It was clear that Rome could count on the loyal if weary support of the bishops.

The Government was consequently placed in an acute dilemma. Briand, now Ministre des Cultes, saw the whole future of the Separation Law in jeopardy – together with his own reputation as the architect of religious peace in France. His aim throughout had been to minimise the political repercussions at grass-roots level. But with no Catholic *associations cultuelles* to represent the Church, this immediately raised a highly emotive issue: the future of the parish churches. To whom could they be entrusted, without violating the Law or arousing local feeling? His first inclination was to try to force Rome into having second thoughts. Together with Clemenceau, he decided to encourage dissident Catholics to form associations, his aim being to panic the Church into taking similar action. Faced with a phalanx of independent associations, all ready to claim the churches, Rome might well capitulate before the prospect of a divided Church.

The instrument lay to hand. There already existed two unauthorised groups who were trying to foster the formation of associations.[2] The elder of these, the Association Cultuelle Catholique Nationale, was avowedly schismatical and already had three schismatical associations under its wing. The younger, and more powerful, was the Ligue des Catholiques de France, the brain-child of the bizarre and imaginative journalist, 'Henri des Houx' (Durand-Morimbau), perhaps the strangest member of the demimonde of French ecclesiastical gossip writers. This group had more ambivalant aims, and included a mixture of orthodox and unorthodox Catholics. It was to them that Clemenceau and Briand decided to give secret financial help.

Feelings were mixed at the former Direction des Cultes as to the wisdom of this policy. The new deputy director, Louis Méjan, feared that it would cause Catholics to question the Government's good faith if the matter came to light. It might even give rise to claims that the Government was promoting schism.[3] Briand himself was well aware of these dangers, and after a few weeks decided to withdraw government support – much to Méjan's relief. Briand may also have been influenced by Rome's imperviousness to the des Houx campaign. Far from being alarmed, the Vatican found these initiatives consoling.[4] The fact that several of the priests involved were widely known as schismatics helped to discredit the movement in French Catholic eyes.

Although the Ligue des Catholiques de France was eventually to claim a membership of well over a hundred associations, it progressively lost all semblance of orthodoxy – especially after Briand withdrew his secret support. Symptomatically its directing committee now included Eugène Réveillaud, whose schismatical aims were well known – he himself having declared them to parliament (see p. 175). It also suffered from the eccentricities of its spiritual leader, the self-styled Archbishop of North America, Joseph-René Vilatte, whose appearance and behaviour inspired the contemporary song, 'The Chicago Schism', whose opening lines acquired a wide if short-lived popularity.

> From Chicago there comes to us
> A huge American ape.

Though destined to die a shriven member of the Church, his singular life-style helped to divest the movement of its claims to religious respectability.

Although a number of its member *associations cultuelles* succeeded in obtaining church property from the old parish councils (*fabriques*), none of their claims survived appeal to higher courts. Indeed the movement helped to convince Catholics that the Conseil d'Etat and the Cour de Cassation were sincerely determined to prevent Church property falling into schismatical hands.

Yet in the meantime there still remained the basic problem as to who could legally represent orthodox Catholics. Briand's solution was both daring and simple. As far as the churches were concerned, he convinced his colleagues that they were best left in the hands of the parish priest (laws of 2 January and 28 March 1907), a proposal that would keep local disturbance to a minimum. And to the astonishment of *bien pensant* pessimists, the Conseil d'État and the Cour de Cassation consistently upheld the right of these priests to occupy the churches, despite the fact that they had no associations to support them. Schismatical priests, armed with the full panoply of an *association cultuelle*, were systematically routed at law, with the result that Réveillaud bitterly complained that the State was once more a buttress of Roman orthodoxy.

On other property, however, Briand could afford to be less indulgent. As soon as 1906 elapsed without a Catholic association in sight, the presbyteries and episcopal palaces were taken over by the public authorities and put to various purposes.[5] Admittedly the injunction was ignored in many *pratiquant* areas; and one of the more entertaining features of local life in the following years was the battle of wits between tolerant mayors and less tolerant prefects. In a fair number of cases, the mayor claimed that he was employing the priest as caretaker of the presbytery, thereby justifying the rent-free presence of the priest. Some even proposed to pay him a wage for his services. But elsewhere there was less indulgence. Many of the episcopal palaces became museums, libraries and other municipal amenities, while a number of presbyteries were rented to the parish clergy, in cases where the Church was prepared to allow it. In fact when the bishops met for their third plenary assembly in January 1908, they agreed to let the clergy rent presbyteries that were unquestionably public property. But they were not prepared to permit this solution in cases where the presbytery belonged to the Church.

Had the Church formed *associations cultuelles*, this complicated and expensive situation would not have arisen, in that the associations would have become the owners of this and other church property. But in their absence the Government was not prepared to leave the presbyteries in the hands of the clergy, as it had in the case of the churches. Instead they were to be given to the local public assistance boards and relief committees, together with all the other property belonging to the Church (law of 13 April 1908). Catholics understandably denounced the measure as confiscation; but Briand pointed out that the Church had only itself to blame for not conforming to the law. And there the matter stayed – until 1941.

Even so, parliament was still prepared to make two notable exceptions. This concerned the awkward category of church property that was encumbered with legal conditions, arising from the wishes of the donor. Many benefactors had made their gifts conditional on the saying of masses for their souls; and this was always an embarrassing issue for secular authorities, who felt somewhat like a bachelor faced with the problem of feeding a newborn baby. Parliament agreed to give such property to Catholic mutual benefit societies, together with the assets of the former diocesan pension funds and clerical rest homes (law of 13 April 1908).

But this, like so much else, foundered on the intransigence of Rome. The Vatican feared that to accept even this modest concession might be interpreted as acceptance of the Law, especially when right-wing papers were calling the mutual benefit societies '*associations cultuelles* in disguise'. The result was that the proposed societies were ground into the carpet by *la mule du pape*, and the property involved was lost with all the rest. In many parishes only the churches remained as material evidence of a great institution, at one time the foremost proprietor of France; and most of these were merely 'occupied', not owned. Only new churches were completely independent of the tolerance of a fickle parliament – together with a handful of chapels still owned by nineteenth-century benefactors. And even these were subject to the whims of the legal proprietor, most of them rich patrons who could afford to be capricious, if so minded. As it happened, the Church was singularly fortunate in the loyalty and obedience of its benefactors.

As far as the rest of the churches were concerned, there still remained the problem of upkeep. All repairs were the responsibility of the occupant; and although the law of 13 April 1908 allowed public authorities to give assistance if they felt so minded, many were impervious to the appeals that were made to them – especially in districts where the church was a neo-gothic or byzantine eyesore. Only churches that were scheduled as historic or cultural monuments were positively entitled to public funds.[6] And there remained many others – quite interesting in their various ways – that were condemned to neglect as a result of the poverty of the parish and the indifference of the local authorities. Eventually, after long campaigning, Maurice Barrès succeeded in persuading Briand to extend the principle of government aid to all churches built before 1800 – thereby rescuing a rich cultural inheritance that was in danger of being lost, merely for want of sufficient stars in the Ministry of Fine Arts catalogue.

The upkeep of the churches was one problem; the upkeep of the parish priests was another which required more urgent attention – the clergy being subject to swifter misfortunes than dry rot and deathwatch beetle. The solution proposed by the plenary episcopal assemblies was a new diocesan collection – the *denier du culte*. To spare the priest the invidious role of collecting for himself, it seemed preferable to keep this collection on a diocesan basis and share it out equitably between the parish clergy.

Where necessary, it could be supplemented with subsidies from a new supra-diocesan fund, set up to enable the richer dioceses to help the poorer.

The contributions to the *denier du culte* varied enormously from parish to parish. In a fashionable Parisian parish such as St Philippe du Roule, scarcely a confetti-throw from the Elysée palace, over 121,000 francs were collected in the first year of operation (1907);[7] whereas in the working-class parish of Notre Dame de la Gare, wedged between the freight yards of the thirteenth *arrondissement*, the total was scarcely more than 1,000 francs, just enough to keep one *desservant* at the Concordatory level of salary (900 francs). In several of the *banlieu* parishes, it was only a fifth of this. When, moreover, the Dunkirk spirit of the immediate crisis was over, enthusiasm rapidly waned. In Paris as a whole the total proceeds dropped from 1,326,612 francs in 1907 to 1,103,261 francs in 1910, with even the well-lined parishioners of St Philippe du Roule dropping their offerings by over a quarter.

Each parish, of course, had other sources of income. In addition to an appropriate share of the *denier du culte*, each parish still continued to draw an income from funeral and marriage services, the hire of seats, and the various items described in Chapter 3 (see pp. 52–3). While a flash parish like St Philippe du Roule garnered as much as 238,000 francs in 1907, Our Lady of the freight yards stopped short of 9000, many *banlieu* parishes giving only a fraction of this.[8]

The Church was clearly going to have difficulty maintaining 42,000 clergy at their accustomed level of salary, modest though this was. With the prospect of hard times ahead, the seminaries found recruitment progressively a problem. Even before the Separation became law, the dark skies of the Combes era saw a distinct drop in seminary entrants – and second thoughts among the more lukewarm candidates for ordination. Ordinations on a national level dropped steadily from 1733 in 1901 to 825 in 1913[9] (as can be seen partly reflected in the third and fourth maps on pp. 12–13). It was not until the late twenties that recruitment began to pick up once more, following the regularisation of the Church's legal position in 1924 (see pp. 219–20). The harvest in fact did not come until six years later, when these seminarists emerged as fullfledged ordinands, their number rising from 981 in 1933 to 1355 in 1938.[10]

The gravity of this situation should have led to a rapid and radical reform of the parochial and diocesan structure. But Pius X was quick to discourage the amalgamation of small parishes (see p. 161), while the existing pattern of dioceses was too deeply embedded in local interests to make reform easy. No town, however anticlerical, wanted to be deprived of its bishop; and although recruitment of the clergy was a problem, every seminarist had a mitre in his knapsack, making it difficult to prune the hierarchy of its plethora of mountain sees without arousing apprehensions among the more ambitious clergy. In Italy the situation was even more wasteful, as Merry del Val freely admitted.[11] But faced with a legion of vested interests, he was not prepared to take unpopular steps in a matter where Vatican diplomacy was not at stake. It was only in the 1950s and 1960s that the Church in France began to make even modest changes in its existing structure. And even after these adjustments, the ecclesiastical map remains much as it was under the Second Empire, the main change being an added system of regional co-ordination – an accretion rather than an alteration.

It is hard not to see the Separation as a vast neglected opportunity, whose possibilities are still draining away like an unstopped oil well. As pointed out in Chapter 3, 400 years of Concordatory life had crystallised in the clerical mind the existing structure; and faced with the discouragement of Rome, would-be innovators were unlikely to get far in the early years of Separation. Once the initial cold shower of Separation was over, inertia and old habits reasserted themselves. Nearly all the parochial amalgamations that took place were forced on the Church by shortage of priests; few were the outcome of conscious planning. At the same time diocesan autonomy continued to be a crippling feature of the French Church, making an equitable spread of manpower over the country difficult to achieve, as well as keeping standards low in the over-numerous diocesan seminaries. Loss of buildings after the Separation brought about some amalgamation between them, but not nearly enough.

Rome worsened the situation by giving *desservants* security of tenure (August 1910) – a privilege that the Concordat had confined to *curés*. Whatever its intention, this concession put yet another obstacle in the way of redeploying manpower. A priest in a comfortable niche, and impervious to persuasion, could only be shifted by a complicated formal procedure.

In the rough seas that lay ahead, a brisk hand on the wheel was essential; yet the bishops' ability to provide this was ruined by the papal ban on general episcopal assemblies. The three assemblies that took place between 1906 and 1908 had only served to strengthen the Pope's suspicions and those of Merry del Val. The disastrous votes of May 1906 (see pp. 199–200); the leaks to the press, despite the papal demand for secrecy; the insidious talk of an accommodation with the law in September 1906; all this and much else determined Rome to put an end to them as soon as possible. Having abolished secret voting in September's assembly, the Vatican then abolished voting altogether in the third and last (January 1908). And shortly after, when Henry Cochin spoke to the Pope about the future organisation of the Church, Pius replied with a sweep of the hand, 'Small assemblies, provincial assemblies, yes. But general assemblies – we don't want any more of *them*!'[12] And that was that. Apart from the periodic meetings of the French cardinals and archbishops, the bishops as a whole were never to meet again on a national basis until 1951, when all those of 1908 were long since dead and mostly forgotten.

Those that replaced them were of a different stamp. The new generation of bishops were the nominations of Rome, not Paris, and were mostly noted for their uncompromising attitude towards the Government. In 1906 Rome tried a brief conciliatory experiment. When a vacancy occurred, the other bishops of the archdiocese were invited to meet and make three suggestions to the Pope, without committing the Pope to accepting any of the three. Even this slender concession, however, was soon withdrawn, after disagreement in the Montauban affair. This arose when the Bishop of Montauban needed a coadjutor; and he and his colleagues all proposed the same candidate. Rome, however, preferred an ardent royalist, the notorious Canon Marty, whose allegiance to Action Française was later to lead Pius XI to demand his resignation.[13] Despite respectful warnings of Marty's unsuitability, Pius X was adamant. Not only did he appoint him, but he punished the bishops' independent mindedness by abolishing the current system of episcopal consultation. Henceforward each bishop was merely invited to submit each year a personal list of three worthy men, from which Rome could compile a general list of suitable candidates, which might or might not be used to fill future vacancies. On this wide basis it was hard for anyone to know whether the bishops' suggestions were being heeded or not.

It moreover became papal policy to look to the French seminary in Rome for future bishops. Like the Alsatian pups in *Animal Farm*, these young men were nurtured in salutary isolation from Gallic influences and could be relied on to do their stuff in times of crisis. Between 1871 and 1905 only five episcopal appointments had their roots in the Roman seminary, whereas in the brief period between 1906 and 1919 seventeen were reared in Rome – a decennial average that was nine times higher than under Leo.[14] The products of these dragon's teeth, moreover, were to pose severe problems in the 1920s. In common with most of Pius X's bishops, they were not only hostile to Pius XI's conciliatory policies, but a sizeable number were also devotees of Action Française. So marked was their sympathy for this movement, that the papal condemnation of Action Française (1926–7) was to be an embarrassing and long-delayed affair.

Without renouncing the Ralliement, Pius X and Merry del Val progressively undermined its spirit and strategy. It had been Leo XIII's policy to encourage an alliance between Catholics and conservative Republicans on the basis of keeping a tactical silence on Catholic demands that might embarrass the conservatives. Divisive issues were to be kept for the while in a bottom drawer – like 'the maximum programme' of the Socialists.

In Merry del Val's view this policy had been disastrous, and he regarded the current predicament of the French Church as its direct result (see p. 124). In June 1909 he announced on the Pope's behalf that 'the most practical and opportune policy was to rally all men of goodwill on to *le terrain nettement catholique et religieux*, according to papal instructions'.[15] This in effect was a reversal of Leo's strategy, in that it threatened to throw royalists and Ralliés together in an alliance against everyone else, thereby creating the kind of ghetto mentality that Leo had been so anxious to avoid.

Symptomatically Action Libérale Populaire, with its republican assumptions, ceased to receive the warm expressions of favour that it had hitherto found in Rome. So much so, that the ultramontane Henri Groussau asked Rome whether he ought to resign from the A.L.P.'s committee.[16] Although he was advised to stay put, it was clear that he had not been oversensitive in asking.[17] *La Croix* too was accused of being insufficiently militant. Although there could be no question of the Assumptionists resuming the direction of the paper, Merry del Val encouraged the editor to refer to Emmanuel Bailly whenever in doubt on matters of general policy and attitude.[18] As Emmanuel Bailly told the editor in January 1911, 'Rome is of the opinion that *La Croix* has become paler, less vigorous, *less Pius X*'.[19]

Equally disturbing were the activities of the Vatican's unofficial intelligence service, the Sodalitium Pianum – or the '*Sapinière*' as it was familiarly called.[20] While always retaining something of a private-eye existence, its chief organiser, Mgr Umberto Benigni, was a member of the Secretariat of State, and its main organ, *La Correspondance de Rome*, enjoyed the circumspect support of Merry del Val. Although the '*Sapinière*' was primarily directed against theologians suspected of Modernism, its agents also reported to Rome clergy who were considered unduly complaisant towards the French Government Like McCarthyism in the 1940's, it became dominated by a group of insensitive vindictive men, who ultimately had to be disowned by the Vatican; but not before they had done untold damage to the intellectual life of the Church.

PRIMAVERA

The First World War brought many changes – notably a change of Pope. As Under-Secretary of State at the time of the Separation, Benedict XV (1914–22) had been the unwilling instrument of Merry del Val's dour policy towards France. Appointed in the last years of Rampolla's ministry, he represented a conciliatory approach to French problems; and it was significant that he appointed Pietro Gasparri as Secretary of State.[21] At the time of the Separation, Gasparri had been Secretary of the Sacred Congregation of Extraordinary Ecclesiastical Affairs; and like his new master he had chafed under the narrow grip of Merry del Val's hard-line strategy. Merry del Val was now retired to being Archpriest of St Peter's, a change that came as a great relief to him, since he had never enjoyed the heavy responsibilities of his former office. It was also something of a relief to his colleagues and subordinates – though not entirely an unmixed blessing, as soon became evident. As Archpriest of the basilica he went out of his way to encourage their attendance at the long services in St Peter's, something which his more easy-going predecessor had left to their unaided discretion.

Benedict XV and Gasparri made tentative attempts to repair the rift that separated Rome and Paris. It was a difficult task in that the war obliged Rome to avoid any gesture that suggested partiality. On the other hand, the war helped to eclipse religious issues as a divisive element in French politics – and so prepared the ground for an eventual understanding. With Catholic priests serving in the trenches, anticlericalism seemed for the time to be an irrelevance. Indeed, when Briand formed his fifth cabinet in October 1915, Denys Cochin and Emile Combes sat side by side as Ministers of State. The war likewise brought a certain rehabilitation of the Right. Their constant opposition to Germany made a congenial contrast to the internationalism of the Socialist Left, at a time when patriotism seemed the cardinal virtue. And France was still sufficiently old-fashioned for the stock of Catholicism to rise and fall with that of the Right.

As in pantomime, however, when the curtain call finds the demon king and the fairy queen holding hands and smiling, the following day's performance generally finds them abusing each other once more in vehement rhyming couplets. Yet France was partly spared such a situation as a result of two factors. On the one hand, the 1919 elections had weakened the anticlerical Left in parliament – putting moderates such as Millerand, Leygues and Briand in office once more. And on the other, the restoration to France of Alsace-Lorraine created a new politico-religious situation which obliged the Government to move with unaccustomed delicacy.

The Second Reich had been anxious to placate the strongly Catholic population of these provinces, and had therefore left intact the privileges that the Church had enjoyed under the Second Empire. Consequently, when the rest of France was in the icy grip of *laicisme*, the Alsatian Church had continued more or less to lead its traditional existence. Now that the provinces were once more part of France, it remained to be seen whether the Church would be allowed to retain its position of happy anomaly. With considerable wisdom, the French Government decided to play safe and avoid straining the loyalty of its long-lost Catholic subjects. The Concordatory regime was left in being, as were certain ecclesiastical advantages that the Reich had bestowed during one of its coaxing moods.

If mercy blesses him that gives and him that takes, it does not always come gratis; and in retaining the Concordatory regime in the reunited provinces, the old familiar question of episcopal appointments posed both sides with problems. For the game to be played in traditional style, it needed a nuncio and an ambassador, or at least some kind of diplomatic contact. During the war Briand had favoured the resumption of relations – if only to prevent Rome forgetting French interests when dealing with the represented powers. But difficulties on both sides had prevented fruition. Now, however, with Millerand, Leygues and Briand forming successive 'moderate' cabinets, the link was made (1920–21); and the sees of Metz and Strasbourg became once more a matter for nostalgic routines, as in the days of Imperial France.

It was not only Alsace-Lorraine that felt its effects. A remarkable outcome of the settlement was a countervailing scheme for the other French sees. Although Rome was left theoretically free to appoint whom it liked, Cardinal Gasparri conceded in an *aide-mémoire* of May 1921 'that in the case of every episcopal nomination, the Holy See will consult with the French representative to discover whether the government has anything to say against the chosen candidate from a political point of view'.[22] It was especially appropriate that the concession should come from Gasparri who had said in 1906 that the French cabinet would be '*fichues bêtes*' if they did not insist on an *exequatur*.

The concession has proved to be weighty. The Government's consultant on episcopal appointments in the 1950s summed up the situation as follows: 'No bishop can be nominated in France without the approval of the government. The Pope has consistently respected this state of affairs – there have been about a dozen refusals in the last decade, and the Holy See has always withdrawn the candidate in question.'[23]

Although there was much head-shaking over this concession, it needs to be seen in perspective. Rome still retained the right of choice; and all that the Government could do was to make objections to specific candidates. It was the Concordatory position in reverse. From Rome's point of view it had the mild advantage of partly disarming any later government inclination to interfere with the bishops; Rome could always point out that the Government had had its chance when the initial appointment was proposed. While clearly limited as a safeguard, it was by no means a one-sided victory for the Government.

As it happened, the situation was one of piquant irony in that Gasparri had perhaps even more reason than the Government to regret the previous absence of such an arrangement. The appointments and promotions of Pius X had put fire into the belly of the French episcopate; and it was now extremely difficult to make them sit down and contemplate the future with cold realism. An uncomfortable number of them were sympathetic to Action Française, for which a papal death warrant was pending; and given the general *esprit exalté* which pervaded them, it was going to be very hard to convince them of the facts of life. For Gasparri, the well-being of the French Church depended on a *modus vivendi* with a modern capitalist Republic, not a cerebral monarchy, based on a back-to-the-land ideology and a nostalgia for *le grand siècle*. It was true, of course, that many of the bishops who admired Maurras did so mainly for his anathemas against the Government, rather than for his ideology, much of which was irreconcilable with Catholic teaching. But this was little consolation to the would-be architect of a lasting peace with France.

Gasparri was well furnished with telling arguments. The *soummissionistes* of 1906 still had intelligent and influential spokesmen. Bishop Henri Chapon of Nice, aided by the Abbé Ferdinand Renaud, had provided Rome with a compelling brief in favour of accepting the *associations cultuelles* on a diocesan basis. To make sure of the ground, they had notably consulted with Briand and Louis Méjan on whether the Government was likely to accept the principle of a single association for each diocese. This diocesan body would take the place of the various parochial associations envisaged by the Separation Law. Chaired by the bishop, and consisting entirely of diocesan clergy, this association would in effect be merely a consultative committee, concerned exclusively with matters of material administration.

After ten months of discussion Briand declared in November 1921 that the proposal could be legally reconciled with the Separation Law and subsequent legislation. And as far as Paris and Rome were concerned there appeared to be no serious obstacle to a settlement. Benedict XV, however, was intimidated by the hostile attitude of Sarto's bishops, many of whom would see such an arrangement as a betrayal of their patrons – and indeed were already saying as much.

Benedict's agonising was to be shortly allayed by death; and his bolder successor, Cardinal Ratti, was prepared to be tough. If hopes were raised in intransigent breasts by his taking of the name Pius, they were quickly dashed by his retaining Gasparri as Secretary of State. With a firmness worthy of his namesake, Pius XI outfaced episcopal opinion, and lifted Sarto's ban (18 June 1924). To minimise the reflection on Sarto's judgement, much was made of the different character of the *associations cultuelles* and the changed nature of the political situation. But as the author of the new associations privately pointed out, there was nothing in them that could not have been achieved seventeen years earlier with a little tact and careful bargaining. What Briand had conceded in the laws of 2 January and 28 March 1907 was far more remarkable than what he was now admitting in 1921. The problem in 1906 had been the papal refusal to accept *any* association that might imply recognition of the Separation law (see Chapters 11 and 12). It was true that, unlike Pius X, Benedict and Pius XI had subsequently had the additional assurance of a long line of favourable judgements by the Conseil d'État and the Cour de Cassation. But, as shown in Chapters 11 and 12, uncertainty on this score was irrelevant to Sarto's decision. If it had had any relevance at all, it should, if anything, have encouraged acceptance (see pp. 173–4).

It was significant that Merry del Val remained to the last an inveterate opponent of a settlement. Writing to a French bishop in December 1921, he exclaimed, 'Oh, dear Lord, how sad and disconcerting it is to see the ease with which people let themselves be tricked into believing that all is changed, tricked into putting their trust in mere appearances, fleeting assurances, dubious interpretations that do not even square with the law, and which can be rescinded tomorrow in the name of this perpetual *laicité*! How can people be so naive in the light of past experience, and not see the danger that threatens our principles, our freedom, and the authority and prestige of the Church? It is our whole future which is at stake – a future whose chances depend on our sticking to the policies we have hitherto followed. Little or nothing has changed behind the mists of a superficial courtesy which is chloroforming our vigilance, and which, in the absence of serious guarantees, could well be preparing further ruin.'[24] And so he continued to think until 1930, when in the course of a surgical operation he is said to have swallowed a tooth and died of asphyxia.[25]

A possible element in Rome's indulgence was the fact that papal independence had survived the test of war. Residence on Entente soil had not deprived the Pope of the respect of the Central Powers. If anything, it was the Entente countries who felt short-changed and were heard to mutter unseemly comments about '*le pape boche*'. Like Leo XIII, however, Gasparri was Concordat-minded, and similarly considered the Roman Question a matter of importance for the Church, directly affecting its ability to pursue vigorous independent policies. Unlike Leo, however, he had very modest ideas of what was territorially necessary to secure this independence. The Lateran Treaty of 1929, which later made the Vatican a sovereign State, was largely Gasparri's brain-child – and the product of many years' thinking. He had long been optimistic that his scheme would one day find eventual acceptance; and these hopes may or may not have encouraged him to be indulgent in his dealings with other countries, including France. A more obvious factor was his Concordat-mindedness, which made a settlement with France an attractive proposition. Even a mutually accepted Separation was paradoxically better than a situation where one side recognised the status quo and the other did not.

In the final analysis, however, the cumulative weight of practical considerations was almost certainly the decisive element. With the *associations diocésaines*, the French Church could now corporately own property instead of being reliant on private individuals. With a legal roof over its head, the French Church could at long last terminate its eighteen years of mentally living out of suitcases. It was even hoped that the associations could recover the residue of church property that had been lost in 1908 (see pp. 210–11). Not all of this had been disposed of; and it was certainly the hope of Briand and of Louis Méjan that this could now be given back to the Church. Unfortunately for the Church, the 1924 elections were a victory for the Cartel des Gauches, whose leadership was in the hands of the old standard-bearers of Republican ideals, the Radicals. Like the Ultras of Restoration France, they had forgotten nothing and learnt nothing during their brief years of political exile. Under Edouard Herriot they tried to rub life into the stiffening limbs of anticlericalism. Mayor of Lyon for half a century, Herriot was to be called 'the symbol of Radicalism'. Indeed the remarkable force of his personality, combined with the basic modesty of his national achievements, embodied to perfection the party whose pervasive presence remained such an abiding feature of the Third Republic. Like the smell of the Métro, the Radicals had an evocative charm for the foreign observer, but added little that was remarkable to the quality of life in the Republic.

With the Radicals in power – albeit for two years – there was little immediate hope of regaining the church property that remained unallocated. All that was obtained was a quantity of property originating in private gifts, where the recurring problem of fulfilling the donors' conditions had exasperated the Government into repeating earlier offers (see pp. 210–11). Even this, however, was partly lost through the intransigence of individual bishops. Rather than offend Sarto's memory, they preferred to refuse it (1926), thereby depriving the Church of its only available chance to recover these losses. Another fifteen years was to elapse before a similar opportunity occurred. And much was to happen in the meantime – notably a German invasion and the fall of the regime.

The chance, when it came, had to be taken from the compromising hands of Marshal Pétain. A decree law of 15 February 1941 gave the Church what Herriott had refused in 1924 – the dwindling residue of unallocated property. With the passage of the years its quantity had steadily diminished, as local authorities progressively found suitable uses for the little that was left. By 1941 it was only worth 22 million francs – barely 1 per cent of what the Church had discarded in 1906, when the change in monetary values is included. It was nevertheless better than nothing for a Church which had to raise nearly all its own finance.

Another bonus that came with the decree law was an opportunity for the bishops to have second thoughts over their high-minded refusal of tied property in 1926 (see p. 222). With new faces under many mitres, gratitude prevailed, and the offer was taken.

REINTEGRATION

The Church has survived its chequered record under Vichy and the Occupation. Like the rest of France, Catholics were divided in their attitudes to Pétain. If there is much the Church would like to forget about those years – especially the effusive compliments paid to Pétain by certain bishops – there were enough Catholic critics and opponents of the regime to make it hard for post-war anticlericals to justify reprisals. The Church was no longer judged merely on the record of its accredited spokesmen. There also remained the quirk of circumstance that de Gaulle was a practising Catholic and Pétain was not. Similarly some of the leading Catholic politicians of the post-war period first came into prominence in the Resistance. It was, moreover, de Gaulle and Georges Bidault – not the Left – who tried to remove some of the more complaisant bishops at the Liberation; and it was likewise the predominantly Catholic M.R.P. which was now the main democratic rival to the Communist Party. Of the first twenty ministries of the Fourth Republic, four were led by the M.R.P., and of the others all but one contained a large contingent of M.R.P. ministers. Although at pains not to be a confessional party, the M.R.P. was generally regarded as a Catholic Left-Centre party with mild aspirations to social reform. Many would contest the inclusion of 'Left' in the description 'Left-Centre'; but symptomatically it elected Marc Sangnier as its first president – a piece of nostalgia perhaps, but not without significance. Clearly much had happened since the 1930s.

That Catholics had such a share in the Promised Land was the result of a combination of long- and short-term factors. Underlying all of them was the gradual submergence of religious issues in the economic and social problems that faced France between the wars. Apart from Herriot's unhappy attempt to open old wounds in the mid-1920s, there were few occasions for Catholics to rally on the terrain of religious defence in the inter-war period. Grievances remained; but there were few new threats that were seen as such at the time.

In the second place, the Second World War, like the First, also served to obscure and overshadow religious issues. Although many bishops showed an embarrassing willingness to profit from 'the Pétain miracle', the division of Catholics in these years illustrated the irrelevance of the old battle-cries to the current situation – despite the attempts of many to prove the contrary. In parallel fashion, the corresponding divisions among Radical and other politicians also served to make the same point. Indeed in the New Jerusalem of Liberated France, the Radicals made a very poor showing, both electorally and in parliament.

That their fortunes compared so badly with the new M.R.P. was primarily the outcome of two additional factors. On the one hand there was a growing public demand for social improvement – of a type that outstepped the old individualistic approach of the Radicals. To many electors, it seemed that the M.R.P. was prepared to offer what they wanted, without committing them to the larger package that was popularly associated with the Socialists. The M.R.P. also had the initial advantage of seeming to be a young vigorous movement with roots in the Resistance and the various youth organisations of the inter-war years.

In fact the post-war decade was the time when both the Church and the M.R.P. were reaping the harvest of the various Catholic Action youth groups that had proliferated in urban and rural life in the twenties and thirties. Committed to social improvement and professional self-fulfilment, these organisations had done a great deal to free French Catholicism from its old conservative attachments, persistent though these were. Thus, armed with a socially progressive image – but a politically 'moderate' programme – these new Catholic elements in French politics stood to gain a sizeable slice of the non-socialist democratic vote.

What assured their success, however, was the new unknown quantity in French politics – the female vote, first acquired in 1945. Not only was Catholicism stronger among women than men; but the M.R.P.'s mixture of social reform and political moderation had a particular appeal to a sex that knew the realities of trying to make ends meet but distrusted violent or radical solutions.

The 1950s, however, found the ideals of the M.R.P. sinking in the morass of Fourth Republican politics, while many of its former supporters drifted to the right or left. When the events of 1958 finished the Fourth Republic, a large section of the Catholic vote turned to Gaullism. This did not go unrewarded at the time – whatever problems it may be creating for the future. Catholic private education now receives state subsidies; and the religious orders, though still not formally authorised in the bulk of cases, enjoy a security they have not had since the 1870s.[26] Whether all this is good for the Church – and good for France – is a continuing matter for debate.

When in 1956 Catholics reviewed the first fifty years of Separation, most of them then thought that the Church had profited from its independence from state help. The clergy had undoubtedly gained in self-reliance and public esteem, as a result of having to fend for themselves. In the same way the need to find adequate finance had made for closer links between the clergy and the laity – a laity moreover that was more aware than formerly of its responsibilities towards the Church. Others pointed out that many of the advantages of Separation had yet to be exploited. In the words of a worker-priest, 'the priest still remains the owl in the belfry, as he did in Concordatory times'; and indeed nothing could be more eloquent of chances missed than the present ecclesiastical map of France.

It was also felt that the secular government was well rid of an expensive and individual role. There were other and more effective ways of controlling clerical influence – as the last fifty years had shown. All agreed, however, that complete Separation was a mythical beast of the legal imagination. Contact between Church and State was unavoidable; and like all forms of contact it needed a code of conduct to keep it pleasurable. Many claimed that such a code had been effectively pieced together in the years since World War I. But whether it had reached the point of satisfactory completion – or still had far to go – remained a matter for sharp controversy.

Under the Fifth Republic the process has continued, but on

a different front. Gaullist favour has mainly shown itself in the less well-charted areas of Church-State relations, where constitutional and legal principles are less obviously at stake. The religious neutrality of the State has become a benevolent neutrality, so much so that stern anticlericals are now demanding a new concordat – to safeguard the independence of the State.

This bizarre reversal of roles may seem a paradox today; but it would certainly not have surprised Combes – nor, for that matter, Napoleon.

Appendix

LOI DU 9 DÉCEMBRE 1905
CONCERNANT LA SÉPARATION DES ÉGLISES ET DE L'ÉTAT

TITRE PREMIER

Principes

ART. PREMIER. – La République assure la liberté de conscience. Elle garantit le libre exercice des cultes sous les seules restrictions édictées ci-après dans l'intérêt de l'ordre public.

ART. 2. – La République ne reconnaît, ne salarie ni ne subventionne aucun culte. En conséquence, à partir du 1er janvier qui suivra la promulgation de la présente loi, seront supprimées des budgets de l'État, des départements et des communes, toutes dépenses relatives à l'exercice des cultes. Pourront toutefois être inscrites auxdits budgets les dépenses relatives à des services d'aumônerie et destinées à assurer le libre exercice des cultes dans les établissements publics, tels que lycées, collèges, écoles, hospices, asiles et prisons.

Les établissements publics du culte sont supprimés, sous réserve des dispositions énoncées à l'article 3.

TITRE II

Attributions des biens – Pensions

ART. 3 – Les établissements dont la suppression est ordonnée par l'article 2 continueront provisoirement de fonctionner, conformément aux dispositions qui les régissent actuellement, jusqu'à l'attribution de leurs biens aux associations prévues par le titre IV et au plus tard jusqu'à l'expiration du délai ci-après.

Dès la promulgation de la présente loi, il sera procédé par les agents de l'administration des domaines à l'inventaire descriptif et estimatif :

1° Des biens mobiliers et immobiliers desdits établissements;

2° Des biens de l'État, des départements et des communes dont les mêmes établissements ont la jouissance.

Ce double inventaire sera dressé contradictoirement avec les représentants légaux des établissements ecclésiastiques ou eux dûment appelés par une notification faite en la forme administrative.

Les agents chargés de l'inventaire auront le droit de se faire communiquer tous titres et documents utiles à leurs opérations.

ART. 4 – Dans le délai d'un an à partir de la promulgation de la présente loi, les biens mobiliers et immobiliers des menses, fabriques, conseils presbytéraux, consistoires et autres établissements publics du culte seront, avec toutes les charges et obligations qui les grèvent et avec leur affectation spéciale, transférés par les représentants légaux de ces établissements aux associations qui, en se conformant aux règles d'organisation générale du culte dont elles se proposent d'assurer l'exercice, se seront légalement formées, suivant les prescriptions de l'article 19, pour l'exercice de ce culte dans les anciennes circonscriptions desdits établissements.

ART. 5 – Ceux des biens désignés à l'article précédent qui proviennent de l'État et qui ne sont pas grevés d'une fondation pieuse créée postérieurement à la loi du 18 germinal an X feront retour à l'État.

Les attributions de biens ne pourront être faites par les établissements ecclésiastiques qu'un mois après la promulgation du règlement d'administration publique prévu à l'article 43. Faute de quoi la nullité pourra en être demandée devant le tribunal civil par toute partie intéressée ou par le ministère public.

En cas d'aliénation par l'association cultuelle de valeurs mobilières ou d'immeubles faisant partie du patrimoine de l'établissement public dissous, le montant du produit de la vente devra être employé en titres de rente nominatifs ou dans les conditions prévues au paragraphe 2 de l'article 22.

L'acquéreur des biens aliénés sera personnellement responsable de la régularité de cet emploi.

Les biens revendiqués par l'État, les départements ou les communes ne pourront être aliénés, transformés ni modifiés jusqu'à ce qu'il ait été statué sur la revendication par les tribunaux compétents.

ART. 6 – Les associations attributaires des biens des établissements ecclésiastiques supprimés seront tenues des dettes de ces établissements ainsi que de leurs emprunts, sous réserve des dispositions du troisieme paragraphe du présent article; tant qu'elles ne seront pas libérées de ce passif, elles auront droit à la jouissance des biens productifs de revenus qui doivent faire retour à l'État en vertu de l'article 5.

Le revenu global desdits biens reste affecté au payement du reliquat des dettes régulières et légales de l'établissement public supprimé, lorsqu'il ne se sera formé aucune association cultuelle apte à recueillir le patrimoine de cet établissement.

Les annuités des emprunts contractés pour dépenses relatives aux édifices religieux seront supportées par les associations en proportion du temps pendant lequel elles auront l'usage de ces édifices par application des dispositions du titre III.

Dans le cas où l'État, les départements ou les communes rentreront en possession de ceux des édifices dont ils sont propriétaires, ils seront responsables des dettes régulièrement contractées et afférentes auxdits édifices.

ART. 7 – Les biens mobiliers ou immobiliers grevés d'une affectation charitable ou de toute autre affectation étrangère à l'exercice du culte seront attribués, par les représentants légaux des établissements ecclésiastiques, aux services ou établissements publics ou d'utilité publique, dont la destination est conforme à celle desdits biens. Cette attribution devra être approuvée par le préfet du département où siège l'établissement ecclésiastique. En cas de non-approbation, il sera statué par décret en Conseil d'État.

Toute action en reprise ou en revendication devra être exercée dans un délai de six mois à partir du jour où l'arrêté préfectoral ou le décret approuvant l'attribution aura été inséré au *Journal officiel*. L'action ne pourra être intentée qu'en raison de donations ou de legs et seulement par les auteurs et leurs héritiers en ligne directe.

ART. 8 – Faute par un établissement ecclésiastique d'avoir, dans le délai fixé par l'article 4, procédé aux attributions ci-dessus prescrites, il y sera pourvu par décret.

A l'expiration dudit délai, les biens à attribuer seront, jusqu'à leur attribution, placés sous séquestre.

Dans le cas où les biens attribués en vertu de l'article 4 et du paragraphe 1 du présent article seront, soit dès l'origine, soit dans la suite, réclamés par plusieurs associations formées pour l'exerci ce du même culte, l'attibution qui en aura été faite par les représentants de l'établissement ou par décret pourra être contestée devant le Conseil d'État statuant au contentieux, lequel prononcera en tenant compte de toutes les circonstances de fait.

La demande sera introduite devant le Conseil d'État, dans le délai d'un an à partir de la date du décret ou à partir de la notification, à l'autorité préfectorale, par les représentants légaux des établissements publics du culte, de l'attribution effectuée par eux. Cette notification devra être faite dans le délai d'un mois.

L'attribution pourra être ultérieurement contestée en cas de scission dans l'association nantie, de création d'association nouvelle par suite d'une modification dans le territoire de la circonscription ecclésiastique et dans le cas où l'association attributaire n'est plus en mesure de remplir son objet.

ART. 9 – A défaut de toute association pour recueillir les biens d'un établissement public du culte, ces biens seront attribués par décret aux établissements communaux d'assistance ou de bienfaisance situés dans les limites territoriales de la circonscription ecclésiastique intéressée.

En cas de dissolution d'une association, les biens qui lui auront été dévolus en exécution des articles 4 et 8 seront attribués, par décret rendu en Conseil d'État, soit à des associations analogues dans la même circonscription ou, à leur défaut, dans les circonscriptions les plus voisines, soit aux établissements visés au paragraphe 1 du présent article.

Toute action en reprise ou en revendication devra être exercée dans un délai de six mois à partir du jour où le décret aura été inséré au *Journal officiel*. L'action ne pourra être intentée qu'en raison de donations ou de legs et seulement par les auteurs et leurs héritiers en ligne directe.

ART. 10. – Les attributions prévues par les articles précédents ne donnent lieu à aucune perception au profit du Trésor.

ART. 11. – Les ministres des cultes qui, lors de la promulgation de la présente loi, seront âgés de plus de soixante ans révolus et qui auront, pendant trente ans au moins, rempli des fonctions ecclésiastiques rémunérées par l'État, recevront une pension annuelle et viagère égale aux trois quarts de leur traitement.

Ceux qui seront âgés de plus de quarante-cinq ans et qui auront, pendant vingt ans au moins, rempli des fonctions ecclésiastiques rémunérées par l'État, recevront une pension annuelle et viagère égale à la moitié de leur traitement.

Les pensions allouées par les deux paragraphes précédents ne pourront pas dépasser 1.500 francs.

En cas de décès des titulaires, ces pensions seront réversibles, jusqu'à concurrence de la moitié de leur montant, au profit de la veuve et des orphelins mineurs laissés par le défunt et, jusqu'à concurrence du quart, au profit de la veuve sans enfants mineurs. A la majorité des orphelins, leur pension s'éteindra de plein droit.

Les ministres des cultes actuellement salariés par l'État, qui ne seront pas dans les conditions ci-dessus, recevront, pendant quatre ans à partir de la suppression du budget des cultes, une allocation égale à la totalité de leur traitement pour la première année, aux deux tiers pour la deuxième, à la moitié pour la troisième, au tiers pour la quatrième.

Toutefois dans les communes de moins de 1,000 habitants et pour les ministres des cultes qui continueront à y remplir leurs fonctions, la durée de chacune des quatre périodes ci-dessus indiquées sera doublée.

Les départements et les communes pourront, sous les mêmes conditions que l'État, accorder aux ministres des cultes actuellement salariés par eux des pensions ou des allocations établies sur la même base et pour une égale durée.

Réserve est faite des droits acquis en matière de pensions par application de la législation antérieure, ainsi que des secours accordés, soit aux anciens ministres des différents cultes, soit à leur famille.

Les pensions prévues aux deux premiers paragraphes du présent article ne pourront se cumuler avec toute autre pension ou tout autre traitement alloué, à titre quelconque, par l'État, les départements ou les communes.

La loi du 27 juin 1885, relative au personnel des facultés de théologie catholique supprimées, est applicable aux professeurs, chargés de cours, maîtres de conférences et étudiants des facultés de théologie protestante.

Les pensions et allocations prévues ci-dessus seront incessibles et insaisissables dans les mêmes conditions que les pensions civiles. Elles cesseront de plein droit en cas de condamnation à une peine afflictive ou infamante ou en cas de condamnation pour l'un des délits prévus aux articles 34 et 35 de la présente loi.

Le droit à l'obtention ou à la jouissance d'une pension ou allocation sera suspendu par les circonstances qui font perdre la qualité de Français, durant la privation de cette qualité.

Les demandes de pension devront être, sous peine de forclusion, formées dans le délai d'un an après la promulgation de la présente loi.

TITRE III

Des édifices des cultes

ART. 12. – Les édifices qui ont été mis à la disposition de la nation et qui, en vertu de la loi du 18 germinal an X, servent à l'exercice public des cultes ou au logement de leurs ministres (cathédrales, églises, chapelles, temples, synagogues, archevêchés, évêchés, presbytères, séminaires), ainsi que leurs dépendances immobilières et les objets mobiliers qui les garnissaient au moment où lesdits édifices ont été remis aux cultes, sont et demeurent propriétés de l'État des départments et des communes.

Pour ces édifices, comme pour ceux postérieurs à la loi du 18 germinal an X, dont l'État, les départements et les communes seraient propriétaires, y compris les facultés de théologie protestante, il sera procédé conformément aux dispositions des articles suivants.

ART. 13. – Les édifices servant à l'exercice public du culte, ainsi que les objets mobiliers les garnissant, seront laissés gratuitement à la disposition des établissements publics du culte, puis des associations appelées à les remplacer auxquelles les biens de ces établissements auront été attribués par application des dispositions du titre II.

La cessation de cette jouissance, et, s'il y a lieu, son transfert, seront prononcés par décret, sauf recours au Conseil d'État statuant au contentieux :

1° Si l'association bénéficiaire est dissoute;

2° Si, en dehors des cas de foce majeure, le culte cesse d'être célébré pendant plus de six mois consécutifs;

3° Si la conservation de l'édifice ou celle des objets mobiliers classés en vertu de la loi de 1887 et de l'article 16 de la présente loi est compromise par insuffisance d'entretien, et après mise en demeure dûment notifiée du conseil municipal ou, à son défaut, du préfet;

4° Si l'association cesse de remplir son objet ou si les édifices sont détournés de leur destination;

5° Si elle ne satisfait pas soit aux obligations de l'article 6 ou du dernier paragraphe du présent article, soit aux prescriptions relatives aux monuments historiques.

La désaffectation de ces immeubles pourra, dans les cas ci-dessus prévus, être prononcée par décret rendu en Conseil d'État. En dehors de ces cas, elle ne pourra l'être que par une loi.

Les immeubles autrefois affectés aux cultes et dans lesquels les cérémonies du culte n'auront pas été célébrées pendant le délai d'un an antérieurement à la présente loi, ainsi que ceux qui ne seront pas réclamés par une association cultuelle dans le délai de deux ans après sa promulgation, pourront étre désaffectés par décret.

Il en est de même pour les édifices dont la désaffectation aura été demandée antérieurement au 1er juin 1905.

Les établissements publics du culte, puis les associations bénéficiaires seront tenus des réparations de toute nature, ainsi que des frais d'assurance et autres charges afférentes aux édifices et aux meubles les garnissant.

ART. 14. – Les archevêches, évêchés, les presbytères et leurs dépendances, les grands séminaires et facultés de théologie protestante seront laissés gratuitement à la disposition des établissements publics du culte, puis des associations prévues à l'article 13, savoir : les archevêchés et évêchés pendant une période de deux années; les presbytères dans les communes où résidera le ministre du culte, les grands séminaires et facultés de théologie protestante pendant cinq années à partir de la promulgation de la présente loi.

Les établissements et associations sont soumis, en ce qui concerne ces édifices, aux obligations prévues par le dernier paragraphe de l'article 13. Toutefois, il ne seront pas tenus des grosses réparations.

La cessation de la jouissance des établissements et associations sera prononcée dans les conditions et suivant les formes déterminées par l'article 13. Les dispositions des paragraphes 3 et 5 du même article sont applicables aux édifices visés par le paragraphe 1 du présent article.

La distraction des parties superflues des presbytères laissés à la disposition des associations cultuelles pourra, pendant le délai prévu au paragraphe 1, être prononcée pour un service public par décret rendu en Conseil d'État.

A l'expiration des délais de jouissance gratuite, la libre disposition des édifices sera rendue à l'État, aux départements ou aux communes.

Les indemnités de logement incombant actuellement aux communes, à défaut de presbytère, par application de l'article 136 de la loi du 5 avril 1884, resteront à leur charge pendant le délai de cinq ans. Elles cesseront de plein droit en cas de dissolution de l'association.

ART. 15. – Dans les départements de la Savoie, de la Haute-Savoie et des Alpes-Maritimes, la jouissance des édifices antérieurs à la loi du 18 germinal an X, servant à l'exercice des cultes ou au logement de leurs ministres, sera attribuée par les communes sur les territoires desquelles ils se trouvent aux associations cultuelles, dans les conditions indiquées par les articles 12 et suivants de la présente loi. En dehors de ces obligations, les communes pourront disposer librement de la propriété de ces édifices.

Dans ces mêmes départements, les cimetières resteront la propriété des communes.

ART. 16. – Il sera procédé à un classement complémentaire des édifices servant à l'exercice public du culte (cathédrales, églises, chapelles, temples, synagogues, archevêchés, évêchés, presbytères, séminaires), dans lequel devront être compris tous ceux de ces édifices représentant, dans leur ensemble ou dans leurs parties, une valeur artistique ou historique.

Les objets mobiliers ou les immeubles par destination mentionnés à l'article 13 qui n'auraient pas encore été inscrits sur la liste de classement dressée en vertu de la loi du 30 mars 1887 sont, par l'effet de la présente loi, ajoutés à ladite liste. Il sera procédé par le ministre de l'Instruction publique et des Beaux-Arts, dans le délai de trois ans, au classement définitif de ceux de ces objets dont la conservation présenterait, au point de vue de l'histoire ou de l'art, un intérêt suffisant. A l'expiration de ce délai, les autres objets seront déclassés de plein droit.

En outre, les immeubles et les objets mobiliers, attribués en vertu de la présente loi aux associations, pourront être classés dans les mêmes conditions que s'ils appartenaient à des établissements publics.

Il n'est pas dérogé, pour le surplus, aux dispositions de la loi du 30 mars 1887.

Les archives ecclésiastiques et bibliothèques existant dans les archevêchés, évêchés, grands séminaires, paroisses, succursales et leurs dépendances seront inventoriées, et celles qui seront reconnues propriété de l'État lui seront restituées.

ART. 17. – Les immeubles par destination classés en vertu de la loi du 30 mars 1887 ou de la présente loi sont inaliénables et imprescriptibles.

Dans le cas où la vente ou l'échange d'un objet classé serait autorisé par le ministre de l'Instruction publique et des Beaux-Arts, un droit de préemption est accordé : 1° aux associations cultuelles; 2° aux communes; 3° aux départements; 4° aux musées et sociétés d'art et d'archéologie; 5° à l'État. Le prix sera fixé par trois experts que désigneront le vendeur, l'acquéreur et le président du tribunal civil.

Si aucun des acquéreurs visés ci-dessus ne fait usage du droit de préemption, la vente sera libre; mais il est interdit à l'acheteur d'un objet classé de le transporter hors de France.

Nul travail de réparation, restauration ou entretien à faire aux monuments ou objets mobiliers classés ne peut être commencé sans l'autorisation du ministre des Beaux-Arts, ni exécuté hors de la surveillance de son administration, sous peine, contre les propriétaires, occupant ou détenteurs qui auraient ordonné ces travaux, d'une amende de seize à quinze cents francs (16 à 1.500 fr.).

Toute infraction aux dispositions ci-dessus ainsi qu'à celles de l'article 16 de la présente loi et des articles 4, 10, 11, 12 et 13 de la loi du 30 mars 1887 sera punie d'une amende de cent à dix mille francs (100 à 10.000 fr.) et d'un emprisonnement de six jours à trois mois, ou de l'une de ces deux peines seulement.

La visite des édifices et l'exposition des objets mobiliers classés seront publiques; elles ne pourront donner lieu à aucune taxe ni redevance.

TITRE IV

Des associations pour l'exercice des cultes

ART. 18. – Les associations formées pour subvenir aux frais, à l'entretien et à l'exercice public d'un culte devront être constituées conformément aux articles 5 et suivants du titre premier de la loi du 1er juillet 1901. Elles seront, en outre, soumises aux prescriptions de la présente loi.

ART. 19. – Ces associations devront avoir exclusivement pour objet l'exercice d'un culte et être composées au moins:

Dans les communes de moins de 1.000 habitants, de sept personnes;

Dans les communes de 1.000 à 20.000 habitants, de quinze personnes;

Dans les communes dont le nombre des habitants est supérieur à 20.000, de vingt-cinq personnes majeures, domiciliées ou résidant dans la circonscription religieuse.

Chacun de leurs membres pourra s'en retirer en tout temps, après payement des cotisations échues et de celles de l'année courante, nonobstant toute clause contraire.

Nonobstant toute clause contraire des statuts, les actes de gestion financière et d'administration légale des biens accomplis par les directeurs ou administrateurs seront, chaque année au moins, présentés au contrôle de l'assemblée générale des membres de l'association et soumis à son approbation.

Les associations pourront recevoir, en outre des cotisations prévues par l'article 6 de la loi du 1er juillet 1901, le produit des quêtes et collectes pour les frais du culte, percevoir des rétributions: pour les cérémonies et services religieux même par fondation; pour la location des bancs et sièges; pour la fourniture des objets destinés au service des funérailles dans les édifices religieux et à la décoration de ces édifices.

Elles pourront verser, sans donner lieu à perception de droits, le surplus de leurs recettes à d'autres associations constituées pour le même objet.

Elles ne pourront, sous quelque forme que ce soit, recevoir des subventions de l'État, des départements ou des communes. Ne sont pas considérées comme subventions les sommes allouées pour réparations aux monument classés.

Art. 20. – Ces associations peuvent, dans les formes déterminées par l'article 7 du décret du 16 août 1901, constituer des unions ayant une administration ou une direction centrale; ces unions seront réglées par l'article 18 et par les cinq derniers paragraphes de l'article 19 de la présente loi.

Art. 21. – Les associations et les unions tiennent un état de leurs recettes et de leurs dépenses; elles dressent, chaque année, le compte financier de l'année et l'état inventorié de leurs biens, meubles et immeubles.

Le contrôle financier est exercé sur les associations et sur les unions par l'administration de l'enregistrement et par l'inspection générale des finances.

Art. 22. – Les associations et unions peuvent employer leurs ressources disponibles à la constitution d'un fonds de réserve suffisant pour assurer les frais et l'entretien du culte et ne pouvant en aucun cas recevoir une autre destination: le montant de cette réserve ne pourra jamais dépasser une somme égale, pour les unions et associations ayant plus de cinq mille francs (5.000 fr.) de revenue, à trois fois et, pour les autres associations, à six fois la moyenne annuelle des sommes dépensées par chacune d'elles pour les frais du culte pendant les cinq derniers exercices.

Indépendamment de cette réserve, qui devra êtra placée en valeurs nominatives, elles pourront constituer une réserve spéciale dont les fonds devront être déposés, en argent ou en titres nominatifs, à la caisse des dépôts et consignations pour être exclusivement affectés, y compris les interêts, à l'achat, à la construction, à la décoration ou à la réparation d'immeubles ou meubles destinés aux besoins de l'association ou de l'union.

Art. 23. – Seront punis d'une amende de seize francs (16 fr.) à deux cents francs (200 fr.) et, en cas de récidive, d'une amende double les directeurs ou administrateurs d'une association ou d'une union qui auront contrevenu aux articles 18, 19, 20, 21 et 22.

Les tribunaux pourront, dans le cas d'infraction au paragraphe 1 de l'article 22, condamner l'association ou l'union à verser l'excédent constaté aux établissements communaux d'assistance ou de bienfaisance.

Ils pourront, en outre, dans tous les cas prévus au paragraphe 1 du présent article, prononcer la dissolution de l'association ou de l'union.

ART. 24. – Les édifices affectés à l'exercice du culte appartenant à l'État, aux départements ou aux communes continueront à être exemptés de l'impôt foncier et de l'impôt des portes et fenêtres.

Les édifices servant au logement des ministres des cultes, les séminaires, les facultés de théologie protestante qui appartiennent à l'État, aux départements ou aux communes, les biens qui sont la propriété des associations et unions sont soumis aux mêmes impôts que ceux des particuliers.

Les associations et unions ne sont en aucun cas assujetties à la taxe d'abonnement ni à celle imposée aux cercles par l'article 33 de la loi du 8 août 1890, pas plus qu'à l'impôt de 4 p. 100 sur le revenu établi par les lois du 28 décembre 1880 et du 29 décembre 1884.

TITRE V

Police des cultes

ART. 25. – Les réunions pour la célébration d'un culte tenues dans les locaux appartenant à une association cultuelle ou mis à sa disposition sont publiques. Elles sont dispensées des formalités de l'article 8 de la loi du 30 juin 1881, mais restent placées sous la surveillance des autorités dans l'intérêt de l'ordre public. Elles ne peuvent avoir lieu qu'après une déclaration faite dans les formes de l'article 2 de la même loi et indiquant le local dans lequel elles seront tenues.

Une seule déclaration suffit pour l'ensemble des réunions permanentes, périodiques ou accidentelles qui auront lieu dans l'année.

ART. 26. – Il est interdit de tenir des réunions politiques dans les locaux servant habituellement à l'exercice d'un culte.

ART. 27. – Les cérémonies, processions et autres manifestations extérieures d'un culte continueront à être réglées en conformité des articles 95 et 97 de la loi municipale du 5 avril 1884.

Les sonneries de cloches seront réglées par arrêté municipal, et, en cas de désaccord entre le maire et le président ou directeur de l'association cultuelle, par arrêté préfectoral.

Le règlement d'administration publique prévu par l'article 43 de la présente loi déterminera les conditions et les cas dans lesquels les sonneries civiles pourront avoir lieu.

ART. 28. – Il est interdit, à l'avenir, d'élever ou d'apposer aucun signe ou emblème religieux sur les monuments publics ou en quelque emplacement public que ce soit, à l'exception des édifices servant au culte, des terrains de sépulture dans les cimetières, des monuments funéraires, ainsi que des musées ou expositions.

ART. 29. – Les contraventions aux articles précédents sont punies des peines de simple police.

Sont passibles de ces peines, dans le cas des articles 25, 26 et 27, ceux qui ont organisé la réunion ou manifestation, ceux qui y ont participé en qualité de ministres du culte et, dans le cas des articles 25 et 26, ceux qui ont fourni le local.

ART. 30. – Conformément aux dispositions de l'article 2 de la loi du 28 mars 1882, l'enseignement religieux ne peut être donné aux enfants âgés de six à treize ans, inscrits dans les écoles publiques, qu'en dehors des heures de classe.

Il sera fait application aux ministres des cultes qui enfreindraient ces prescriptions des dispositions de l'article 14 de la loi précitée.

ART. 31. – Sont punis d'une amende de seize francs (16 fr.) à deux cents francs (200 fr.) et d'un emprisonnement de six jours à deux mois ou de l'une de ces deux peines seulement ceux qui, soit par voies de fait, violences ou menaces contre un individu, soit en lui faisant craindre de perdre son emploi ou d'exposer à un dommage sa personne, sa famille ou sa fortune, l'auront déterminé à exercer ou à s'abstenir d'exercer un culte, à faire partie ou à cesser de faire partie d'une association cultuelle, à contribuer ou à s'abstenir de contribuer aux frais d'un culte.

ART. 32. – Seront punis des mêmes peines ceux qui auront empêché, retardé ou interrompu les exercices d'un culte par des troubles ou désordres causés dans le local servant à ces exercices.

ART. 33. – Les dispositions des deux articles précédents ne s'appliquent qu'aux troubles, outrages ou voies de fait dont la nature ou les circonstances ne donneront pas lieu à de plus fortes peines d'après les dispositions du Code pénal.

ART. 34. – Tout ministre d'un culte qui, dans les lieux où s'exerce ce culte, aura publiquement, par des discours prononcés, des lectures faites, des écrits distribués ou des affiches apposées, outragé ou diffamé un citoyen chargé d'un service public sera puni d'une amende de cinq cents francs à trois mille francs (500 fr. à 3.000 fr.) et d'un emprisonnement d' un mois à un an, ou de l'une de ces deux peines seulement.

La vérité du fait diffamatoire, mais seulement s'il est relatif aux fonctions, pourra être établie devant le tribunal correctionnel dans les formes prévues par l'article 52 de la loi du 29 juillet 1881. Les prescriptions édictées par l'article 65 de la même loi s'appliquent aux délits du présent article et de l'article qui suit.

ART. 35. – Si un discours prononcé ou un écrit affiché ou distribué publiquement dans les lieux où s'exerce le culte contient une provocation directe à résister à l'exécution des lois ou aux actes légaux de l'autorité publique, ou s'il tend à soulever ou à armer une partie des citoyens contre les autres, le ministre du culte qui s'en sera rendu coupable sera puni d'un emprisonnement de trois mois à deux ans, sans préjudice des peines de la complicité, dans le cas où la provocation aurait été suivie d'une sédition, révolte ou guerre civile.

ART. 36. – Dans le cas de condamnation par les tribunaux de simple police ou de police correctionnelle en application des articles 25 et 26, 34 et 35, l'association constituée pour l'exercice du culte dans l'immeuble où l'infraction a été commise sera civilement responsable.

TITRE VI

Dispositions générales

ART. 37. – L'article 463 du Code pénal et la loi du 26 mars 1891 sont applicables à tous les cas dans lesquels la présente loi édicte des pénalités.

ART. 38. – Les congrégations religieuses demeurent soumises aux lois des 1er juillet 1901, 4 décembre 1902 et 7 juillet 1904.

ART. 39. – Les jeunes gens qui ont obtenu à titre d'élèves ecclésiastiques la dispense prévue par l'article 23 de la loi du 15 juillet 1889 continueront à en bénéficier conformément à l'article 99 de la loi du 21 mars 1905, à la condition qu'à l'âge de vingt-six ans ils soient pourvus d'un emploi de ministre du culte rétribué par une association cultuelle et sous réserve des justifications qui seront fixées par un règlement d'administration publique.

ART. 40. – Pendant huit années à partir de la promulgation de la présente loi, les ministres du culte seront inéligibles au conseil municipal dans les communes où ils exerceront leur ministère ecclésiastique.

ART. 41. – Les sommes rendues disponibles chaque année par la suppression du budget des cultes seront réparties entre les communes au prorata du contingent de la contribution foncière des propriétés non bâties qui leur a été assigné pendant l'exercice qui précédera la promulgation de la présente loi.

ART. 42. – Les dispositions légales relatives aux jours actuellement fériés sont maintenues.

ART. 43. – Un règlement d'administration publique rendu dans les trois mois qui suivront la promulgation de la présente loi déterminera les mesures propres à assurer son application.

Des règlements d'administration publique détermineront les conditions dans lesquelles la présente loi sera applicable à l'Algérie et aux colonies.

ART. 44. – Sont et demeurent abrogées toutes les dispositions relatives à l'organisation publique des cultes antérieurement reconnus par l'État, ainsi que toutes dispositions contraires à la présente loi et notamment :

1° La loi du 18 germinal an X, portant que la convention passée le 26 messidor an IX entre le pape et le gouvernement français, ensemble les articles organiques de ladite convention et des cultes protestants, seront exécutés commune des lois da la République;

2° Le décret du 26 mars 1852 et la loi du 1er août 1879 sur les cultes protestants;

3° Les décrets du 17 mars 1808, la loi du 8 février 1831 et l'ordonnance du 25 mai 1844 sur le culte israélite;

4° Les décrets des 22 décembre 1812 et 19 mars 1859;

5° Les articles 201 à 208, 260 à 264, 294 du Code pénal;

6° Les articles 100 et 101, les paragraphes 11 et 12 de l'article 136 et l'article 167 de la loi du 5 avril 1884;

7° Le décret du 30 décembre 1809 et l'article 78 de la loi du 26 janvier 1892.

Sources

UNPUBLISHED PRIMARY SOURCES

Ecclesiastical Archives

Archives Historiques de l'Archevêché de Paris, cited as 'Archiepisc Paris'.

Archivio dei Padri Assunzionisti, Rome, cited as 'Assumpt'. In addition to a wide range of manuscript material, these archives also contain in typescript the collected letters of Vincent Bailly and Ernest Picard (cited as 'Bailly T S' and 'Picard T S').

Archivio Segreto Vaticano, cited as 'Segr. Vatican'. For the pre-1878 period only. Documents for the post–1878 period are unobtainable except by special authorisation of the Secretary of State.

Archives de la Société de Jésus, Province de Paris, Chantilly. The Rev. Joseph Dehergne, S.J., has kindly provided me with copies of relevant material.

Archives de l'Institut Supérieur de Théologie Saint Augustin, Enghien, Belgium. Private papers of Henri Groussau (cited as 'Groussau MSS').

French Public Archives

Archives Nationales (now Archives de France), cited as 'A. N.'

F^{19} : Archives of the former Direction des Cultes.

AP : Private letters, to and from various political figures.

C : Chambre des Députés.

At the time of consultation, the following documents were still held in the Archives de l'Assemblée Nationale :

MS *procès-verbaux* of the Commission of the Chambre des Députés for the Separation of Church and State : C.D., 8. 1074–1080.

Correspondence and papers of Mgr Montagnini, Papal *chargé d'affaires* in Paris : C.D., c. 1027–1036; cited as 'Montagnini MSS'.

A commission of the Chamber was appointed to examine these papers after their confiscation in December 1906. The translation from Italian into French also contained in the dossiers is that of the commission, and is as accurate as the legibility of the accompanying Italian originals will allow. Historians have hitherto used the small collection of extracts previously distributed to the press, based on the first Parquet translations, and republished in part as *Les fiches pontificales* (Paris, 1908). The incompleteness of the press extracts occasionally distorts their significance.

Archives du Ministère des Affaires Etrangères, cited as 'MAE'.

Archives du Conseil de la République (now Archives du Sénat) MS *procès-*

verbaux of the Commission of the Sénat for the Separation of Church and State : SSE 259.22.

Archives de la Charente-Maritime.

The private papers of Emile Combes, cited as 'Combes MSS, A. Ch-M'. (Consulted immediately after their donation by his grandson, M. Émile Bron. They had not yet been formally classified and the individual items were not then numbered.)

Bibliothèque Nationale, Cabinet des Manuscrits.

Provincial archives of the Grand Orient de France, FM², Boîtes Oranges (non communicables), 20th-century material made available by kind permission of the Grand Orient de France.

N.A.F., 12 711 Auguste Scheurer-Kestner's diary, VIII.

N.A.F., 15 713 Papers of Albert Houtin.

N.A.F., 24 401–6 Papers of Mgr Lucien Lacroix, one-time Bishop of Tarentaise.

Various letters, to and from active participants.

Belgian Public Archives

Archives du Ministère des Affaires Etrangères et du Commerce Extérieur, cited as 'Belg.' Despatches of the Belgian representatives in Madrid, Paris and the Holy See, notably those of Baron Maximilien d'Erp, who was Belgian Minister Plenipotentiary to the Holy See from 1896 to 1915 (cited as 'Belg., SS') See comment on p. 266, note 7.

Italian Public Archives

Archivio Storico del Ministro degli Affari Esteri, cited as 'Ital. Aff. Est.'
Archivio Centrale dello Stato, cited as 'Ital. Centr.'

Private archives

MS notebooks of Francis de Pressensé, kindly lent by M. Marcel Faucon.

MS letters of the Baron Denys Cochin, kindly lent by his grandson, M. Denys Cochin, and M. Marc Bonnefous.

MS diary of the Abbé Landrieux, Cardinal Langénieux's personal secretary and later Bishop of Dijon, kindly lent by the Abbé Patrick Heidsieck.

MS notes on the *associations cultuelles,* kindly lent by Canon Ferdinand Renaud.

Notes and letters of J. E. C. Bodley, kindly lent by Mrs J. E. C. Bodley. (Most of these have subsequently been donated to the Bodleian Library, Oxford.)

Verbal information

Surviving participants in the events of the period, and relatives and friends of others no longer living, have helped me with a variety of reminiscences and comment. I have acknowledged their kindness at the beginning of this book and in the footnotes; but I ought here to single out as a major source of information and encouragement over ten years the late M. Paul Grunebaum-Ballin (1871–1969), legal collaborator of Charles Dumay and Aristide Briand at the time of the Separation (see p. 269, note 32).

PUBLISHED PRIMARY SOURCES (INCLUDING MEMOIRS)

Additional sources are listed in the bibliographies of the following, Jean-Marie Mayeur, *L'abbé Lemire, 1853–1928, Un prêtre démocrate* (Paris, 1968), Louise Violette Méjan, *La Séparation des Églises et de l'Etat. L'oeuvre de Louis Méjan* (Paris, 1959), Pierre Sorlin, *Waldeck-Rousseau* (Paris, 1966).

Arnaud, François. *Conférence sur la loi de séparation des Eglises et de l'État et ses consequences pour l'arrondissement de Barcelonnette.* Barcelonnette, 1906.

D'Avenel, the Vicomte Georges. 'La Reforme Administrative. III Les Cultes', *La Revue des deux mondes,* 15 May 1890, pp. 332–69.

B. . ., Mgr. 'Faudra-t-il louer nos églises?' *La Semaine religieuse* (Montpellier), 4 Feb 1905, p. 74.

Barbier, the Abbé Emmanuel. *Histoire du Catholicisme libéral et du catholicisme social en France (1871–1914),* Vol. 4. Paris, 1923.

Barrès, Maurice. *Scènes et doctrines du nationalisme.* 2 vols. Paris, defin. edn., 1925.

Baudrillart, Mgr Alfred. *Quatre cents ans de Concordat.* Paris, 1905.

Becamel, Marcel. 'Lettres inédites d'Emile Combes.' *La Revue du Tarn,* 15 Sept 1958, pp. 223–52.

Benoist, Charles. *Souvenirs de Charles Benoist,* Vol. 3: *Vie parlementaire. Vie diplomatique 1902–1933.* Paris, 1933.

Berry, Georges. *Un page d'histoire. La Séparation des Eglises et de l'État à la Chambre des Députés.* Paris, 1905.

Besnard, Eric. 'La Séparation et les Eglises. Notre enquête', *Le Siècle,* 24, 26, 27, 28, and 29 Nov 1904, 1, 3, 4, 5, 7, 9, 10, 12, 13, 16, 18, 21, 22, 23, 24, 25, 26, and 27 Dec 1904, 1, 2, 3, 4, 5, 10, 17, 19, 20, 26, and 30 Jan 1905, 7, 8, 11, 12, 13, 14, 16, 17, 24, and 25 Feb 1905, 6, 8, 13, 14, 16, 18, 19, 21, and 22 Mar 1905.

Bonnet, Mgr Joseph. *Lettre pastorale sur le laicisme et mandement pour le carême.* Viviers, 1905.

Bricout, the Abbé. 'La Séparation de l'Eglise et de l'Etat et le projet Briand', *La Revue du clergé français,* 1 Sep 1904, pp. 5–24.

De Broglie, the Duc Albert. *Le Concordat.* Paris, 1893.

'L'Eglise et la France moderne', *La Revue des deux mondes,* 15 May 1897, pp. 282–319.

Brugerette, the Abbé Joseph. 'M. Briand chez Mgr Lacroix', *La Revue de Paris,* 1 Oct 1930, pp. 650–59.

Brunetière, Ferdinand. 'Voulons-nous une église nationale?' *La Revue des deux mondes,* 15 Nov 1901, pp. 277–94.

'Quand la Séparation sera votée', *La Revue des deux mondes,* 1 Dec 1905, pp. 688–708.

Buisson, Frédéric. 'A qui l'Eglise?' *Le Radical*, 22 Feb 1905.

Bureau, Paul. 'Deux doctrines sur la Séparation,' *Le Bulletin de la semaine*, 17 May 1905.

C.... J. 'La Politique', *Le Gaulois*, 28 Nov 1891.

De Cabrières, Mgr François. 'Le Concordat', *L'Eclair* (Montpellier), 17 Dec 1891.

Le Discours d'Auxerre (4 *septembre* 1904). *Lettre de Mgr l'Evêque de Montpellier au clergé du diocèse*. Montpellier, 1904.

'Lettre de Monseigneur l'Evêque sur la question des "associations cultuelles",' *La Semaine religieuse* (Montpellier), 11 Mar 1905, pp. 150–52.

Caillaux, Joseph. *Mes Mémoires*, Vol 1: *Ma Jeunesse orgueilleuse*. Paris, 1942.

De Cassagnac, Paul Adolphe. 'Le Carcan', *L'Autorité*, 23 Oct 1902.

De Cassagnac, Paul-Julien. 'L'Alternative effrayable,' *L'Autorité*, 11 Aug 1905.

'Le Livre d'or de M. Brunetière et de ses amis,' *L'Autorité*, 29 Mar 1906.

De Castellane, the Comte Boni. *Rapports de l'Eglise et de l'Etat en France, de l'origine de la monarchie française jusqu'a nos jours*. Paris, 1905.

Chapon, Mgr Henri. 'Chronique locale', *La Semaine religieuse* (Nice), 9 Jan 1904, pp. 33–8.

'Allocution de Mgr l'Evêque de Nice à son clergé à l'occasion de la nouvelle année', *La Semaine religieuse* (Nice), 7 Jan 1905, pp. 4–7.

Charriaut, Henri. *Après la Séparation, enquête sur l'avenir des Eglises*. Paris, 1905.

[Charriaut, Henri.] 'La Séparation de l'Église et de l'État. Notre enquête', *Le Figaro*, 4, 5, 6, 7, 8, 9, 10, 12, 13, 14, 16, 18, 20, 22, 24, and 27 Aug 1904, 2, 4, 7, 9, 12, 16, 20, and 23 Sep 1904.

Clemenceau, Georges. 'Les Conséquences de la Liberté', *L'Aurore*, 26 Feb 1905.

Clément, Mgr Maurice. *Vie du cardinal Richard*. Paris, 1924.

Combarieu, Abel. *Sept ans à l'Elysée. Paris*, 1932.

Combes, Émile. *Mon ministère, Mémoires 1902–1905*, with Introduction and notes by Maurice Sorre. Paris, 1956.

Crispi, Francesco. *Questioni internazionali. Diario e documenti*. Edited by T. Palamenghi-Crispi. Milan, 1913.

Crouzil, the Abbé Lucien. 'La Propriété des églises paroissiales', *La Revue du clergé français*, 1 Nov 1904, pp. 449–73.

'L'Affaire des cardinaux verts d'après des documents inédits', *Le Bulletin de Littérature Ecclésiastique*, 1930, Nos. 3–4 (Mar–Apr), pp. 64–86.

Deixonne, Maurice. 'Un printemps de la laicité?' *Le Populaire de Paris*, 24 Apr 1957.

Delahaye, Jules. 'Les grands catholiques', *L'Autorité*, 25 Mar 1906.

Delamaire, Mgr François. *Séparation dans l'Oppression*. Périgueux, 1905.

Domenach, Jean-Marie. 'Conscience politique et conscience religieuse', *L'Esprit*, 1958, No. 3 (Mar), pp. 341–58.

Douais, Mgr Célestin. *La Séparation et le pape, lettre de Mgr. l'Evêque de Beauvais à un députe*. Beauvais, 1905.

Dubillard, Mgr François. *Instruction pastorale sur les rapports de l'Eglise et de l'Etat et mandement pour le Saint Temps du Carême de 1905*. Quimper, 1905.

'Lettre circulaire au clergé au sujet de la suppression du budget des cultes', *La Semaine religieuse* (Quimper), 18 Aug 1905, pp. 540–44.

Dubois, Mgr Louis. *Concordat et Séparation, lettre de Mgr l'évêque de Verdun à ses diocésains*. Verdun, 1905.

Duval, Robert. 'Quelques Anti-Séparatistes', *L'Univers*, 23 Mar 1905.

Exposé documenté de la rupture des relations diplomatiques entre le Saint-Siège et le Gouvernement français. Vatican Press, 1904.

'Félix II.' 'Pourquoi le Pape hésite,' *Le Figaro*, 8 Aug 1906.

Ferrata, Cardinal. *Mémoires. Ma Nonciature en France*. Paris, 1922.

Foucault, Mgr Alphonse. *Lettres sur la Séparation de l'Église et de l'État, adressées au président d'un cercle d'études sociales*. St. Die, 1905.

Fonsegrive, Georges. *Le Journal d'un évêque*, Vol. 2, Paris, 1897.

'Chronique politique', *La Quinzaine*, 16 Mar 1905, p. 275.

La France ecclésiastique – Almanach – Annuaire du clergé. Paris, 1871–1872 and 1899.

Frémont, the Abbé Georges. *Le Conflit entre la République et l'Église, lettres à un officier français sur la separation de l'église et de l'état*. Paris, 1905.

Freneuse, Louis. 'L'Avenir des Eglises et la Séparation. III: L'Église catholique. – Organisation', *Le Signal*, 20 July 1905.

Fulbert-Petit, Mgr Marie-Joseph. *Instruction pastorale sur la pacification religieuse*. Besançon, 1902.

Fuzet. Mgr Edmond. *Lettre pastorale à l'occasion de son entrée dans son archidiocèse*. Rouen, 1900.

Lettre pastorale publiant l'indulgence du jubilé. Rouen, 1901.

Discours de Mgr l'archevêque de Rouen, primat de Normandie, prononcé à la distribution des prix du petit séminaire du Mont-aux-Malades, le 20 juillet 1903, sur la législation des petits séminaires et le projet de loi concernant l'instruction secondaire, déposé par M. Chaumié, ministre de l'Instruction publique et des beaux-arts. Rouen, 1903.

Lettre pastorale sur les devoirs que les circonstances actuelles imposent à notre clergé et nos fidèles. Rouen, 1903.

Sur l'intervention du prêtre dans la politique et la dénonciation du Concordat. Rouen, 1904.

Lettre de Monseigneur l'Archevêque de Rouen au clergé de son Archidiocèse sur le projet d'organisation des Associations cultuelles. Rouen, 1905.

Lettre au clergé de son archidiocèse relative à l'inventaire du mobilier des Eglises. Rouen, 1905.

Les Associations cultuelles en Allemagne. Paris, 1906.

Gayraud, the Abbé. Hippolyte. *La République et la Paix religieuse*. Paris, 1900.

La Séparation des Églises et de État. Paris, 1904.

'Associez-vous! Associez-vous!' *L'Univers*, 18 Nov 1904.

'Séparation et liberté', *La Revue du clergé français*, 15 Jan 1905, pp. 337–58.

'Avant la bataille', *L'Univers*, 8 Feb 1905.

'Mon optimisme,' *L'Univers*, 15 Mar 1905.

'Que feriez-vous?' *L'Univers*, 12 Apr 1905.

'A propos de la Séparation', *La Revue du clergé français*, 1 Nov 1905, pp. 449–76.

Grand Orient de France. *Grand Orient de France. Assemblée Générale, 1903*. Paris, 1903.

Grunebaum-Ballin, Paul. *La Séparation des Églises et de l'État, étude juridique sur le projet Briand et le projet du gouvernement*. Paris, 1905.

La Tentative de paix religieuse d'Aristide Briand. Cahiers laïques No. 31, Jan–Feb 1956.

D'Haussonville, the Comte Othenin. 'La Séparation des Églises et de l'État', *Le Figaro*, 9, 17, 23, and 30 Jan 1905 and 3 Mar 1905.

'La Rupture du Concordat', *Le Figaro*, 12 Sep 1905.

'La Séparation et le clergé', *Le Figaro*, 22 Sep 1905.

'La Séparation et les Catholiques', *Le Figaro*, 26 Sep 1905.

'Les Associations cultuelles', *Le Figaro*, 22 Oct 1905.

'Les Unions diocésaines', *Le Figaro*, 6 Nov 1905.

'Les Associations diocésaines', *Le Figaro*, 13 Nov 1905.

'Le Lendemain de la Séparation', *Le Figaro*, 29 Nov 1905.

Hemmer, the Abbé Hippolyte. 'Reflexions sur la situation de l'Église de France au début du vingtième siècle', *La Quinzaine*, 1 May 1905, pp. 1–18, and 1 June 1905, pp. 289–314.

Hervé, Edouard. 'Plutôt la Séparation', *Le Soleil*, 6 Nov 1891.

Honorat, Henry. 'Le Clergé et la Séparation. Interview de l'abbé Viollet', *La Petite République*, 24 Aug 1905.

Houtin, Albert. *Evêques et diocèses*, Vol. 2. Paris, 1909.

Mon Expérience, Vol. 2: *Une Vie de prêtre 1867–1912*. Paris, 1926.

[Houtin, Albert.] 'La Séparation. Ce que décidèrent les évêques'. *Le Temps*, 24 and 25 Aug 1906.

'La Séparation. Le texte des statuts organiques adoptés par les évêques', *Le Petit Temps*, 26 Aug 1906.

D'Hulst, Mgr Maurice. *Mélanges oratoires*, Part 2. Paris, 1891.

[Keller, Émile.] 'Les derniers projets de loi sur la séparation de l'Église et de l'État', *Le Correspondant*, 10 Mar 1905, pp. 1006–22.

Klein, the Abbé Félix. *Au pays de la vie intense*. Paris, 1904.

'La séparation aux États-Unis', *Le Correspondant*, 10 Apr 1905, pp. 3–33.

La Route du petit Morvandiau. Souvenirs de l'abbé Felix Klein, Vol. 6: *Au début du siècle*. Paris, 1950.

De L. . ., P. 'Le Pape et la Séparation', *L'Autorité*, 17 Sep 1905.

Le Camus, Mgr Émile. *Lettre à ses prêtres sur la situation faite à l'Eglise de France*. La Rochelle, 1902.

Lettre de Monseigneur l'Evêque de La Rochelle et Saintes au clergé de son diocèse. La Rochelle, 1905.

Lecomte, Maxime. *La Séparation au Sénat*. Paris, 1906.

Lecot, Cardinal Victor. *Lettre pastorale de Son Eminence, le Cardinal-Archevêque de Bordeaux sur les obligations des chrétiens dans le temps présent et mandement pour le saint temps de Carême de l'an de grâce 1905*. Bordeaux, 1905.

'Lettre au clergé du diocèse', *L'Aquitaine*, 28 July 1905, pp. 470–72.

Leduc, H. 'Consultations et renseignements. Des édifices affectés au culte et aux établissements ecclésiastiques', *La Revue du clergé français*, 1 Mar 1902, pp. 86–104.

Legrand, Jules. 'Après le vote', *La République française*, 9 Dec 1905.

Lemire, the Abbé Jules. *Le cardinal Manning et son action sociale*. Paris, 1893.

Leo XIII. *Leonis Papae XIII, Allocutiones, Epistolae, Constitutiones*, Vol. 2. Paris, 1887.

Sanctissimi Domini nostri Leonis papae XIII Allocutiones, epistolae, constitutiones, aliaque acta praecipua, Vol. 5: *1891–1894*. Bruges, *1898*.

Le Poloucis ('Sigismund Lacroix'). 'Le Pape et la Séparation', *Le Radical*, 26 Feb 1905.

Lesourd, Paul. 'Journal inédit de Georges Goyau', *La Pensée catholique*, 1954, No. 31, pp. 74–88, No. 32, pp. 62–74, No. 33, pp. 77–91, and No. 34. pp. 70–80.

Libres Entretiens sur la Séparation des Églises et de l'État. Published by L'Union pour l'Action morale, Nov 1904–May 1905.

Lissorgue, the Abbé. 'La Séparation', *La Croix du Cantal*, 13 Aug 1905.

Le Livre blanc du Saint-Siège. Paris, 1906.

Loisy, Alfred. *Mémoires pour servir à l'histoire religieuse de notre temps*, Vol. 2: *1900–1908*. Paris, 1931.

Loth, Arthur. 'La Revendication des Églises', *La Vérité française*, 1 Oct 1904.

De Maizière. 'La Séparation. Conversation avec l'Evêque de Quimper', *Le Gaulois*, 2 Mar 1905.

De Mandat-Grancey, the Baron E. 'A propos de l'incident de Mgr Le Nordez', *L'Action française*, 15 June 1904, pp. 429–43, and 1 July 1904, pp. 30–42.

Le Clergé français et le Concordat. Paris, 1906.

Mater, André. *La Politique religieuse de la République française*. Paris, 1909.

Mignot, Mgr Eudode. *Le Concordat et la Séparation de l'Église et de l'État*. Albi, 1905.

'Nad.' 'Lettre parlementaire', *Le Salut publique*, 11 June 1903.

De Narfon, Julien. *Vers l'Eglise libre*. Paris, 1905.

'Les Traitements ecclésiastiques et le casuel', *Le Gaulois*, 24 Jan 1905.

'Associations "paroissiales" non "cultuelles". Conversation avec M. l'abbé Odelin,' *Le Gaulois*, 15 Aug 1905.

'Nos églises demain. Conversation avec l'archevêque d'Aix', *Le Gaulois*, 1 Oct 1905.

'La Nomination des Evêques et l'article 17 du Code Civil. Conversation avec M. de Lamarzelle,' Supplement to *Le Gaulois*, 3 Dec 1905.

'Les papiers Montagnini', *Le Figaro*, 1 Apr 1907.

La Séparation des Églises et de l'État. Paris, 1912.

[De Narfon, Julien.] 'Notre enquête sur la dénonciation du Concordat', *Le Gaulois*, 2 June 1903.

'Les Evêques et la Dénonciation du Concordat,' *Le Gaulois*, 16 June 1903.

Nède, André. 'Les Evêques et la Concordat. Conversation avec Mgr Le Camus', *Le Figaro*, 11 Sep 1903.

Oury, Mgr Frédéric. *Lettre pastorale de Mgr l'archevêque d'Alger au clergé et aux fidêles de son diocèse touchant les périls et les devoirs de l'heure présente*. Alger, 1905.

Paléologue, Maurice. *Un Grand tournant de la politique mondiale*. Paris 1934.

Parsons, Léon. 'La Séparation des Églises et de l'État. Une enquête extraparlementaire', *La Grande Revue*, 15 June 1904, pp. 509–41.

Perraud, Cardinal Alphonse. *Quelques réflexions au sujet de l'Encyclique du 16 février 1892*. Paris, 1892.

Picot, Georges. 'La Pacification religieuse 1832–1892', *La Revue des deux mondes*, 1 July 1892, pp. 156–81.

Piou, Jacques. *D'une guerre à l'autre*. Paris, 1932.

Pius X. *Actes de S.S. Pie X*, Vol. 2. Paris, 1907.

Proust, Marcel. 'La Mort des Cathédrales. Une Conséquence du projet Briand sur la Séparation', *Le Figaro*, 16 Aug 1904.

Reinach, Joseph. *Histoire de l'Affaire Dreyfus*. 7 vols. Paris, 1901–8.

Renouard, Mgr Firmin. *Le Projet de loi sur la Séparation des Églises et de l'État*. Limoges, 1905.

Ribot, Alexandre. Preface to Georges Noblemaire, *Concordat ou Séparation*. Paris, 1904.

Samuel, René, and G. Bonet-Maury, *L'Annuaire du Parlement*. Paris, 1902, 1903–1904, and 1905.

La Semaine religieuse (Mende), 'Associations paroissiales', 3 Mar 1905, p. 139.

La Semaine religieuse (Quimper), 'L'Inventaire du mobilier des églises,' 12 May 1905, p. 294.

Servonnet, Mgr Pierre. *Lettre de Mgr. l'Archevêque de Bourges ordonnant des Prières spéciales à l'occasion des solennités de la Pentecôte et de la prochaine séance parlementaire*. Bourges, 1903.

Suarez, Georges. *Briand*, Vol. 1. Paris, 1943.

Théry, Gustav. *Mémoire présenté à Mgr. l'Archevêque de Cambrai sur le projet de loi relatif à la Séparation de l'Église et de l'État*. Cambrai, 1904.

De la Tour, Imbart. 'L'Obsession du schisme', *Le Bulletin de la semaine*, 21 Mar 1905.

Triger, Robert. *De la propriété des églises*. Le Mans, 1905.

Turinaz, Mgr Charles. *Projet de séparation de l'Église et de l'État. Exposé de ce projet et de ses conséquences adressé à ses diocésains*. Nancy, 1905.

'Lettre de Mgr. l'Evêque à MM les doyens, au sujet de l'inventaire du mobilier des églises', *La Semaine religieuse* (Nancy), 20 May 1905, p. 504.

Veuillot, Pierre. 'Précision', *L'Univers*, 21 Mar 1905.

De Vogué, the vicomte Melchior. 'A propos d'un débat religieux', *La Revue des deux mondes*, 1 June 1894, pp. 675–90.

ANONYMOUS ARTICLES

L'Action, 'Vers la Séparation. La seconde étape. La Commission favorable', 12 June 1903.

La Dépêche (Toulouse), 'Nos Dépêches par fil spécial. La Séparation', 30 Sep 1904.

L'Eclair, 'Le Concordat. Les Evêques devant les menaces de M. Combes', 25 May 1903.

'Notre enquête sur la dénonciation du Concordat', 1 Sep 1903.

Le Gaulois, 'Un Projet de concordat pour les ordres religieux', 23 April 1901.

Le Matin, 'Le Testament de Lavigerie', 2 Sep 1904.

La Patrie, 'Après la Séparation. Interview de Mgr Pechenard', 14 Dec 1905.

L'Univers, 'Dans le diocèse de Dijon. Une note de *L'Osservatore Romano*', 1 Mar 1905

'Autour de la Séparation', 10 and 28 Mar 1905, and 3 Apr 1905.

SOME SECONDARY SOURCES

Much fuller lists may be found in the excellent bibliographies in Jean-Marie Mayeur, *L'Abbé Lemire, 1853–1928, Un Prêtre démocrate* (Paris, 1968) and Pierre Sorlin, *Waldeck-Rousseau* (Paris, 1966).

Alquier, Georges. *Le Président Emile Combes*. Castres, 1962.

Anderson, Robert. 'The Conflict in Education. Catholic Secondary Schools (1850–70): a reappraisal', *Conflicts in French Society* (ed. Theodore Zeldin). London, 1970.

Andreotti, Giulio. *Pranzo di Magro per il Cardinale*. Rome, 1954.

Appolis, Émile. 'En marge de la Séparation: les associations cultuelles schismatiques', *La Revue d'Histoire de l'Église de France*, XLIX (1963), 47–88.

Aubert, Roger. 'Documents relatifs au mouvement catholique italien sous le pontificat de S. Pie X', *Rivista di Storia della Chiesa in Italia*, XII (1958) 202–43, 334–70.

Baudrillart, Alfred. *Vie de Mgr d'Hulst*, Vol. 2. Paris, 1914.
Bazoche, M. *Le Régime légal des Cultes en France*. Paris, 1948.
    Le Régime légal des Cultes en Alsace-Lorraine. Paris, 1950.
Beauguitte, André. *Le Chemin de Cocherel*. Paris, 1960.
Binchy, D. A. *Church and State in Fascist Italy*. Oxford, 1941.
Boulard, Fernand. *Essor ou declin du clergé français?* Paris, 1950.
    An Introduction to Religious Sociology: Pioneer Work in France. London, 1960.
    and Remy, Jean. *Pratique religieuse urbaine et regions culturelles*. Paris, 1968.
Brogan, Sir Denis. *The Development of Modern France*. London, 1940.
Brugerette, Joseph. *Le Prêtre et la société contemporaine*, Vol. 2: *Vers la Séparation de l'Église et de l'État*. Paris, 1935.
Buehrle, Maria. *Rafael Cardinal Merry del Val*. London, 1957.
Capéran, Louis. *L'Anticléricalisme et l'Affaire Dreyfus, 1897–1899*. Toulouse, 1948.
Clément, Maurice. *Vie du cardinal Richard*. Paris, 1924.
Combès, G. *L'abbé Louis Birot*. Paris, 1949.
Cordonnier, Charles, *Mgr Fuzet*, Vol. 2. Paris, 1950.
Coutrot, A., and Dreyfus, F. *Les Forces religieuses dans la Société française*. Paris, 1965.
Crispi, Francesco. *Questioni internazionali. Diario e documenti*. Edited by T. Palamenghi-Crispi. Milan, 1913.
Crouzil, Lucien. *Quarante ans de Séparation*. Paris, 1964.
Daniel, Yvon. *L'Equipement paroissial d'un diocèse urbain*. Paris, 1957.
Dansette, Adrien. *Histoire religieuse de la France contemporaine*, Vol. 2: *Sous la Troisième République*, Paris, 1951.
    Destin du Catholicisme français, 1926–1956. Paris, 1957.
Debidour, A. *L'Église catholique et l'État en France sous la Troisième République*, Vol. 2: (*1889–1906*), Paris, 1909.
Delattre, Pierre. *Les établissements des Jésuites en France, 1540–1900*, 5 vols. Paris, 1940–57.
Denis, Michel. *L'Église et la République en Mayenne, 1896–1906*. Paris, 1967.
Ducray, Camille. *Paul Déroulède, 1846–1914*. Paris, 1914.
Engel-Janosi, Friedrich, *Österreich und der Vatikan, 1846–1918*, 2 vols. Vienna, 1958–60.
Gadille, Jacques. *La Pensée et l'action politiques des évêques français au début de la III Republique, 1870–1883*. 2 vols. Paris, 1967.
Goldberg, Harvey. *The Life of Jean Jaurès*. Wisconsin, 1962.
Headings, Mildred J. *French Freemasonry under the Third Republic*. Baltimore, 1949.
Isambert, Francois-André. *Christianisme et classe ouvrière*. Paris, 1961.
Jarry, Eugène. 'L'Orientation politique de *La Croix* entre les années 1895–1900', *La Documentation Catholique*, 23 August 1954, pp. 1031–59.
Kerlévéo, Jean. *L'Église Catholique en regime français de Séparation*, vol. 1: *L'occupation des églises par le desservant et les fidèles*, Aire-

sur-la-Lys, 1951, vol. 2: *Les prérogatives du curé dans son église*, Paris, 1956, vol. 3: *Le prêtre catholique en droit français*, Paris, 1962.

Lapaquellerie, Yvon. *Émile Combes ou le surprenant roman d'un honnête homme*. Paris, 1929.

Laperrière, Guy. *La "Séparation" à Lyon (1904–1908)*. Lyon, 1973.

Larkin, Maurice J. M. 'Loubet's visit to Rome and the question of Papal prestige', *The Historical Journal*, IV (1961), 97–103.

'The Vatican, French Catholics, and the associations cultuelles', *The Journal of Modern History*, XXXVI (1964), 298–317.

'The Church and the French Concordat, 1891 to 1902', *The English Historical Review*, LXXXI (1966), 717–39.

'French Catholics and the Question of the Separation of Church and State, 1902 to 1906', unpublished Ph. D. dissertation, University of Cambridge, 1958.

Lecanuet, Edouard. *L'Église de France sous la Troisième République*, Vol. 3: *Les Signes avant-coureurs de la Séparation*, and Vol. 4: *La Vie de L'Église sous Léon XIII*. Paris, 1930.

Ligou, Daniel. *Frédéric Desmons et la Franc-Maçonnerie sous la 3me République*. Paris, 1966.

McManners, John. *Church and State in France, 1870–1914*. London, 1972.

Marcilhacy, Christianne. *Le Diocése d'Orléans sous l'Episcopat de Mgr Dupanloup 1849–1878*. Paris, 1962.

Le Diocèse d'Orléans au milieu du XIX siècle. Paris, 1964.

Martini, Angelo. *Studi sulla Questione Romana e la Conciliazione*. Rome, 1963.

Mayeur, Jean-Marie. *La Séparation de l'Église et de l'État*. Paris, 1966.

'Géographie de la resistance aux inventaires. Fevrier-mars 1906', *Annales*, Nov-Dec 1966, pp. 1259–72.

'Droite et Ralliés a la Chambre des Députés au début de 1894', *Revue d'histoire moderne et contemporaine*, April–July 1966, pp. 117–35.

L'Abbé Lemire, 1853–1928. Un Prêtre démocrate. Paris, 1968.

Méjan. Louise Violette, *La Séparation des Églises et de l'État. L'Oeuvre de Louis Méjan*. Paris, 1959.

'Contribution a l'étude de la Séparation des Églises et de l'État en France jusqu'aux préliminaires législatifs du régime actuel.' Unpublished *thèse complémentaire*, Aix-en-Provence, 1959.

Mollat, G. *La Question Romaine*. Paris, 1932.

Murray, Rev. John Courtenay, S.J. 'Bellarmine on the Indirect Power', *Theological Studies* (Woodstock, Maryland), IX (1948).

'*Leo XIII*: Separation of Church and State', *Theological Studies*, XIV (1953).

Partin, Malcolm O. *Waldeck-Rousseau, Combes, and the Church: the Politics of Anticlericalism, 1899–1905*. Durham, N.C., 1969.

Paul, Harry W. *The Second Ralliement. The Rapprochement between Church and State in France in the Twentieth Century*. Washington, 1967.

Poulat, Emile. *Intégrisme et Catholicisme intégral*. Paris, 1969.

(ed.). *Le 'Journal d'un prêtre d'après-demain' (1902–1903)*. Paris, 1961.

Prost, Antoine. *Histoire de l'Enseignement en France, 1800–1967*. Paris, 1968.

Renard, Edmond. *Le cardinal Mathieu*. Paris, 1925.

Schurer, Wilhelm. *Aristide Briand und die Trennung von Kirche und Staat in Frankreich*. Basel, 1939.

Sedgwick, Alexander. *The Ralliement in French Politics, 1890–1898*. Cambridge, Mass., 1965.

Shapiro, David; Watson, D. R.; and Anderson, Malcolm. *The Right in France, 1890–1919. Three Studies*. London, 1962.

Siegfried, Agnès. *L'Abbe Frémont*. 2 vols. Paris, 1932.

Soderini, Edouardo. *Leo XIII, Italy and France*. London, 1935.

Sorlin, Pierre. *Waldeck-Rousseau*. Paris, 1966.

'La Croix' et les Juifs (1880–1899). Paris, 1967.

La Société Française, vol 1 : *1840–1914*. Paris, 1969.

Spadolini, Giovanni. *Giolitti e i Cattolici (1901–1914)*. Florence, 1970.

Sweeney, Francis (ed.). *Vatican Impressions*. New York, 1962.

[Touveneraud, Pierre]. 'Les origines et les grandes étapes du journal, *La Croix*', *Pages d'Archives*, Oct 1965.

Tharaud, Jérome and Jean. *La Vie et la Mort de Déroulède*. Paris, 1925.

Thierry, Jean-Jacques. *La Vie quotidienne au Vatican au temps de Léon XIII à la fin du XIX siècle*. Paris, 1963.

Ullman, Joan C. *The Tragic Week. A Study of Anticlericalism in Spain, 1875–1912*. Cambridge, Mass., 1968.

Ward, James E. 'Leo XIII and Bismarck : the Kaiser's Vatican Visit of 1888', *The Review of Politics*, XXIV (1962) 392–414.

'The French Cardinals and Leo XIII's Ralliement Policy', *Church History*, XXXIII (1964) 3–16.

'The Algiers Toast : Lavigerie's Work or Leo XIII's?' *The Catholic Historial Review*, LI (1965) 173–91.

'Leo XIII : "The Diplomat Pope" ', *The Review of Politics*, XXVIII (1966) 47–61.

'Cardinal Richard versus Cardinal Lavigerie : Episcopal Resistance to the Ralliement'. *The Catholic Historical Review*, LIII (1967) 346–71.

Winnacker, R. A. 'The Délégation des Gauches : a successful attempt at managing a parliamentary coalition', *The Journal of Modern History*, IX (1937), 449–70.

Notes

INTRODUCTION

1 The term 'Dreyfusian Revolution' was initially popularised by Georges Sorel in an ironical sense (*La Révolution Dreyfusienne*, 1909); but like so many of the sardonic remarks in history, it has subsequently acquired a life of its own at face value.

2 'The Dreyfusian Revolution' is, of course, an entirely independent issue from the campaign to establish the innocence of Dreyfus – a campaign which is rightly remembered for the devotion and self-sacrifice of those who set it in motion.

3 It also saw the disestablishment of the Calvinist Église Réformée, the Lutheran Église de la Confession d'Augsbourg and the Jewish religion – all of which had been officially state supported during the nineteenth century.

4 The only other work to cover the Separation in depth is Louise Violette Méjan's very useful doctoral thesis, *La Séparation des Églises et de l'État: l'oeuvre de Louis Méjan* (Paris, 1959), which was written in the year following my own unpublished Ph.D. thesis, 'French Catholics and the question of the Separation of Church and State, 1902 to 1906' (Cambridge). Although her book is much more detailed than mine, its use of archival material is mainly confined to a selection of papers from the Direction des Cultes; and its main corpus of evidence is a collection of her father's notes, some of which are rather misleading on the origins of the Separation bill. Although the book is a mine of valuable detail, it leaves a number of the more important issues unresolved, especially those affecting Vatican policy.

Of less specialised appeal is Jean-Marie Mayeur's percipient and well-informed *La Séparation de l'Église et de l'État* (Paris, 1966). Like other books in its series, it is a collection of documents and extracts, linked by explanatory narrative and comment. Given its brevity, it does not have room to do more than give an outline of the main problems, though it contains some original evidence and comments. There still remain the brief histories contained in Adrien Dansette's standard *Histoire religieuse de la France contemporaine*, Vol. 2 (Paris, 1951) and Antonin Debidour's *L'Église catholique et l'État en France sous la Troisième République*, Vol. 2 (Paris, 1909), neither of which has the space to do more than summarise the main events. Edouard Lecanuet' *L'Église de France sous la Troisième République* (Paris, 1910–30) stops short of the Separation – as does Malcolm Partin's *Waldeck-Rousseau, Combes and the Church: the Politics of Anticlericalism, 1899–1905* (Durham, N.C., 1969).

A very welcome addition to the outline histories is John McManners's *Church and State in France, 1870–1914* (London, 1972), which incorporates many of the findings of the current generation of church historians – including a few of my own conclusions, for what they are worth, culled from the articles listed on p. 252 below.

5 See comments on p. 242 below.

CHAPTER 1: GRASS-ROOTS CATHOLICS AND THE SECULAR DROUGHT

1 Encyclical, *Au milieu des sollicitudes,* 16 Feb. 1892.
2 This general chapter is mostly based on published secondary sources, notably the following books by Canon Fernand Boulard: *Essor ou Déclin du Clergé Français?* (Paris, 1950), *An Introduction to Religious Sociology. Pioneer Work in France* (London, 1960), and, with Jean Remy, *Pratique Religieuse Urbaine et Régions Culturelles* (Paris, 1968). Canon Boulard has very kindly supplied me with additional information, some of which is summarised in Figure 1. See also François-André Isambert, *Christianisme et classe ouvrière* (France, 1961).
3 This obligation applied to Catholics having attained 'the age of reason' – traditionally reached at the age of seven.
4 The period of grace in which this duty could be performed varied from four to six weeks, with Easter Sunday as the central date.
5 Approximately 23·9 per cent of all French adults; 25·5 per cent of baptised adults. Boulard, *Pratique religieuse,* pp. 30–31.
6 Approximately 31·9 per cent of baptised adults, ibid, p. 30.
7 See Figure 1, p. 8.
8 Boulard, *Pratigue religieuse,* p. 31.
9 Experts I have tried to tempt with this hypothesis have rightly refused to be drawn.
10 Boulard, *Pratique religieuse,* pp. 64–5.
11 First holy communion was usually made between the ages of seven and ten, depending on regional practice.
12 See the comparative table in Boulard, *Pratique religieuse,* Tableau A.
13 Boulard, *Pratique religieuse,* Chapter V.
14 Cited in Boulard, *Introduction,* p. 32.
15 Thomas Gilby, 'Our Place in the Church', lecture given to the Glasgow Circle of the Newman Association, 1962.
16 James Joyce, *A Portrait of the Artist as a Young Man* (London, reprint, 1946) pp. 151–2.

CHAPTER 2: THE VIEW FROM ROME

1 Like Chapter 1, this chapter is largely based on secondary sources, notably, Angelo Martini, *Studi sulla Questione Romana e la Conciliazione* (Rome, 1963); G. Mollat, *La Question Romaine* (Paris, 1932); Edouardo Soderini, *Leo XIII, Italy and France* (London, 1935); Jean-Jacques Thierry, *La Vie quotidienne au Vatican au temps de Léon XIII à la fin du XIX Siècle* (Paris, 1963); Francis Sweeney (ed.), *Vatican Impressions* (New York, 1962); D. A. Binchy, *Church and State in*

Fascist Italy (Oxford, 1941), the opening chapters on the 1870–1922 period; and the important series of articles by James E. Ward, listed in the bibliography (p. 253). Primary source material is specifically indicated in the notes.

2 Retailed by the late Mgr Philip Hughes and Dr James E. Ward.

3 MS diary of the Abbé Landrieux, secretary to Cardinal Langénieux of Reims. Kindly lent by the Abbé Patrick Heidsieck. In choosing investments, Leo relied heavily on the advice of Signor Pacelli, the uncle of Pius XII. While Pacelli thrived on the relationship, his advice was not always profitable to the Pope. When Pacelli moved into an expensive house opposite Giomini's, the papal tailor's, it was rumoured that someone had chalked on Giomini's wall, 'Here they dress the Pope', and on Pacelli's wall, 'Here they strip him.' Ibid., entry of 18 May 1900.

4 Mollat, op. cit., p. 398.

5 These and the following expressions appear in the encyclical, *Immortale Dei* (1 Nov 1885). For a discussion of this issue, see the latter part of the stimulating article by John C. Murray, 'Bellarmine on the Indirect Power', *Theological Studies*, IX (1948) p. 515.

6 Encyclical, *Au milieu des sollicitudes* (16 Feb 1892).

7 Encyclical, *Longinqua oceani* (6 Jan 1895).

8 *Au milieu des sollicitudes.*

9 Ibid.

10 This issue is well examined in Alexander Sedgwick's [*The*] *Ralliement* [*in French Politics*] (Cambridge, Mass., 1965).

11 Related by Pius X to Baron d'Erp, audience of 16 Aug 1906, Archives of the Belgian Ministère des Affaires Etrangères et du Commerce Exterieure (hereafter designated 'Belg.'), Erp to Favereau, 407/100, 16 Aug 1906, Belg., P. 1354, dossier 903.

12 Soderini, op. cit., p. 3.

13 Mollat, op. cit., p. 367.

14 Letter to Cardinal Rampolla, 8 Oct 1895, cited in Binchy, op. cit., p. 15.

15 Canon Edmond Renard, [*Le cardinal*] *Mathieu* (Paris, 1925) p. 369.

16 Report from Herbert von Bismarck to Otto von Bismarck, 15 and 16 Oct 1888, examined by James E. Ward, 'Leo XIII and Bismarck: the Kaiser's Vatican visit of 1888', *The Review of Politics*, XXIV (1962) p. 405.

17 See Mollat, op. cit., p. 394, and Binchy, op. cit., pp. 52–3. Bonomelli's proposal appeared in an anonymous article in *Rassegna Nazionale*, 1 Mar 1889, subsequently reissued as a brochure.

18 Monbel to Flourens, D. 168, 10 Nov 1887, *Documents diplomatiques français* (1871–1914), 1st series, VI *bis* (Paris, 1938) pp. 134–5.

19 The interview is well described in James E. Ward's entertaining article, cited in note 16 above.

20 Despatch cited in note 18.

21 Monbel to Goblet, 30 Oct 1888, cited by Ward, 'Leo XIII and Bismarck', p. 410.

22 Remarks to a French diplomat in 1886, Binchy, op. cit., pp. 33–4.

23 Monbel to Goblet, 1 Jan 1889, cited by Ward, 'Leo XIII and Bismarck', p. 413.

24 Cambon to Ribot, D.18, 2 Dec 1892, *D.D.F.*, 1st series, x p. 102.
25 Landrieux MS diary, entry of 13 Nov 1895.
26 Reported by Lozé, French ambassador in Vienna, to Hanotaux, D.89, 13 May 1896, *D.D.F.*, 1st series, XII p. 601.
27 Landrieux MS diary, entry of 3 Dec 1898.
28 Barrère to Delcassé, 30 May 1899, *D.D.F.*, 1st series, XV pp. 325–6.
29 The issue is dealt with in detail by Martini, op. cit., pp. 25–51.
30 Navenne to Delcassé, 30 Aug 1898, *D.D.F.*, 1st series, XIV p. 511, cited by Martini, op. cit., p. 28.
31 Landrieux MS diary, entry of 7 Mar 1902.

CHAPTER 3: THE CONCORDATORY REGIME

1 This chapter is mainly based on the archives of the Direction des Cultes – Archives Nationales, F[19]. A more detailed examination of the subject is contained in my article, 'The Church and the French Concordat, 1891 to 1902', *The English Historical Review*, LXXXI (1966) 717–39.
2 Letter of 12 May 1801, quoted in [*Le*] *Livre blanc* [*du Saint-Siège. La Séparation de l'Église et de l'État en France. Exposé et Documents*] (Paris, 1906) p. 46.
3 The whole process described in this paragraph can be followed for the 1891–1902 period in A.N., F[19] 1956.
4 A.N., F[19] 2610.
5 Taken to the nearest month, and compiled from information in A.N., F[19] 1956. For the date of settlement, I have taken the date of the nuncio's acceptance (written or verbal) of the Government's nominee. The list includes six appointments to Algerian and West Indian dioceses. I have been unable to classify four of the forty-eight, owing to incomplete information, but they were certainly agreed upon in less than twelve months.
6 Ibid. This list includes an appointment to Réunion.
7 Ibid. This list includes two appointments to Algiers. Two of the nineteen could not be classified, but they were certainly agreed upon in less than six months.
8 Combes MSS, Archives de la Charente-Maritime. (I consulted them before they were given catalogue-numbers.)
9 Edouard Lecanuet, *L'Église de France* [*sous la Troisième République*], IV: *La vie de l'Église sous Léon XIII* (Paris, 1930) p. 112.
10 Recalled in Combes's Senate speech of 21 Mar 1903, 'Procès-verbaux du Sénat, 21 mars 1903', *Journal Officiel*, 21 Mar 1903, p. 501C. That this was also the traditional view of the Direction des Cultes is indicated by a Note of 8 Mar 1892, Cabinet du Directeur, A.N., F[19], 1956. For Combes's supplementary arguments, see Combes to Navenne, 21 Feb 1896, A.N., F[19] 1956.
11 The Vatican's position in this matter was to be best explained in a letter of the Papal Secretary of State, Cardinal Rampolla, to the nuncio, Mgr Benedetto Lorenzelli, 15 Feb 1903, *Livre blanc*, pp. 123–6.

12 Lists contained in A.N., F19 2610. The difference in the grand totals of bishops listed in 1896 and 1899 is explained by vacancies. The figures for both years include the three Algerian sees.

13 Paul Grunebaum-Ballin, [*La*] *Tentative* [*de paix religieuse d'Aristide Briand*], (*Cahiers Laiques*, no. 31, Jan-Feb 1956) p. 10.

14 Letter to a member of the regular clergy, 6 Jan 1896, quoted in Alfred Buadrillart [*Vie de Mgr.*] *d'Hulst*, II (Paris, 1914) 436–7.

15 Letter to d'Hulst, 20 Jan 1889, ibid, 422–3.

16 A.N., F19 2610.

17 E.g., Cabrière's letter of 27 Mar 1906 to Emmanuel Bailly, Assumpt., HD 34.

18 Adrien Dansette, *Histoire religieuse* [*de la France contemporaine*], II: *sous la Troisième République* (Paris, 1951) 136.

19 Figures compiled from information in [*La France ecclésiastique*] *Almanach-Annuaire* [*du Clergé pour l'an de Grâce*] 1899 (Paris, 1899).

20 The situation in the diocese of Angers is well described in a communication by the Abbé Louis Gallard to the Société d'Histoire Moderne et Contemporaine, 6 Dec 1970, 'Eglise riche ou église pauvre? Étude sur les revenus du diocese d'Angers à la veille de la loi de Séparation de 1905. *Bulletin de la Société d'Histoire Moderne et Contemporaine*. Being a relatively *bien pensant* diocese, its clergy fared better than in many others. If all sources of revenue are included, a *desservant* could count on an income of c. 2000 fr. and a *vicaire*, c. 1000 fr.

21 The running costs of the parish itself were the concern of the parish council (*fabrique*). In the diocese of Angers, c. 80 per cent of these costs were covered by the hire of church seats, ibid, p. 3.

22 *Almanach-Annuaire 1899*. Seminaries received some state aid under other headings.

23 The evidence and its implications are discussed in the Abbé Lucien Crouzil, 'De le propriété des églises paroissiales'. *La Revue du clergé français*, XL (1 Nov 1904), notably 463.

24 The Church's viewpoint was well summarised by the Papal Secretary of State, Cardinal Rampolla, in an interview with the French ambassador to the Holy See. Poubelle to Hanotaux, 6 April 1897, A.N., F19 1944.

25 For a full statement of the Government's viewpoint, see *L'Avenir adminstratif*. *Recueil*, 22 May 1892, p. 161.

26 See undated memorandum of the Directeur-Général des Cultes, A.N., F19 6129.

27 Statement of the Ministre des Cultes, Charles Dupuy to the Chambre des Députés, 20 Jan 1893, 'Procès-Verbaux de la Chambre des Députés, 20 janvier 1893', *Journal officiel*, p. 146b.

28 A.N., F19 2610.

29 A.N., F19 6135–6.

30 Annotated copy of a catechism circulated in the archdiocese of Aix, A.N., F19 6135.

31 A.N., F19 2540 and 6135–6.

32 Letter to René Goblet of 9 Dec 1894, Baudrillart, *d'Hulst*, II 431–3. The

idea had been discussed earlier in some detail by the Vicomte Georges d'Avenel, 'La Réforme Arminiistrative III. Les Cultes', *La Revue des deux mondes*, 3e période, xc, 15 May 1890, 332–69.

33 Letter to a young priest, 22 Sep 1895, Baudrillart, *d'Hulst*, II 436.

34 Jules Lemire, [*Le cardinal*] *Manning* [*et son action sociale*] (Paris, 1893) pp. 264–5.

35 Communication of 18 Aug 1802, *Livre blanc*, p. 25.

36 Communication of 25 June 1804, ibid, p. 26.

37 Domenico Ferrata [*Mémoires. Ma*] *Nonciature* [*en France*] (Paris, 1922) p. 226.

38 Communication of 18 July 1804, *Livre blanc*, p. 27.

39 A decree of 28 Feb 1810 amended Article 1 (see note 41 below), Article 26 which required a property qualification for ecclesiastics, and Article 36 which concerned the administration of vacant dioceses.

40 A number of articles were officially recognised as no longer in force. See memorandum on the Organic Articles, probably compiled in the early 1880s, in A.N., F^{19} 2005. 'Depuis l'Empire', the teaching staff of seminaries were no longer expected to subscribe to the Four Articles of 1682 (Article 24). (This had easily been the most offensive of the Organic Articles – in theory, at least – since it struck at the very concept of papal supremacy.) At the same time, episcopal candidates ceased to be examined in doctrine under state auspices (Article 17). Furthermore, under the Third Republic, bishops no longer swore an oath of loyalty to the Government (Article 6 of the Concordat and Article 18 of the Organic Articles). Similarly, the Direction des Cultes gave up vetting entrants to seminaries (Article 25). Other articles were considerably modified by subsequent legislation. Article 11, for instance, forbad the setting up of any collective religious body other than seminaries and cathedral chapters, yet even under the First Empire several orders of regular clergy were officially permitted to establish houses in France.

41 Purely spiritual matters had been exempted by a decree of 28 Feb 1810.

42 A.N., F^{19} 5629.

43 A.N., F^{19} 5628.

44 Landrieux MS diary, entry of July 1899.

45 A.N., F^{19} 2468–69 and 2540.

46 Memorandum cited in note 40.

47 A.N., F^{19} 3180.

48 These and the following figures for 1871 and 1898 are compiled from information in *Almanach-Annuaire 1871–1872* and 1899. Each archiepiscopal see had its own diocese, bearing the same name, and these figures refer only to the diocese, not the archdiocese as a whole.

49 The vast majority of French parishes were *succursales* – which differed from the more important and generally older class of parish, the *cure*, in being served by a *desservant*, not *a curé*.

50 A.N., F^{19} 2209 (suppression of *succursales*); F^{19} 2279 (suppression of

vicariats); F[19] 2219 (rejected requests for the erection of *vicariats* into *succursales*).

51 Adrien Dansette, *Destin du catholicisme français 1926–1956* (Paris, 1957), table on p. 64. (The arithmetic appears to be slightly at fault in certain details given in this table.)

52 These and the following figures are compiled from information in *Almanach-Annuaire 1899*.

53 E.g., advertisements in *L'Ami du clergé*.

54 This is not to belittle the important pioneer work that had already started in some dioceses. E.g., see Christianne Marcilhacy, *Le Diocèse d'Orléans sous l'Episcopat de Mgr. Dupanloup 1849–1878* (Paris, 1962).

55 See in particular Dansette, *Destin*, chap. 1, especially pp. 63–75.

CHAPTER 4: THE DREYFUS AFFAIR – BEFORE AND AFTER

1 See notably Sedgwick, *Ralliement*.

2 Eugène Jarry, 'L'Orientation politique de *La Croix* entre les années 1895 and 1900', *La Documentation Catholique*, 23 Aug 1954, p. 1059.

3 Jarry, op. cit., p. 1037.

4 Letter to his brother, Emmanuel Bailly, Assumpt., Bailly TS.

5 P. Debauge, 'La fortune de la France', *La Croix*, 4 Feb 1893, cited in Pierre Sorlin, [*La*] *Croix et* [*les*] *Juifs* (Paris, 1967) p. 61.

6 *La Croix*, 17 Jan 1890, cited in Sorlin, *Croix et Juifs*, p. 34.

7 Letter of 8 May 1906 to Emmanuel Bailly, Assumpt., Bailly TS, XV, no. 4673.

8 For details, see Sorlin, *Croix et Juifs*.

9 Jarry, op. cit., p. 1042.

10 Letter of 14 Apr 1898 to Emmanuel Bailly, Assumpt., Picard TS, VIII, no. 3885.

11 Letter of 20 Jan 1898, Assumpt., MI 67.

12 Letter of 14 Jan 1898, Assumpt., Picard TS, VIII, no. 3842.

13 Sedgwick, *Ralliement*, p. 111.

14

	Old Chamber	*New Chamber*
Ralliés	30	38
Opportunists and allies	250	254
Radicals	128	104
Radical Socialists	68	74
Socialists	52	57
Right	53	54

André Daniel, *L'Année Politique, 1898* (Paris, 1899) p. 217.

15 The Socialists had initially regarded the Affair as a bourgeois issue with no relevance for the working classes. Jaurès, Pressensé and their friends had difficulty in arousing Socialist interest, which came late and in fragmented form.

16 Given French fears of German military strength, many felt that death would have been a more appropriate sentence.

17 'J'accuse', *L'Aurore*, 13 Jan 1898.
18 *Le Pèlerin*, 12 Sep 1891, 30 Aug 1892, 25 Feb 1892, 15 Jan 1893, cited in Sorlin, *Croix et Juifs*, pp. 171 and 312.
19 'Le Paysan', 'Ne grossissons pas!' *La Croix*, 6 Sept 1898.
20 'La Nuit. La France ne périt point', *La Croix*, 4–5 Sep 1898.
21 Louis Capéran, *L'Anticléricalisme et l'Affaire Dreyfus, 1897–1899* (Toulouse, 1948) p. 249.
22 Entry of 21 Feb 1899, *My Secret Diary of the Dreyfus Case 1894–99* (London, 1957) pp. 152–3.
23 19 Feb 1899.
24 Maurice Barrès, *Scènes et doctrines* [*du nationalisme*] (Paris definitive ed., 1925) I 245.
25 Pellieux had also led the inquiry into the conduct of Major Esterhazy, which had resulted in the culprit's acquittal.
26 The best known are contained in C. Ducray, *Paul Déroulède 1846–1914* (Paris, 1914); Jérome and Jean Tharaud, *La Vie et la mort de Déroulède* (Paris, 1925); Barrès, *Scènes et doctrines*; Joseph Reinach, *Histoire de l'Affaire Dreyfus* 7 vols (Paris, 1901–8).
27 *La Vie Catholique*, 24 Feb 1899.
28 Letter of Vincent Bailly to Emmanuel Bailly, 12 Nov 1899, Assumpt., Bailly TS, XII, no. 3340.
29 E.g., issue of 27 Sep 1898.
30 'Miriam', 'Sauveurs', *La Croix*.
31 Letter of 17 Feb 1899, Assumpt., Picard TS, VIII, no. 3964.
32 The following account is based on evidence in Vincent Bailly's letter of 26 Feb 1899 to Emmanuel Bailly, Assumpt., Bailly TS, XII, no. 3301.
33 'Le Moine', 'L'Emeute', *La Croix*, 23 Feb 1899.
34 Letter of 20 Feb 1899, Assumpt., Picard TS, VIII, no. 3965.
35 Letter cited in note 32.
36 Letter of Emmanuel Bailly to Vincent Bailly, 1 Mar 1899, Assumpt., MJ 44.
37 Letters of Emmanuel Bailly to Vincent Bailly, 21 and 23 March 1899, Assumpt., MJ 51–52.
38 Letter of Vincent Bailly to Picard, 19 Sep 1899, Assumpt., Bailly TS, XII, no. 3283.
39 Letter of Vincent Bailly to Picard, 25 Sep 1899, Assumpt. Bailly TS, XII, no. 3285.

CHAPTER 5: MÉMOIRES D'OUTRE-COMBES

1 See the definitive political biography, by Pierre Sorlin, *Waldeck-Rousseau* (Paris, 1966).
2 Ibid., pp. 415–16.
3 Ibid., pp. 406–10.
4 John McManners, *Church and State in France, 1870–1914* (London, 1972) p. 125.
5 The origins of the practice are described in a report of 4 Nov 1904, sent by the Directeur de la Sûreté-Générale to Émile Combes. Combes MSS, A. Ch.-M.

6 Sorlin, *Waldeck-Rousseau*, p. 425.
7 Letter of Vincent Bailly to Emmanuel Bailly, 12 June 1900, Assumpt., Bailly TS, XII, no. 3496.
8 Landrieux MS diary, entry of Jan 1900. Ten months later, Lorenzelli was to express his complete disillusionment, ibid., entry of 28 Nov 1900.
9 The promotion of Bishops Fuzet of Beauvais and Germain of Rodez to the archbishoprics of Rouen and Toulouse and the following episcopal appointments: Mando to Angoulême, Henry to Grenoble, Herscher to Langres, and Lacroix to Tarentaise. On Rome's particular reluctance to accept Fuzet, ibid., entry of Jan 1900.
10 Andrieu for Marseille – though the Government at first tended to underestimate his intransigency. In 1902 the Direction des Cultes still classified him as '*douteux*' rather than '*mauvais*'. A.N., F^{19} 5610.
11 Archbishop Gouthe-Soulard of Aix and Bishop Cotton of Valence. See Waldeck-Rousseau to Delcassé, 12 Feb 1900, A.N., F^{19} 5613.
12 Waldeck-Rousseau rejected current suggestions for a concordat concerning the religious orders, Sorlin, *Waldeck-Rousseau*, p. 427.
13 See Pierre Delattre, *Les établissements des Jésuites en France, 1540–1900*, 5 vols, (Paris, 1940–57).
14 Ibid., II 1603–4, III 1369–72, IV 337–9, 1397–9.
See also the statistics for the École St Géneviève, contained in the Archives de la Société de Jésus de la Province de Paris, Chantilly.
15 Anderson, op. cit., p. 59.
16 'Journal', VIII 100, Bibliothèque Nationale, N.A.F., 12,711.
17 Notably members of the Union Républicaine of the Senate, 10 Nov 1898, reported in J.D., 'Les élèves des congréganistes', *Le Radical*, 12 Nov 1898.
18 A demand made by a number of Masonic lodges.
19 See notably the article cited in note 17.
20 See Capéran, op. cit., pp. 263–76.
21 Letter to Picard, 22 June 1901, Assumpt., Bailly TS XIII, no. 3599.
22 Instructions, 8 July 1900, Assumpt., HJ 36.
23 Letter of Vincent Bailly to Picard, 24 Apr 1900, Assumpt., Bailly TS, XII, no. 3418.
24 Tribunal correctionel, 9me Chambre, 23 Feb 1904.
25 Verbal instructions from Cardinal Gotti to Emmanuel Bailly, 7 Mar 1900, 'Les Origines et les grandes étapes du journal, *La Croix*', *Pages d'Archives*, Oct 1965, pp. 531–3.
26 Letter of Emmanuel Bailly to Cardinal Vincenzo Vannutelli, 2 Apr 1900, Assumpt., PZ. 55.
27 Letter to Picard, 31 March 1900, *Pages d'Archives*, Oct 1965, p. 535.
28 Note of 29 Mar 1900, Assumpt., PZ. 54.
29 Renard [*Le Cardinal*] *Mathieu* (Paris, 1925), p. 416.
30 Maupetit gave a detailed account of the interview in a letter to Léon Harmel, 29 Mar 1900, Assumpt., PZ. 53.
31 Letter of 21 Feb 1902, Assumpt., MM 137.

32 The main group were represented as follows:

Socialists	53
Radical-Socialists	110
Gauche Radicale	77
Union Démocratique ('Left wing' of former Opportunists)	88
Progressistes ('Right wing' of former Opportunists)	91
Action Libérale (Catholic Ralliés)	52
Nationalists	58
'La Droite' (monarchists)	12

33 The whole issue is thoroughly discussed in Sorlin, *Waldeck-Rousseau*, p. 484.

34 Combes's private life is described in 'Yvon Lapaquellerie', *Émile Combes ou le surprenant roman d'un honnête homme* (Paris, 1929), and Georges Alquier, *Le Président Émile Combes* (Castres, 1962).

35 I am very grateful to his great nephew, M. Yvon Bizardel, for information on this aspect of Combes's experience.

36 Letter to Combes, 4 Jan 1889, Combes MSS, A. Ch.-M.

37 Marcel Becamel, 'Lettres inédites d'Emile Combes,' *La Revue du Tarn*, 15 Sep 1958, pp. 223–52.

38 His country cousin mentality is very evident in his memoirs: Émile Combes, [*Mon Ministère*] *Mémoires* [*1902–1905*] (Paris, 1956).

39 Ibid., p. 193.

40 Combes MSS, A. Ch.-M.

41 Letter to Combes, 9 Sep 1905, Combes MSS, A. Ch.-M.

42 Letter of Princess Bibesco to Combes, 27 Jan 1907, Combes MSS, A. Ch.-M.

43 Bib. Nat., F.M. Impr. 2, *Grand Orient de France. Assemblée Générale.*

44 Audience to Picard, reported in Emmanuel Bailly's letter of 29 Dec 1902 to Vincent Bailly, Assumpt., MM 173.

45 Audience to Féron-Vrau, 10 Nov 1901. Assumpt., PZ 105.

46 These and the following figures are drawn from Mildred J. Headings, *French Freemasonry under the Third Republic* (Baltimore, 1949). See also Daniel Ligou, *Frédéric Desmons et la Franc-Maçonnerie sous la 3me République* (Paris, 1966).

47 21 Sep 1903. *Grand Orient de France. Assemblée Générale*, 1903, pp. 21–33.

48 This is evident from the archives of the provincial lodges, Bib. Nat., FM², Boîtes Oranges (non communicables), made available by kind permission of the Grand Orient de France.

49 Ministère de l'Instruction Publique, note for Monsieur le Ministre, 26 Oct 1903, Combes MSS, A. Ch.-M.

50 Waldeck-Rousseau's policies towards the religious orders are extensively examined in Sorlin, *Waldeck-Rousseau*, pp. 423–49.

51 Interview in October 1899, reported in Vincent Bailly's letter to Emmanuel Bailly, 2 Nov 1899, Assumpt., Bailly TS, XII, no. 3335.

52 Michel Denis, *L'Église et la République en Mayenne, 1896–1906* (Paris, 1967) p. 254.
53 Direction de l'Enseignement Primaire, note pour Monsieur le Ministre, 20 Oct 1903, Combes MSS, A. Ch.-M.
54 See, among much else, Dansette, *Histoire religieuse*, II, 312–14.
55 Note cited in note 49, Combes MSS, A. Ch.-M.
56 See two undated notes, Combes MSS, A. Ch.-M.

CHAPTER 6: THE SEPARATIST MINORITY

1 Although it was during Rouvier's ministry that it was adopted by parliament, the determining events took place under Combes.
2 See p. 263, note 38.
3 Abel Combarieu, *Sept ans à l'Elysée* (Paris, 1932) p. 205.
4 Théophile Delcassé (Foreign Affairs), Maurice Rouvier (Finance), Jacques Chaumié (Education), and Émile Maruéjouls (Public Works).
5 Camille Pelletan (Navy) was personally in favour of Separation, but could be relied on to muffle his enthusiasm in the interests of cabinet solidarity.
6 Twenty-two had specifically included it in their electoral manifestos; and of those who had not, eleven were to join their colleagues in signing Francis de Pressensé's Separation bill of 7 Apr 1903.
7 15 Aug 1904, John McManners, op. cit., p. 143.
8 Fifty-two had specifically included it in their electoral manifestos.
9 The arch-*mangeur de curés* among the Socialistes Révolutionnaires in parliament.
10 There appears to be no surviving minutes of the meetings of the Délégation des Gauches, but its deliberations were briefly summarised in the main political newspapers. For a general analysis of its function, see R. A. Winnacker, 'The Délégation des Gauches: a successful attempt at managing a parliamentary coalition', *The Journal of Modern History*, Dec 1937, pp. 449–70.
11 *Mémoires*, p. 279, note 48.
12 The details of Pressensé's life given in this chapter are based on the following: his MS notebooks, kindly lent by M. Marcel Faucon; information kindly given by Pressensé's niece, Mlle Geneviève Boegner; various letters in the Bibliothèque Nationale, N.A.F., and the Archives Nationales; [*Le*] *Bulletin officiel de la Ligue* [*des Droits de l'Homme et du Citogen*]; various obituary notices, Jan–Feb 1914.
13 Initially published in *La Revue des Deux Mondes*, 4th pd., vol. 135 (1896), 1 May, 5–41, 15 May, 366–401.
14 Victor Basch, funeral oration, reproduced in *Bulletin officiel de la Ligue*, 1 Feb 1914.
15 Ibid.
16 Ibid.
17 *Histoire de l'Affaire Dreyfus*, VI 494.
18 Ligue conference, 24 Jan 1901, reproduced in *Bulletin officiel de la Ligue*, 1 Feb 1901.

19 The composition of Pressensé's bill predated that of Eugène Réveillaud's bill – see pp. 112–13 below, especially note 21.

20 The full text of the bill appears in *Le Journal Officiel, Documents parlementaires – Chambre des Députés,* Annexe no. 897 (séance du 7 avril 1903), pp. 452–7.

21 The full text appears in ibid, Annexe no. 1073 (séance du 25 juin 1903), pp. 955–7. Louis Méjan's memory was at fault in thinking that its elaboration predated that of Pressensé's; see Méjan's note in Lucie Violette Méjan, *La Séparation* [*des Églises et de l'État. L'oeuvre de Louis Méjan*] (Paris, 1959) pp. 115–18. Méjan's reminiscences consistently exaggerate the contribution of Réveillaud's bill to the final text of the Separation Law. He likewise exaggerates his own part in the elaboration of Briand's draft (see ibid, chapter 3). The manuscript minutes of the Chamber commission on the Separation make it abundantly clear where the roots of the Separation Law lie, and contradict a number of his assertions. Archives de l'Assemblée Nationale, C.D., 8 1074–80 (now transferred to the Archives Nationales). Mlle Lucie Méjan was unfortunately unable to consult these minutes before publishing her thesis.

22 See various letters published in *Bulletin officiel de la Ligue,* 1903, notably from Gabriel Monod, 28 June 1903, and Camille Rabaud, 15 June 1903.

23 Ibid.

24 The following personal details are mainly taken from André Beauguitte, *Le Chemin de Cocherel* (Paris, 1960).

25 The fact that Briand was subsequently acquitted by the Cour d'Appel of Rennes did not save his career in St Nazaire. Briand's acquittal in Rennes was supposedly secured by a friend, bearing a close physical resemblance to Briand, who lured the prosecution into claiming that Briand was also in the field on another occasion when Briand could prove that he was in Paris. Ibid., pp. 67–70.

26 This was the view of his lively but not always accurate biographer, Georges Suarez, *Briand,* I (Paris, 1943) 423. Mme Billiau, who possesses the major part of Briand's papers, has been unable to find anything to substantiate Jaurès's role in this particular. Certainly Briand had not included Separation in his electoral manifesto of 1902 – but neither, paradoxically, had Jaurès. Both, however, were signatories of Pressensé's bill.

27 In accordance with normal procedure, each of the nine *bureaux* of the Chamber elected two or three of its number to sit on the commission.

28 In the fifth *bureau.*

29 The details of these manoeuvres were supplied by deputies to political correspondants and published in the newspapers of 12 and 13 June 1903. See in particular 'Séparation des Eglises et de l'État, *La Petite République,* 13 June 1903, and 'Nad', 'Lettre parlementaire', *Le Salut Public,* 12 June 1903.

30 Paul Grunebaum-Ballin, *Tentative,* p. 4.

31 *L'Humanité*, 23 Jan 1914.

32 Mlle Geneviève Boegner.

33 Proposed by Gabriel Deville, Socialist deputy for the Seine, who defeated Maurice Barrès in the by-election of March 1903. Commission minutes, C.D. 8. 1074–80.

34 Ibid.

CHAPTER 7: THE NEW VIEW FROM ROME

1 Salvatore Cortesi, 'When the Pope dies', *Vatican Impressions*, p. 200.

2 Landrieux MS diary. Entry of 30 July 1903. Landrieux, who accompanied Cardinal Langénieux to the conclave, conversed with a number of cardinals before and during the conclave. The Abbé Heidsieck has published extracts from this part of the diary: 'Le Conclave de 1903 – journal d'un conclaviste', *Études*, 1958, pp. 157–83.

3 There are a number of pious biographies of both men, useful for personal anecdote but lacking in historical perspective. Not untypical of the genre is Maria Buehrle's *Rafael Cardinal Merry del Val* (London, 1957), which is somewhat overfond of reconstructed dialogue – 'Merry del Val relaxed . . . "Babs, why don't we meet for lunch at Madame Tussaud's?" ' etc. (p. 78).

4 Cited in Binchy, op. cit., p. 55.

5 Camille Barrère, French ambassador to the Holy See, to Delcassé, D. 112, 11 June 1904, Archives du Ministère des Affaires Etrangères, 'Saint Siege – relations avec l'Italie', II 108 – hereafter designated 'MAE, SS/Ital'.

6 14 June 1904.

7 Erp to Favereau, 353/42, 19 Aug 1904, Archives of the Belgian Ministère des Affaires Etrangères, 'Saint Siège' – hereafter designated 'Belg. SS'. Baron Maximilien d'Erp was Belgian Minister Plenipotentiary to the Holy See from 1896 to 1915. He had a longer acquaintance with Vatican milieux than either Pius X or Merry del Val, and enjoyed to an unusual degree the confidence of both of them. As a practising Catholic, representing what Pius X liked to call 'the most Catholic government in Europe' he was the constant recipient of the opinions and preoccupations of the Vatican. In consequence his despatches provide a remarkable and hitherto neglected record of Vatican attitudes towards the situation in France. And, taken in their entirety, they trace the evolution of papal international policy over nearly twenty years. A selection of his despatches, dealing specifically with Italy, have been published by Canon Roger Aubert, 'Documents relatifs au mouvement catholique italien sous le pontificat de S. Pie X', *Rivista di Storia della Chiesa in Italia*, XII (1958) 202–43, 334–70.

8 Erp to Favereau, 237/62, 26 June 1905, Belg., SS 25.25.

9 Audience of 23 Mar 1905, Erp to Favereau, 115/35, 23 Mar 1905, Belg., SS 25.14.

10 D.144, translation conveyed by Legrand to Rouvier, 20 Aug 1905, MAE., SS/Ital. p. 183.

11 Erp to Favereau, 513/129, 26 Nov 1906, Belg., SS 25.106.
12 The subject of Giulio Andreotti's *Pranzo di magro per il cardinale* (Rome, 1954).
13 See the extensive correspondence between the Italian Foreign Ministry and its various ambassadors, Jan–Mar 1906, Archivio Storico del Ministro degli Affari Esteri – hereafter designated 'Ital. Aff. Est.'
14 E.g., as reported in Erp to Favereau, 393/119, 15 Dec 1905, Belg., SS.
15 Interview with Fathers Ernest and Franc, 20 Dec 1906, Assumpt., PZ 64.
16 Ibid.
17 Audience to Mgr P. Fagès, reported in P. Fagès to Cardinal Richard, 8 Apr 1904, Archives Historiques de l'Archevêche de Paris, 1 DX 29, hereafter designated 'Archiepisc. Paris'.
18 Audience to Baron d'Erp, 6 Nov 1904, Erp to Favereau, 384/110, 6 Nov 1904, Belg. SS 24.55.
19 E.g. Interview between Combes and Lorenzelli, 10 Jan 1903, described in Combes to Delcassé, 10 Jan 1903, *Livre blanc*, pp. 120–2.
20 The whole issue is covered extensively in A.N., F^{19} 1956.
21 See Delcassé to Waldeck-Rousseau, 18 Sep 1901 (and see Nisard to Delcassé, 9 Nov 1901); Waldeck-Rousseau to Delcassé, 26 May 1902, A.N., F^{19} 1956.
22 Conversation with Baron d'Erp, 5 June 1903, Erp to Favereau, 197/49, 5 June 1903, Belg., SS 23.45.
23 A.N., F^{19} 1956.
24 A.N., F^{19} 2610. See especially Mazeran to Dumay, 17 Dec 1896. However, one of his successors as *curé* of Compiègne, who knew him well, told me that *'il était d'un commerce très agréable, un excellent administrateur et un prêtre très régulier'*, letter of 4 Nov 1957.
25 A.N., F^{19} 2610 contains several letters of accusation, remarkable for their virulence rather than precision.
26 See the bulky 'Notes sur le chanoine Casanelli d'Istria actuellement vicaire capitulaire du diocese d'Ajaccio', signed by the Dean of the Chapter and the other *vicaire capitulaire*, Foata (who subsequently obtained the see), 20 Aug 1877, Archivio Segreto Vaticano, 1877, Rubrica 248, Fasc. 2.
27 Lorenzelli to Combes, 26 Nov 1903, A.N., F^{19} 1956.
28 Combes to Lorenzelli, 19 Mar 1904, A.N., F^{19} 1956.
29 Merry del Val to Lorenzelli, 30 Mar 1904, *Livre blanc*, pp. 129–30.
30 Undated pencil note, perhaps intended for Delcassé, Combes MSS, A. Ch.-M.
31 Renard, *Mathieu*, p. 427.
32 Dumay to Combes, 9 Nov 1903, A.N., F^{19} 2610, and also Combes MSS, A. Ch.-M.
33 See notably 'Situation des suppressions de traitement au 12 octobre 1904', Combes MSS, A. Ch-M; similar figures in A.N., F^{19} 6129. Of these totals, Combes restored 284 before the end of his ministry, and Waldeck-Rousseau 73.

CHAPTER 8: LE FESTIN DE PIERRE

1 Loubet himself was personally well disposed towards the Church, and frequently accompanied his wife to church on Sundays.
2 I have treated the matter in some detail in my article, 'Loubet's visit [to Rome and the question of Papal prestige]', *The Historical Journal*, IV (1961) 97–103.
3 Interview between Lorenzelli and Delcassé, 1 July 1902, *Livre blanc*, p. 57; Rampolla to Nisard, 1 June 1903, ibid., p. 137.
4 Barrère to Delcassé, D, no. 8, 10 Jan 1904, *D.D.F.*, 2nd series, IV (Paris, 1932) 235.
5 MS letter of Denys Cochin to a priest (possibly the R. P. de la Brière), dated 11 June but of a later year. Renard is the only writer who speaks of this episode, apart from L. V. Méjan who takes her information from Renard (*Mathieu*, p. 437; Méjan, *La Séparation*, pp. 41–2). Renard's account, which contains some slight inaccuracies, is presumably based on the papers of Cardinal Mathieu, Cochin's intermediary with Merry del Val. The Holy See clearly had reasons for saying nothing of the mission in the *Livre blanc*. McManners bases his account (op. cit., pp. 138–9) on my article, 'Loubet's visit'.
6 Denys Cochin is best known as the first prominent representative of Catholic interests to be offered a place in a post–1879 French government; he was a minister of State in Briand's government of October 1915. He was at the time of Loubet's visit to Rome a deputy for the eighth *arrondissement* of Paris and a member of the Catholic parliamentary group, *Action Libérale*. His letters – cited hereafter as 'Cochin MSS' – have been kindly lent by his grandson, M. Denys Cochin, M. Marc Bonnefous, at present engaged in writing a thesis on the Cochin family, kindly helped in locating those letters of interest to me.
7 Letter cited in note 5 above.
8 'X', 'M. Delcasse au Vatican', *Le Figaro*, 7 Apr 1904. My italics.
9 Combes to Delcassé, 7 Apr 1904, Combes MSS, A. Ch.-M.
10 *Le Figaro*, 8 Apr 1904.
11 Letter cited in note 5 above.
12 Interview between Merry del Val and Baron d'Erp. Erp to Favereau, 256/51, 23 May, 1904, Belg., SS 24.19. Nine years earlier the King of Portugal had incurred the wrath of Crispi by declining Umberto's invitation to make such a visit; and it was now known that the Italian Government was preparing to renew the invitation. See extensive correspondence between Tittoni and the Italian ambassador in Lisbon. Dec 1903–May 1904, Ital. Aff. Est., P. Pos. 3.
13 The Prince of Monaco's responsibility for the leak was revealed by the textual peculiarities of the published copy of the letter. Erp to Favereau, 252/49, 20 May 1904, Belg., SS 24. 18.
14 Cochin MSS. Undated letter of Denys Cochin to his wife, written in April 1904.
15 Letter cited in note 5 above.
16 Mgr d'Hulst to Cardinal Richard, 26 Sep 1891, Archiepisc. Paris, 2

AII 7. Each was apparently faithful to his partner, while the alleged relationship lasted.

17 Cardinal Serafino Vannutelli to Cardinal Richard, 30 Jan 1904, Archiepisc. Paris, 2 AII 7.

18 Prefect of La Mayenne to Combes, 24 Sep 1904, A.N., F^{19} 1961.

19 Michel Denis, op. cit., pp. 251–3. This book contains a detailed study of the whole Geay affair.

20 Interview between Mgr della Chiesa and Baron d'Erp, Erp to Favereau, 22 July 1904, Belg., SS 24.33.

21 Merry del Val to Geay, 2 July 1904, and to Le Nordez, 9 July 1904, reproduced in *Exposé documenté* [*de la Rupture des relations diplomatiques entre le Saint Siège et le Gouvernement francais*] (Rome, 1904) pp. 27 and 43.

22 Robert de Courcel, French *chargé d'affaires* to Merry del Val, 23 July 1904, ibid., pp. 30–2, 50–51.

23 Merry del Val to Courcel, 26 July 1904, ibid., 52–6.

24 Letter of Cardinal Serafino Vannutelli, ibid., p. 17.

25 Courcel to Merry del Val, 3 June 1904, ibid., pp. 18–19.

26 See the selection in Combes MSS, A. Ch-M. They throw a harsher light on Geay than the rather indulgent view of Michel Denis, op cit.

27 Geay to Combes, 8 Oct 1902, Combes MSS, A. Ch-M.

28 21 Sep 1903, *Grand Orient de France. Assemblée Générale*, 1903, pp. 21–33.

29 The text is in Combes MSS, A. Ch-M. Contrary to what historians have hitherto maintained, it is very different from Combes's own bill. They may perhaps have been misled by the unaccompanied copy of Dumay's letter contained in A.N., F^{19} 1978^2.

30 Paul Grunebaum-Ballin, *Tentative*, p. 3.

31 Combes, *Mémoires*, pp. 228–36.

32 *L'Humanité*, 21 Oct 1904. I am grateful to the late M. Paul Grunebaum-Ballin for much useful information on the political pressures which forced Combes into presenting his bill. M. Grunebaum-Ballin was commissioned by Dumay to prepare the dossiers on the Diion-Laval affair (see pp. 134–5 above), and later compiled the section of Briand's report which dealt with regimes of Separation in other countries.

33 Paul Grunebaum-Ballin gathered this from one of the leaders of the Union Démocratique, Georges Leygues, whom he saw most days on their mutual homeward walk.

34 When the whole affair became public, various Masons in the provinces found themselves ostracised by sections of the local population. The archives of the provincial ateliers contain various appeals from Masonic tradesmen who lost their clientele as a result of the affair. Bib. Nat., FM^2, Boîtes Oranges (non communicables).

35 Combes MSS, A. Ch-M.

36 27 Nov 1904. L.V. Méjan, *La Séparation*, p. 139, note 1.

37 Grunebaum-Ballin, *Tentative*, p. 5.

38 Sir Denis Brogan, *The Development of Modern France* (London, 1940) p. 282.

39 *La Dépêche*, 30 Apr 1905.

40 Until their recent transfer to the Archives Nationales, the archives of the Assemblée Nationale held Montagnini's correspondence and papers Nos. C. 1027–1036 (hereinafter designated by their individual numbers only, e.g. 'Montagnini MSS, Sc.3, p. 68'). A commission of the Chamber was appointed to examine these papers after their confiscation in December 1906. The translation from Italian into French also contained in the dossiers is that of the commission, and is as accurate as the legibility of the accompanying Italian originals will allow. Historians have hitherto used the small collection of extracts previously distributed to the press, based on the first Parquet translations, and republished in part as *Les fiches pontificales* (Paris, 1908). The incompleteness of the press extracts occasionally distorts their significance. Leygues's financial difficulties are indicated in Montagnini to Merry del Val, 24 Mar 1905, Sc.4, p. 119.

41 Letter of 9 Apr 1905, Sc. 7, p. 138.

42 *Le Figaro*, 1 Apr 1907.

43 Ibid., 31 Mar 1907.

44 This is not to deny the very substantial advantages that the Church obtained from various amendments proposed by Georges Leygues and the Union Démocratique (see Chapter 8 below). But as demonstrated in Chapter 8, these amendments had solid political motives behind them – and did not require financial lubrication to bring them into existence.

CHAPTER 9: CATHOLICS AND THE SEPARATION

1 The episode is fully described in Montagnini's letters to Merry del Val Jan-Apr 1905, Montagnini MSS.

2 Montagnini to Merry del Val, 7 Mar 1905, Montagnini MSS, Sc.7, p. 144.

3 Merry del Val to Montagnini, Montagnini MSS, Sc.4, p. 57.

4 Montagnini to Merry del Val, 22 Mar 1905, Montagnini MSS, Sc.4, p. 112.

5 Merry del Val to Montagnini, 17 Mar 1905, Montagnini MSS, Sc.4, p. 111.

6 Montagnini to Merry del Val, 3 Apr 1905, Montagnini MSS, Sc.4, p. 121.

7 The whole gamut of Catholic attitudes to Separation is examined at length in my unpublished Ph.D. dissertation, 'French Catholics and the Question of the Separation of Church and State, 1902 to 1906', which is available in the University Library of Cambridge.

8 The Vicomte Melchior de Vogüé and the Abbé Jules Lemire were notable examples. The Abbé Lemire is the subject of an exemplary biography by Jean-Marie Mayeur, *L'abbé Lemire, 1853–1928, Un Prêtre démocrate* (Paris, 1968).

9 'Le Carcan', *L'Autorité*, 23 Oct 1902.

10 See especially 'Nouvelles parlementaires', ibid., 11 Feb 1905, and Cassagnac, 'Alternative effroyable', ibid., 11 Aug 1905.

11 Denys Cochin to a priest (probably the R. P. de la Brière), 11 June, no year. Cochin MSS.

12 See the report of Archbishop Ireland of St. Paul, referred to in the diary of Georges Goyau, 20 May 1906, 'Journal inédit de Georges Goyau', presented by Paul Lesourd, *La Pensée Catholique*, no. 33 (1954) pp. 77–91.
13 For Merry del Val's misgivings, see Baron d'Erp's reports for 1906, Belg., SS.
14 Letter to the former priest, Hyacinthe Loyson, 5 Dec 1904.
15 Letter to Julien de Narfon, 18 Dec 1903, Narfon, *La Séparation des Églises et de l'État* (Paris, 1912) p. 51.
16 Letter of Vincent Bailly to Ernest Baudouy, Assumpt., Bailly TS, XV, no. 4469.
17 Letter of Emmanuel Bailly to Vincent Bailly, 4 Dec 1902, Assumpt., MM 171.
18 A remark cited approvingly by Emmanuel Bailly, ibid.
19 Pressensé had stated the principle in his bill (Art. 21); and Briand and the Commission had retained it in their successive drafts.
20 The various decisions of the Conseil d'État and the Cour de Cassation, upholding this view, were based on the following assumption. Under the *ancien régime* each local community was Catholic and built its church to fulfil its particular communal needs. Had these church builders of the *ancien régime* been alive in 1905, few of them would still be practising Catholics; Catholic worship was no longer a need of the commune as such.
21 Pressensé's bill had made this obligatory for the first five years, in order to minimise the initial disruption. Briand extended the period to ten years – preceded by two years rent-free occupation. Briand also limited the rent to a maximum of 10 per cent of the average annual revenue of the parish.
22 Robert Triger, *De la propriété des églises* (Le Mans, 1905).
23 *Semaine Religieuse* (Perigueux, 1905), reported in *L'Univers*, 19 Apr 1905.
24 Interview with Eric Besnard, 2 Jan 1905, *Le Siècle*, 3 Jan 1905.
25 Rough draft of a letter to Merry del Val, Dec 1904, Archiepisc. Paris, I DX 16. He subsequently told Montagnini that most of his clergy felt that they should stay in the churches 'until they were driven out by force'. Montagnini to Merry del Val, 25 Dec 1904, Montagnini MSS, Sc.7, p. 64.
26 Audience of 30 Oct 1904, Landrieux MS diary.
27 Montagnini to Merry del Val, 15 Dec 1904, Montagnini MSS, Sc.7, p. 62.
28 Speech in the Chamber of Deputies, 10 Feb 1905. Rome let him know that this was far from being the Vatican's view. Agnès Siegfried, *L'Abbé Fremont, 1852–1912*, II (Paris, 1932) 420.
29 C.D.8 1074–80. The amendment itself was formulated by a Radical-Socialist, Albert-le-Roy.
30 Robert Triger, op. cit.
31 The instructions of the Holy Congregation for Extraordinary Ecclesiastical Affairs stipulated that the local authority would have to make

a declaration '*suivant laquelle il constate qu'ils n'entendent nullement nier les droits immuables de l'Église*'.

32 The property attributable to the *associations cultuelles* was eventually officially valued at 411,743,387 francs. See statistics in Appendices 4–7 of the report of the Commission of the Senate for the Law of 13 Apr 1908. *Annexe au procès verbal du Sénat, 19 mars 1908*. This figure includes the 2233 presbyteries mentioned on p. 155. Combes's bill had characteristically limited the *associations cultuelles* to the free use, not the ownership, of this church property – and then only for ten-year periods, renewable at the discretion of the public authorities.

33 Commission meeting, 17 May 1905, C.D.8. 1074–80.

34 C.D.8. 1074–80. Once again the actual wording of the amendment was provided by the Radical-Socialist, Albert-le-Roy. Pressensé's bill had proposed a flat-rate pension of 600 fr. for all priests over 45 with 20 years' state-paid service. Briand's primitive draft of October 1903 had retained these conditions, but increased the pension to a possible maximum of 1200 fr. Réveillaud's bill, on the other hand, had proposed a generous multi-tiered pension scheme which included everyone – priests under 35 getting quarter pay. The idea of transitional benefits over four years originated with Combes's somewhat ungenerous flat-rate of 400 fr. proposed in his bill.

35 Draft reply, Dec 1904. Archiepisc. Paris. 1 DX 16.

36 Mgr Gasparri to Montagnini, 13 Feb 1906, Montagnini MSS, Sc.3, p. 114.

37 A.N., F[19] 1986.

38

Socialists	74
Radical-Socialists	132
Radicals	115
Union Démocratique	90
Progressistes	66
Action Libérale	64
Nationalists	29
Assorted Right-wing	21

39 Mgr Gasparri to Cardinal Coullié, 14 Apr 1906, copy in Montagnini MSS, Sc.14, p. 115. See also explanatory note, Mgr Guthlin, 18 Apr 1907, MAE SS/Fr., IX, 59.

40 Vincent Bailly to Emmanuel Bailly, 8 May 1906, Assumpt., Bailly TS, XV, no. 4673.

41 Interviewed by *Le Gaulois*, reproduced in *La Semaine Religieuse* (Viviers), 13 Jan 1905.

42 'L'Église libre', *l'Observateur Francais*, 2 Dec 1891.

43 *Le Figaro*, 23 Sep 1904.

44 Reproduced in Henri Charriaut, *Après la Séparation, enquête sur l'avenir des Eglises* (Paris, 1905) p. 248.

45 Unidentified news-cutting of 1904.

46 E.g. *La Revue du Clergé Francais*, 15 Jan 1905.

47 Interview accorded to *La Croix du Cantal*, published 13 Aug 1905.

48 Merry del Val to the Archbishop of Chambéry, 6 June 1907, papers of

Mgr Lacroix, Bishop of Tarentaise, Bibliothèque Nationale, N.A.F., 24402–6.

49 Interview cited in note 47.

50 *Le Figaro*, 8 Aug 1904.

51 *Le Clergé francais et le Concordat* (Paris, 1906).

52 *Le Figaro*, 9 Sep 1904.

53 *La Petite République*, 24 Aug 1905.

54 The whole question has been expertly examined by Émile Poulat in his introduction to *Journal d'un prêtre* [*d'après – demain* (1902–1903)] (Paris, 1961).

55 Ibid., p. 40.

56 Ibid., p. 49.

57 Now presented in book-form by Émile Poulat, see note 54 above.

58 For the modern reader, the happy ending with its establishment of a semi-monastic co-operative weakens the prophetic impact of the novel.

59 S.G., 'Demain', *La Justice Sociale*, 30 May 1903, cited in Poulat, *Journal d'un prêtre*, p. 40.

60 Poulat, *Journal d'un prêtre*, pp. 116–18.

61 Pressensé's fear of a financially strong Church stemmed from his experiences in the Dreyfus crisis and the electoral campaign of 1902. Pressensé had specifically limited the buildings that the parish associations could occupy to a church and a presbytery – one of each. Diocesan associations were similarly limited to a cathedral and a bishop's palace. The rule could not be circumvented by subdividing the parish into two; for, according to Pressensé's bill, no new parish or diocese could be created whose size fell below the existing average at the time of Separation. He had also pegged the fees for marriages, seats and the like to the level current at the Separation, thereby cutting off an additional source of revenue. As though the associations' wings were not sufficiently clipped, he subjected their revenue to an annual 10 per cent tax – in favour of the public assistance fund. While the idea greatly appealed to Pressensé's Socialist conscience, Briand recognised that it would strike conservative Catholics as adding insult to injury. Briand therefore preferred to adopt proposals that were more akin to Réveillaud's.

62 Article 19 allowed them *'le produit des quêtes et collectes pour les frais du culte, percevoir des retributions: pour les cérémonies et services religieux même par fondation; pour la location des bancs et sièges; pour la fourniture des objets destinés au service des funérailles dans les édifices religieux et à la décoration de ces édifices'*.
The *associations cultuelles* were also exempted from the *impôt foncier* and the doors-and-windows tax – as the parish councils had been under the Concordatory regime. This concession, like so much else, was the result of pressure from the Union Démocratique.

63 Pressensé softened the penalties prescribed by the Penal Code, and Briand lowered them still further – borrowing Réveillaud's milder prescriptions in a couple of instances.

Catholic anxiety mainly stemmed from the fact that the *associations cultuelles* were to be made civilly responsible for the good conduct of their parish priests. The unamended version of the bill had even empowered the authorities to terminate the use of the churches put at their disposal – a sanction which Briand had retained from Pressensé. Once again the Union Démocratique came to the Church's rescue and persuaded the Commission to drop it as too provocative.

64 'A propos de l'incident de Mgr Le Nordez', 15 June 1904, pp. 429–43, 1 July 1904, pp. 30–42.

65 Reproduced in *Messidor*, 10 Apr 1907. The original appears to be missing from the Montagnini MSS.

66 A.N., F[19] 2610.

67 His literary collaborator, the Abbé Albert Houtin, noted that 'One day he said to Dumay, "Well now, when are you going to make me Bishop of Versailles?" A few moments later, in the same conversation, he mentioned to Dumay that he was going to give a lecture at the University of Fribourg. Since he had not asked for the authorisation to go, Dumay was absolutely furious.' Houtin MSS, Bibliothèque Nationale, N.A.F., 15713, p. 213.

68 Interview given to *Le Peuple Français*, reported in 'Le Projet de M. Combes', 13 Jan 1905.

69 Joseph Brugerette, 'M. Briand chez Mgr. Lacroix', *La Revue de Paris*, 1 Oct 1930, p. 651.

70 Ibid., p. 652.

71 On Dumay's relations with the Abbé Denis, see A.N., F[19] 2003.

72 *Le Journal*, 19 Feb 1905. The rumours were based on a travestied account of some remarks made by a French prelate in Rome to *L'Eclair* – 'Déclaration d'un prélat', 22 July 1904.

73 Both Montagnini and Vincent Bailly guessed who the source was.

74 Montagnini to Merry del Val, 7 Nov 1905, Montagnini MSS, Sc.4. p. 74.

75 Montagnini to Merry del Val, 29 Oct 1905, Montagnini MSS, Sc.4, p. 60.

76 Renard, *Mathieu*, p. 455.

CHAPTER 10: SOME MORE PRINCIPLES

1 In addition to the thousands who were supernumerary to the state payroll.

2 Some of the conclusions of these three chapters – 10, 11 and 12 – have been summarised in my article 'The Vatican, French Catholics, and the *associations cultuelles*', *The Journal of Modern History*, XXXVI (1964) 298–317.

3 Audience of 2 Jan 1907, reported by Emmanuel Bailly, Assumpt., QG 77.

4 See notably the comments of Abbé Odelin, vicar-general of Paris, in Julien de Narfon, 'Associations "paroissiales" non "cultuelles": conversation avec M. l'abbé Odelin", *Le Gaulois*, 15 Aug 1905.

5 'Procès-verbaux de la Chambre des Députés, 20 avril 1905', *Journal officiel*, p. 1608a.

6 'La séparation: le texte des statuts organiques adoptés par les évêques,' *Le Petit Temps*, 26 Aug 1906, the appendix to an anonymous article by the Abbé Albert Houtin, 'La séparation: ce que décidèrent les évêques', *Le Temps*, 24 and 25 Aug 1906, based on information supplied by Mgr Lacroix, Bishop of Tarentaise.

7 'A qui l'église?' *Le Radical*, 22 Feb 1905. Buisson was probably playing to his electoral gallery.

8 'La séparation: conversation avec l'évêque de Quimper,' *Le Gaulois*, 2 Mar. Dubillard had already said to Eric Besnard on 10 Feb that the Separation Law would lead to schism ('La séparation et les églises: notre enquête', *Le Siecle*, 12 Feb), while his pastoral letter of 16 Feb warned his diocese against the danger of forming associations, for this reason (see *ibid.*, 1 Mar 1905).

9 Debate in the Chamber of Deputies.

10 Remarks to the Commission, 11 Apr 1905, C.D.8. 1074–80. The origin of the amendment has been the subject of much speculation. Mlle Méjan reproduces some of it (*La Séparation*, pp. 176–7), including a note of Louis Méjan, in which he states that it was the result of discussion between Jean Jaurès and various Catholics, including Denys Cochin. There seems to be no evidence for a discussion of this kind, and it is clear from a letter from Cochin to Georges Goyau of 6 Aug 1920 (Cochin MSS) that Cochin had nothing to do with the formula. Georges Suarez (*Briand*, II 46–7) describes a meeting on 17 Apr between Briand and Archbishop Fuzet at a dinner given by the journalist Bonnefon de Puyverdier ('Jean de Bonnefon'), which Mlle Méjan questions (p. 176, n. 1). This meeting did in fact take place, though Suarez's account is inaccurate in many respects. Briand and Fuzet himself, while admitting their meeting, both later denied that Fuzet played any part in the drafting of the amendment as was widely rumoured (see Briand's letter in reply to Clemenceau, *L'Aurore*, 2 Nov 1905, and Fuzet's letter in *Le Bulletin religieux de l'archdiocèse de Rouen*, 3 Nov 1905), but in any case the principle of Pressensé's amendment had been virtually adopted by the commission on 12 Apr, five days before the dinner took place.

11 C.D.8. 1074–80.

12 Interview with Baron d'Erp. Erp to Favereau, 175/48, 28 Apr 1905, Belg., SS 25.21.

13 The Separation Law specified the following minima sizes for *associations cultuelles*: in communes of less than 1000 inhabitants, seven members; 1000 to 20,000 inhabitants, fifteen members; above 20,000, twenty-five members.

14 Debate in the Chamber of Deputies, 5 Nov 1906.

15 Mlle L. V. Méjan, like her predecessors, assumes that the motive was hostility to the Church and quotes various opinions to this effect (pp. 180–87). But she also quotes, while missing its real significance, the remark of Alexandre Ribot: *'c'est une question de parti que vous voulez soulever devant la Chambre. . . . La procédure n'est là qu'un masque pour cacher l'opération politique que vous voulez faire'* (p.

182). I am grateful to M. Paul Grunebaum-Ballin, who was closely acquainted with Leygues at this time, for fully explaining what his motives were. Ironically enough, Leygues had taken the idea of substituting the Conseil d'État *statuant au contentieux* from Paul Grunebaum-Ballin's legal study, *La Séparation des Églises et de l'État* (Paris, 1905) – but for what Grunebaum-Ballin regarded as mildly disreputable reasons. Leygues's motives were not, however, exclusively political. His Concordatory sympathies inclined him to prefer the Conseil d'État to the civil courts, since he felt that the State could not entirely dissociate itself from the activities of a powerful organisation like the Church. Even so, the fact that his reasons were not specifically anticlerical is abundantly clear from his other amendments to the bill (see Chap. 9), which were eminently favourable to the Church.

16 C.D.8. 1074–80.

CHAPTER 11: A NEGOTIATED SETTLEMENT?

1 Professor of law in the Institut Catholique of Lille and a parliamentary member of Action Libérale. Persistent, but with narrow perspectives, he was aptly described by Briand as 'that other *petit père* Combes'. Immersing himself in a detailed study of the shortcomings of Article 4, he became so obsessed with its potential dangers that he seems never to have clearly envisaged what would happen if the Church refused to form associations. His faith and single-mindedness, however, went down well in Rome. Montagnini described him to Merry del Val as 'the most reliable and the most orthodox' of the Church's parliamentary defenders, while the Assumptionists classed him with Piou and Mun.

2 Emmanuel Bailly to Vincent Bailly, 12 Apr 1904, Assumpt., MO 53.

3 Interview with Theillier de Poncheville, Jan 1910, Assumpt., QG 81.

4 Letter of Vincent Bailly to Emmanuel Bailly, 16 Dec 1905, Assumpt., Bailly TS, xv, no. 4428.

5 Interview between Merry del Val and Fathers Ernest and Franc, 24 Dec 1906, Assumpt., PZ 65.

6 Ibid.

7 Reported in Emmanuel Bailly's letter to Mgr de Cabrières, 17 Mar 1906 (accidentally dated 17 Feb), Assumpt., QG 75.

8 Audience of 20 Mar 1906, Assumpt., PZ 63.

9 'Résumé d'une conversation avec un évêque retour de Rome le 9 mars 1906 à Paris.' Lacroix MSS, Bibliothèque Nationale, N.A.F. 24406, pp. 241–2. Needless to say, Lacroix was highly critical of Rome's attitude.

10 Julien de Narfon was later to maintain that the religious situation in Spain was a major factor behind the rejection of the French associations. *La Séparation des Églises et de l'État* (Paris, 1912) p. 225.

11 On the general situation in Spain, see Joan C. Ullman, *The Tragic Week. A Study of Anticlericalism in Spain, 1875–1912* (Cambridge, Mass., 1968).

12 Count della Failles to Favereau, 308/89, 1 Oct 1905, Belg., SS 25.39.

13 On Rome's efforts, see Montagnini to Merry del Val, 7 Aug 1904, Montagnini MSS, Sc.4, p. 66 bis.
14 To make matters worse, Merry del Val's brother was inadvertently responsible for a near-shipwreck of the marriage. As Alfonso's private secretary, he had been responsible for drafting a letter to the Bishop of Barcelona, in which the King undertook to oppose the building of Anglican chapels in Spain. Alfonso apparently signed it without giving it adequate attention; and the bishop released it to the press at a particularly delicate moment in Anglo-Spanish negotiations. Sir Arthur Nicolson assumed that the match was broken off; and it was only after humiliating explanations that it was deemed to be on again. Cambon to Delcassé D. 89, 20 May 1905, MAE SS/Esp. Port., p. 136.
15 See the following letters from Montagnini to Merry del Val, Montagnini MSS: on Rouvier's conversation with Cochin, letter of 10 Feb 1905; on Delcassé's attitude, letter of 13 May 1905, Sc.7, p. 204; on Loubet's conversation with Mignot, letter of 3 July 1905, Sc.7, p. 217.
16 Second letter in note 15 above.
17 Merry del Val to Montagnini, 18 May 1905, Montagnini MSS, Sc. 7, p. 205.
18 Interview with Baron d'Erp, 27 Oct 1905. Erp to Favereau, 334/100, 28 Oct 1905, Belg., SS 25.46.
19 Ibid.
20 Canon Combès, *L'Abbé Louis Birot* (Paris, 1949) pp. 213–14.
21 Although Montagnini probably destroyed or lost much of his correspondence with Merry del Val, it is perhaps significant that what has survived appears to contain no mention of this mission, the existence of which is revealed only in Cochin's letters to Montagnini (e.g., see note 23 below), and in private correspondence elsewhere.
22 Cochin's impression of the situation is revealed in the letter cited on p. 268, note 5, above, and in his introduction to Henri Chapon, *L'Église de France et la loi de 1905* (Paris, 1921) pp. xii-xiii.
23 Undated letter of Cochin to Montagnini, Montagnini MSS, Sc. 3, p. 105.
24 Letter from Cardinal Labouré of Rennes to the editor, Paul Féron-Vrau, 7 Mar 1906, Assumpt., PZ 60–1.
25 See Canon Masquelier's letter to Merry del Val, 15 Mar 1906, Assumpt., PZ 62.
26 Audience, 20 Mar 1906, Assumpt., PZ 63.
27 Rouvier's ministry fell as a result of the inventory of church property, prescribed by the Separation Law (see pp. 193–6). Having survived the spectre of the Separation debates of 1905, it was ironic that Rouvier should succumb to what was a relatively anodyne aspect of the law. An unfortunate demonstrator was killed at Boeschepe on 6 Mar; and the ministry, questioned in parliament on the following day, was put in a minority.
28 Montagnini to Merry del Val, 15 Mar 1906, Sc.3, p. 39, and 18 May 1906, Sc.15, p. 73.

29 Second letter cited in note 28 above.
30 Cochin to Montagnini, 17 Feb 1906, Montagnini MSS, Sc. 4, p. 170.
31 Letter cited on p. 268, note 5.
32 Ibid.
33 Ibid.

CHAPTER 12: EMINENCES GRISES ET CARDINAUX VERTS

1 12 Dec 1905, reported in Emmanuel Bailly's letter to Vincent Bailly, 13 Dec 1905, Assumpt., MP. 166.
2 Note of Mgr Guthlin, 8 Nov 1906, MAE SS/Fr., IX 68. The French bishops declined both offers.
3 Merry del Val to Cardinal Richard, 26 Jan 1906 – contents summarised in Richard's letter to the Archbishop of Toulouse, 18 Feb 1906, Archiepisc. Paris. Contrary to some assertions, it was Merry del Val who insisted that the preparatory working party should be representative of the various shades of episcopal opinion on the matter.
4 Conversation of 12 May 1906, reported in letter of Emmanuel Bailly to Vincent Bailly, 14 May 1906, Assumpt., MQ 106.
5 Notably Bishop Turinaz of Nancy, *La Semaine Religieuse* (Nancy), 20 May 1905.
6 *L'Autorité*, 15 June 1905.
7 Note of Albert Houtin, Houtin MSS, Bib. Nat., N.A.F., 15713.
8 The distribution of these disturbances is examined in Jean-Marie Mayeur, *La Séparation de l'Église et de l'État* (Paris, 1966) pp. 111–45. and end-map. See also his 'Géographie de la résistance aux inventaires. Février-mars, 1906', *Annales*, Nov–Dec 1966, pp. 1259–72.
9 See, among others, Michel Denis, op. cit., p. 205.
10 A.N., 50 AP 1.
11 Letter of Vincent Bailly to Fr Athanase Vanhove, 17 Feb 1906, Assumpt., Bailly TS, XV, p. 259.
12 Audience of 20 Mar 1906, notes of Emmanuel Bailly, Assumpt., PZ 63.
13 Merry del Val to Montagnini, 16 Feb 1906, Montagnini MSS, Sc.25, p. 34.
14 The context was the attitude to be taken to the latest French circular on Catholic religious meetings; but these remarks of Merry del Val also have a much wider significance.
15 My italics.
16 Interviews with Fathers Ernest and Franc, 20 Dec 1906, Assumpt., PZ 64, p. 11.
17 E.g. Ferdinand Brunetière's petition to Cardinal Richard, urging moderation, Feb 1906, Archiepisc. Paris, 1 DX 11.
18 Reported in letter of Vincent Bailly to Pierre-Fournier Merklen, 13 Feb 1906, Assumpt. Bailly TS, XVI, no. 4788.
19 Letter of Emmanuel Bailly to Bishop de Cabrières, 17 Mar 1906 (accidentally dated 17 Feb), Assumpt., QG 75.

20 Conversation between Merry del Val and Baron d'Erp, 15 Dec 1905, Erp to Favereau, 395/121, 15 Dec 1905, Belg., SS 25. 54.

21 Merry del Val to Cardinal Richard, 14 Feb 1906, cited by Archbishop Fulbert-Petit in his speech to the May episcopal assembly, *Le Petit Temps*, 26 Aug 1906.

22 27 Feb 1906, Montagnini MSS, Sc.3, p. 68. Montagnini neglected to destroy this letter as instructed.

23 These and the following details are reported in a letter from Emmanuel Bailly to Bishop de Cabrières, 17 Mar 1906 (accidentally dated 17 Feb), Assumpt., QG 75.

24 Ibid. The epithet '*soumissioniste*', in this context, originated with Merry del Val, according to Emmanuel Bailly. Merry del Val was also anxious that Bailly should persuade Cabrières to make a firm speech at the opening of the assembly, emphasising the moral impossibility of accepting the associations.

25 Ibid.

26 Reported in a letter of Emmanuel Bailly to Vincent Bailly, 14 May 1906, Assumpt., MQ 106.

27 Merry del Val to Cardinal Richard, 10 Mar 1906, Archiepisc. Paris, 1 A 8.

28 The impressive number of green-uniformed *académicians* among them had provoked Comte Costa de Beauregard to give them this title. The Beauregard family was particularly well esteemed at Rome. The Montagnini MSS contain a protracted correspondence between Mgr. Canali and Montagnini concerning Comte Ollivier de Beauregard. Montagnini was instructed to thank him for 'the fine chocolate Easter egg' which Beauregard had sent to Pius X in 1905 and which His Holiness had given to 'some good sisters in Rome'. The following year Beauregard wrote wistfully to Montagnini: 'I have been in Rome for nearly a month, and I count it singularly strange that I cannot yet display some papal decoration on my uniform'. One of Montagnini's last occupations before his expulsion was the negotiation of some satisfaction for him (Montagnini MSS, Sc.6, p. 21).

While papal decorations were not easily accorded, they were a not inconsiderable source of revenue for the Vatican. Thus Potrou was induced by Montagnini '*à la plus large générosité possible, en considération des besoins du Saint Siège*', and paid 2300 fr. for his promotion from Knight to Commander (Montagnini MSS, Sc.20, p. 72). Canali informed Montagnini, 4 Aug 1905, that '*Le Saint Siège s'impose en tout la plus stricte economie*', and regretted its inability to provide a pension for a deserving widow: '*Veuillez donc consoler la pauvre femme avec la bénédiction du Saint Père qui certainement lui apportera la fortune materielle*' (Sc.11, p. 20).

29 Interview with Baron d'Erp, Erp to Favereau, 153/41, 30 Mar 1906, Belg., SS 25. 71.

30 See details in Larkin, 'The Vatican, French Catholics, and the *associations cultuelles*', p. 313.

31 Archiepisc. Paris, uncatalogued at the time of consultation.

32 Merry del Val to Cardinal Richard, 12 Apr 1906, Archiepisc. Paris, 1 DX 11. Richard had recommended a postponement, so as not to discourage the Catholics who had participated in the *inventaires* disturbances, and who might see the assembly's discussions as a possible pointer to betrayal, Richard to Pius X, 15 Mar 1906, ibid., 1 DX 11.

33 Conversation with Emmanuel Bailly, 12 May 1906, reported in letter from Emmanuel Bailly to Vincent Bailly, 14 May 1906, Assumpt., MQ 106.

34 There are various accounts of what took place at the assembly, despite the secrecy enjoined upon it: (1) Houtin's account (see pp. 204–5 below); (2) Canon Charles Cordonnier's account, based on the notes of Archbishop Fuzet of Rouen, in *Mgr. Fuzet*, II (Paris, 1950) 161; (3) Canon Edmond Renard's account, possibly based on information given by Cardinal Gasparri, in *Le Cardinal Mathieu* (Paris, 1925) pp. 457 ff.; (4) The Memorandum of Bishop Touchet of Orleans, given to Montagnini, Sc.10 p. 74 (a fuller account by Touchet was sent by Montagnini to Rome). Less substantial accounts exist elsewhere. There are discrepancies of detail between these accounts, and unfortunately the archiepiscopal archives of Paris do not appear to contain a copy of the official minutes sent to Rome.

35 Given the secrecy of the ballot, their identities were not known at the time; and the general assumption was that these discordant votes belonged to two of the older or more feeble bishops forgetting their spectacles or misunderstanding the question. It was admittedly not the sprightliest of gatherings. One archbishop, too ill to attend, sent his coadjutor as a healthier substitute – a man, who in his own words, was prepared to come, 'in spite of my eighty-six years, my semi-deafness', and 'the risk of congestion'.

36 From Merry del Val's point of view, a particularly disturbing feature of the assembly had been the role played by Mgr Amette, auxiliary bishop of Paris, who had lately emerged as a leading *soumissioniste*. When Cardinal Richard had initially requested his appointment – with eventual succession to the see – Rome had reluctantly acquiesced out of deference to Richard, whom both Pius X and Merry del Val regarded as a virtual saint. It seemed that Rome's worst suspicions were now being realised. With Richard in his eighty-seventh year, there was every chance that Amette would be *de facto* leader of the Church in France in a couple of years or so; and, in the Vatican's view, the outlook for the future looked far from bright. Merry del Val's misgivings over Amette are reported in Emmanuel Bailly's letter to Vincent Bailly, 14 May 1906, Assumpt., MQ 106, and in Merry del Val's interview with Fathers Ernest and Franc, 20 Dec 1906, Assumpt., PZ 64.

37 *Mathieu*, pp. 467–8. He lists the majority as Cardinals Merry del Val, Steinhuber, Vives and the Vannutelli brothers; the minority as Cardinals Ferrata, Mathieu, Pietro and Rampolla.

38 Fragment of a letter from Rome, probably written by a member of the Paris *archevêché* staff, Archiepisc. Paris, 1 DX 9. This account main-

tains that Pietro abstained and Steinhuber voted for the associations. Allegations that Merry del Val 'packed' this subcommittee do not stand close examination. See Larkin, 'The Vatican, French Catholics, and the *associations cultuelles*', pp. 314–15.

39 Italian ambassador to Tittoni, 21 Aug 1906, Ital. Aff. Est., Affari Politici, Serie P, 33/P3.

40 *L'Osservatore Romano*, 29 Nov 1906.

41 Ullman, op. cit., p. 44.

42 Ferrante to Tittoni, 415/214, 9 Sep 1906, Ital. Aff. Est., Affari Politici, P. Pos. 3.

43 'Félix II', 'Pourquoi le pape hésite', *Le Figaro*, 8 Aug 1906.

44 Recounted in Erp to Favereau, 416/104, 25 Aug 1906, Belg., SS 25. 93.

45 Lacroix to Houtin, 16 Aug 1906, Houtin MSS. Bib. Nat., N.A.F., 15712, pp. 330–31.

46 Repeated in Lacroix's letter of 18 Aug 1909 to the editor of *Le Bulletin de la Semaine*, N.A.F. 24403, 133.

47 Houtin MSS, Bib. Nat., N.A.F., 1513, p. 161.

48 With a literal-mindedness, worthy of *Gravissimo officii* itself, Lacroix later publicly denied that '*j'aurais divulgué à la presse les secrets de la première assemblée des évêques*'. Lacroix to *Le Temps*, 11 Apr 1907.

49 Letter of 26 Aug 1906, Montagnini MSS, Sc. 25 p. 76.

50 Letter of 6 June 1906, Archiepisc. Paris, 1 A 8.

POSTSCRIPT: DIVORCE AND COHABITATION – A BRIEF SYNOPSIS

1 Both were much-quoted phrases of Pius X. This synopsis is based mainly on the following: L. V. Méjan, *La Séparation*; Dansette, *Histoire religieuse*, II; A. Coutrot and F. Dreyfus, *Les Forces Religieuses dans la Société Française* (Paris, 1965); Lucien Crouzil, *Quarante Ans de Séparation* (Paris, 1946); M. Bazoche, *Le Régime légal des Cultes en France* (Paris, 1948); Émile Appolis, 'En marge de la Séparation: les associations cultuelles schismatiques', *La Revue de l'Histoire de l'Église de France*, XLIX (1963), 47–88.

2 The question of the schismatical associations is extensively treated in Appolis, op. cit. and L. V. Méjan, *La Séparation*.

3 Louis Méjan's rôle in these events is described in detail in L. V. Méjan, *La Séparation*. Mlle Méjan gives a somewhat alarmist interpretation of Briand's intentions, especially in her earlier account of the Commission *extra-parlementaire*, which discussed the implementation of the Separation Law. She there accuses Briand of 'wanting to laicise the Catholic Church' (pp. 224–9), whereas Briand's concern was merely to prevent an episcopal *coup de main*, which would deprive the parishes of their legal personality. He feared that the bishops might refuse to allow the formation of parochial associations, and might then attempt to organise everything through a single diocesan association, which would deprive the parishes of any say in their own affairs.

4 Note of Mgr Guthlin, 8 Oct 1906, forwarded to MAE by Barrère, SS/Fr., IX, 45. See also G. de Raymond to Favereau, 440/110, 24 Sep 1906, Belg., SS 25. 96.
5 The Separation Law had allowed the clergy longer initial periods of free occupation (see pp. 154–5), but it had assumed in each case the existence of an *association cultuelle* which would be the legal occupant.
6 Article 16 of the Separation Law.
7 About £5000 – or £23,000 in modern terms. These and the following figures are drawn from Archiepisc. Paris, 3 c II, 1.
8 Ibid.
9 Boulard, *Essor ou déclin*, p. 465.
10 Ibid.
11 Interview with Baron d'Erp, 27 Jul 1906, Erp to Favereau, 28 Jul 1906, Belg., SS 25.87.
12 Letter from Henry to Denys Cochin, 16 Jan. 1908, Cochin MSS. The incident is also referred to in Dansette, *Histoire religieuse*, II 376.
13 Marty died in fact before the demand was sent.
14 Dansette, *Histoire religieuse*, II 378. In fairness to Pius X, it should be remembered that Leo was tied by the Concordatory method of appointment.
15 Letter to Colonel Keller, 19 June 1909, ibid, II 381–2.
16 Jan 1910, Assumpt., QG 81. Féron-Vrau, had similar misgivings in 1913, Assumpt., PZ 78.
17 Emmanuel Bailly encouraged the Pope to believe that Action Libérale was having a pernicious effect on French Catholic youth, e.g. audience notes of July 1909, Assumpt., HA 91.
18 E.g. letter of Merry del Val to Paul Féron-Vrau, 5 May 1912, Assumpt., PZ 74.
19 Letter to Paul Féron-Vrau, 28 Jan 1911, Assumpt., PZ 73.
20 This organisation has been treated in fascinating detail by Émile Poulat, *Intégrisme et Catholicisme intégral* (Paris, 1969).
21 Benedict had initially appointed Cardinal Domenico Ferrata, who as nuncio in Paris had been a principal instrument of Rampolla's francophile policies; but Ferrata died shortly afterwards.
22 Coutrot, op. cit., p. 117.
23 The late Professor Gabriel Le Bras, ibid.
24 Typescript copy of an undesignated letter from Merry del Val to an unidentified French bishop, 27 Dec 1921. Archiepisc. Paris I D XII 38. Bishop Landrieux of Dijon reported him as opposing the Associations as 'a disavowal of Pius X and the destruction of his own work'. Landrieux MS diary, entry of 15 June 1920.
25 Accounts vary; some say that he swallowed his tongue. But whatever the truth, his death was recognised as the outcome of a professional bungle. The Vatican has been the victim of its medical attendants several times in the twentieth century. When not incompetent, they have sometimes shown an unhealthy readiness to sell their intimate knowledge of the Vatican to the press.

26 As in the late 1880s and 1890s, there had been a gradual homeward flow in the inter-war years, which had later gathered pace under Pétain.

The subsidies to Catholic education mainly took the form of paying the salaries of teachers whose qualifications and teaching programmes conform to those that are current in state education. This is legally justified as aid to a privately run supplement to the state system – and therefore not a violation of Article 2 of the Separation Law, which stipulated that '*La République . . . ne subventionne aucun culte*'.

Index

(Excluding the Appendix and Sources)